PREDICTIVE ANALYTICS IN HUMAN RESOURCE MANAGEMENT

This volume is a step-by-step guide to implementing predictive data analytics in human resource management (HRM). It demonstrates how to apply and predict various HR outcomes which have an organisational impact, to aid in strategising and better decision-making.

The book:

- Presents key concepts and expands on the need and role of HR analytics in business management.
- Utilises popular analytical tools like artificial neural networks (ANNs) and K-nearest neighbour (KNN) to provide practical demonstrations through R scripts for predicting turnover and applicant screening.
- Discusses real-world corporate examples and employee data collected first-hand by the authors.
- Includes individual chapter exercises and case studies for students and teachers.

Comprehensive and accessible, this guide will be useful for students, teachers, and researchers of data analytics, Big Data, human resource management, statistics, and economics. It will also be of interest to readers interested in learning more about statistics or programming.

Shivinder Nijjer is a faculty member at Chitkara Business School, Chitkara University, Punjab, India. She has also previously worked as a software engineer with Infosys Technologies Limited. She has a PhD in predictive analytics and has contributed extensively to publications in the field of management information systems and business analytics. She has published various research articles in eminent ABDC-ranked and Scopus indexed journals. She is also a reviewer for Scopus indexed journals. She has also been actively involved in designing and delivery of analytics courses for students.

Sahil Raj is a faculty member at School of Management Studies, Punjabi University, Patiala, India. He has a PhD in information systems and has previously worked with Ranbaxy Laboratories. His recent publications include *Management Information Systems* (2017) and *Business Analytics* (2015). He has also published numerous research papers, and is a reviewer and on the editorial board of many national and international journals. He has been invited as an expert speaker and trainer in analytics by various national institutions.

PREDICTIVE ANALYTICS IN HUMAN RESOURCE MANAGEMENT

A Hands-on Approach

Shivinder Nijjer and Sahil Raj

Routledge
Taylor & Francis Group

LONDON AND NEW YORK

First published 2021
by Routledge
2 Park Square, Milton Park, Abingdon, Oxon OX14 4RN

and by Routledge
52 Vanderbilt Avenue, New York, NY 10017

Routledge is an imprint of the Taylor & Francis Group, an informa business

British Library Cataloguing-in-Publication Data
A catalogue record for this book is available from the British Library

Library of Congress Cataloging-in-Publication Data
Names: Nijjer, Shivinder, author. | Raj, Sahil, author.
Title: Predictive analytics in human resource management : a hands–on
    approach / Shivinder Nijjer and Sahil Raj.
Identifiers: LCCN 2020023839 (print) | LCCN 2020023840 (ebook)
Subjects: LCSH: Personnel management—Data processing. | Personnel
    management—Statistical methods.
Classification: LCC HF5549.5.D37 N55 2020 (print) | LCC
    HF5549.5.D37 (ebook) | DDC 658.30072/7—dc23
LC record available at https://lccn.loc.gov/2020023839
LC ebook record available at https://lccn.loc.gov/2020023840

ISBN: 978-0-367-90321-3 (hbk)
ISBN: 978-0-367-46086-0 (pbk)
ISBN: 978-1-003-02682-2 (ebk)

Typeset in Bembo
by Apex CoVantage, LLC

Visit the eResources: www.routledge.com/9780367460860

Dedicated to Guru Ji,
my mom Jasbir,
and my son Birfateh. . . .

CONTENTS

ILLUSTRATIONS

Figures

Tables

FOREWORD

Analytics is the new buzzword in all industries. It has been a well-accepted fact that data and analytics has become a game-changer for almost all industries in the present era. Although the growth of analytics adoption in varied industries is substantial, analytics is an ever-evolving field, with each day bringing in a new advent of application analytics. With the industries witnessing Industry 4.0 revolution, there is an increased demand to redefine their HR practices to equip it to cope up with these changes. However, one of the most under-valued areas of analytics is in the field of HRM. It is a known fact that only one-fourth of industry HR leaders globally believe that their firms are sufficiently equipped to apply HR analytics. There is an imperative need on the HR managers to be skilled in analytics.

The book *Predictive Analytics in Human Resource Management: A Hands-on Approach* by Dr Shivinder Nijjer and Dr Sahil Raj provides a hands-on approach to application of analytics in different areas of HRM. The case studies in different chapters of the book enable readers to become well-versed with the concepts used in HR analytics. In addition, real-world examples from corporations also serve as an aid to understand how to apply analytics in HRM. The book is a very good read for post-graduate students and executives who wish to understand the scope and application of HR analytics. The positive aspects of the book lie in the hands-on exercises described in the chapters. For coding enthusiasts who wish to get into HR analytics, this book should serve as a good primer. The book also has the potential to be a supplementary reading.

Dr DP Goyal
Director
Indian Institute of Management
Shillong, India

FOREWORD

This book *Predictive Analytics in Human Resource Management: A Hands-on Approach* by Dr Shivinder Nijjer and Dr Sahil Raj is an exemplary contribution for the scholars of business management. Human resources have been the backbone of organisations for ages, and its management using data analytics transforms conventional ways of managing human resources into a contemporary data-driven competency in a business environment. This helps an organisation to bridge the gap between employee recruitment and their performance to meet the desired strategic objectives of an organisation. This book makes use of a very engaging approach for its readers using real-life business problems/cases in various domains of human resource management such as selection and recruitment, absenteeism, performance and compensation, and employee safety through evolutionary predictive analysis tools. The authors have deployed a very interactive and exhaustive approach to understand complex techniques in a very effective manner.

I highly recommend this book to all the scholars in business management and industry practitioners for enhancing their capability in modern data-driven tools and techniques for more informed decision-making in a business environment.

Dr Vipul Gupta
Coordinator, Centre for Business Analytics & Excellence
LM Thapar School of Management
Thapar Institute of Engineering and Technology
Patiala, Punjab, India

FOREWORD

As an HR (human resources) professional and a passionate teacher, I have always been fascinated with the data metrics and absolute need to use quantitative methods to draw out HR management (HRM) plans. Data science and use of Big Data has emerged as a modern-day tool for better and swift decision-making. The immense potential of analytical science has dawned upon most organisations as a predictive tool for better decision-making, not only in operations or strategy, but also in the field of HRM. Predictive analytics in HRM is one of the most recent key trends for the last three to four years. Talent acquisition and management require a predictive tool for forecasting and planning, besides an analytical tool on the existing trends. Digital talent dashboards are key to retain competitive edge, and a book like this will be an essential tool for all HR professionals.

The book *Predictive Analytics in Human Resource Management: A Hands-on Approach* by Dr Shivinder Nijjer and Dr Sahil Raj is an essential guide to understand and use data analytics. This book is written using easy-to-understand terms and does not require familiarity with statistics or programming. Dr Shivinder is an expert in the analytical field, and therefore has highlighted all chapters and underlying themes in a lucid manner. The book is easily accessible and discernible to non-experts, and students in the lookout for analytical application in HR fields, as the book provides motivation to the necessity of analysing data. It explains how to visualise and summarise data, and how to find natural groups and frequent patterns in a dataset. The book also explores predictive tasks, through classification or regression and applies these across all HRM functions. Finally, the book discusses popular data analytic applications, like mining the web, information retrieval, and social networks. The book by Dr Shivinder offers huge potential to be used as a textbook for primary courses in business analytics. The simple explanations of sourcing of data, validation, and analysis will be very helpful for those in their maiden journey of data analytics. The book also provides a step-by-step illustration of the application of R software for prediction in different areas of HRM, be it talent acquisition, management or employee performance, and engagement management. It can undoubtedly serve as a supplementary reading or professional aid for managers. The holistic approach for application of analytics in business management enunciated by the book will be extremely useful for the teaching community, as well as by working professionals.

Dr Kulwant Kumar
Dean
Chitkara Business School
Chitkara University
Punjab, India

PREFACE

Managing human resources is one of the most trivial issues for organisations. In the present era of intense competition, no organisation can afford to take its human resources for granted. It is the only human resource that can provide a competitive edge to the organisation. But managing human resources requires a lot of effort and innovative strategies. The domain of human resource management has evolved a lot – from being a static area focusing on traditional aspects, the new age human resource management focuses on the application of analytics. Analytics is being applied in all the allied areas of management, and human resource management is not an exception to this trend. One of the key application areas of analytics is predictive analytics. The organisations are extensively applying predictive analytics to overcome the cut-throat competition in the market. Human resource managers are also moving from traditional human resource management concepts to predictive human resource management. Although still at the nascent stage, predictive analytics is still linked extensively with predicting the future demand of products and services. But of late, organisations have started acknowledging the potential of predictive analytics in human resource management.

This book is an endeavour to highlight the application of predictive analytics in the area of human resources. Human resource management has seen a tremendous change over the years. From waiting for the things to happen, human resource managers are predicting the future events. This book unveils all the critical aspects of predictive human resource management. The readers will get a real insight into the domain of predictive human resource management. Still, there is a perception that that analytics requires a great deal of statistical knowledge to understand. But this book tries to elaborate on all the aspects of predictive human resource management with simple and easy-to-understand examples. The case studies with each important concept will further help the readers to comprehend the concepts of predictive human resource management. Hands-on exercise with executable code of R software will also help the readers to play with the real data. Once the readers will run these codes, this will help them to delve deep into the enticing world of analytics. Various important analytical tools like artificial neural networks, decision trees, and K-nearest clustering are also explained in detail. This book is the result of four years of fruitful journey. When we started researching this area, we had no clue that our research in this unchartered territory will result in this book. We are thankful to Taylor and Francis Group for giving us the opportunity to publish our work. This project is made possible only due to Shoma Choudhury and Anvitaa Bajaj, for their valuable feedback which helped to embellish the content in this book

We hope and wish that this book will help the readers to develop a keen interest in the domain of predictive human resource management. We know that still there are a lot of areas of human resources that were not covered in this book. Moreover, the dynamic area of predictive analytics requires constant updating. We are eagerly waiting for the feedback from our readers regarding this book. This feedback will help us to come up with the second edition of this book.

ACKNOWLEDGEMENTS

Respond to every call that excites your spirit.

— *Rumi*

Any task that I accomplish is solely to HIS credit. No more words needed.

I have always had the urge to write and even higher urge to read; probably that's why God chose to place me in the profession of teaching. However, the motive of any learning in my life is *not* earning; it is and forever will be delivering and nurturing, and that's the reason why I have written this book. I believe one is never perfect, a master at any subject, but one can be skilled enough to initiate learning among others. This work is simply a reflection of this thought – I have tried my best to deliver what I have learnt, in as simple words as I could.

I take this platform to express my gratitude for my loving family – my husband Sardar Arshdeep Singh (who is constantly available for discussions related to book, even after our petty fights), my little one Birfateh Singh (who happily adjusted his time for me so I can continue to work on my book in odd hours), my mother (my backbone) Jasbir Kaur and my father Sardar Inderpal Singh (both parents took to my son so I can devote ample time for the book). Their support, timely nudges and encouragements were my 'go-to' place whenever I felt I am unable to justify my work, and I must admit I have always found a solution thereafter. I also owe timely completion of this work to my nephew Pritam Singh, admiring my work wide-eyed and involved in deciding each little detail for my book. And I also extend hearty thanks to my sister Bhalinder, who was always the decision-maker, when I was in doubt. I must also thank the lovely people in my life who exhibit strong faith in my abilities – Jasdeep and Navdeep (my sisters-in-law), and Sardar Jagdeep Singh (my brother cum brother-in-law).

I would also like to extend sincere thanks to Dr Sahil Raj, who showed me the way to write a book on my research work.

I am grateful to all the eminent literates who agreed to foreword this piece of work for me. They make me feel blessed.

I am also humbly thankful and grateful to the editors and entire team involved in publication of this work for their continuous support.

Shivinder Nijjer

ABBREVIATIONS

AI	artificial intelligence
AIG	American International Group
ANN	artificial neural network
AUC	area under curve
BI	business intelligence
BMI	body mass index
CART	classification and regression tree
CEO	chief executive officer
Cv	cross-validation
DC plan	defined contribution plan
DELTA	data, enterprise, leadership, targets, and analysts
DSS	decision support system
ERP	enterprise resource planning
FE Bureau	financial express bureau
GDP	gross domestic product
GLM	generalised linear model
GPA	grade point average
GUI	graphic user interface
HCL	Hindustan Computers Limited
HP	Hewlett-Packard
HR	human resource
HRD	human resource development
HRIS	human resource information systems
HRM	human resource management
hROI	human return on investment
IBEF	India Brand Equity Foundation
IBM	International Business Machines

INR	Indian rupee
IoT	Internet of Things
IPSS	International Packet Switching Service
IT	information technology
JAD	joint application design
KNN	K-nearest neighbour
KPI	key performance indicator
KPMG	Klynveld Peat Marwick Goerdeler
KSA	knowledge, skills and abilities
LAMP	logic, analytics, measures, and process
LMS	learning management system
LOFT	luck, opportunity, frustration, and threat
MAE	mean average error
MBTI	Myers-Briggs type indicator
MLP	multilayer perceptron
NLP	natural language processing
OHI	organisational health index
OHSAS 18001	Occupational Health and Safety Management certification
PO fit	person-organisation fit
PoS	point of sale
PoS tagging	part of speech tagging
PowerBI	power business intelligence
PTI	Press Trust of India
RBV	resource-based view
RFID	radio frequency identification
RMSE	root mean square error
ROC	receiver operating curve
ROI	return on investment
SAS	Statistical Analysis System
SSE	sum of squared errors
STP	software technology parks
TCS	Tata Consultancy Services
TPS	transaction processing system
TRA	total rewards allocation
US	United States
USP	unique selling proposition

1

ANALYTICS IN HRM

After reading this chapter, users will be able to understand the following key concepts:

- Understand the meaning of business analytics and its need and value in business management
- Understand the meaning, scope, and context of human resource management
- Understand the meaning, need, and role of HR analytics in business management
- Understand adoption of systems approach/process view for application of analytics
- Understand steps in the application of analytics to a business problem
- Identify business problems through an illustrative example of the issue of turnover and retention management in the Indian IT industry

Opening case

Human resource management (HRM) has always been concerned with getting the best out of people, empowering and motivating them, and driving workplace performance. But the question has always been how to empower and motivate them, or make them perform well. Leading organisations today are adopting human resource (HR) analytics – a set of sophisticated analytical tools and techniques – to find an optimal answer to this question. One such business firm, Harrah's Entertainment, an American firm functional in gaming hotels and casinos, applies analytics to understand how HR-related decisions and outcomes translate to customer services and therefore revenue generation. It uses analytics to determine an optimal number of staff required at the front end and back desk operations. Further, through HR analytics, the company understands what organisational factors and benefits make healthy and happy employees, since it directly has an effect on employee behaviour with the hotel guests and visitors. To improve the health and wellness of the employees, Harrah's frequently conducts wellness programmes and then uses metrics to evaluate the impact of these programmes on employee engagement. Analytics assesses how the improvements in employee engagement metrics correspond to an increase in firm revenue. Similarly, other major companies value employee engagement and use analytics to understand how it contributes to firm revenue. Best Buy (Davenport, Harris, and Shapiro, 2010), a retail chain, has also deployed analytics in this context and shown that a 0.1% increase in employee engagement levels leads to a US$100,000 increase in revenue of that store. Analytics has found widespread adoption in many other areas of HRM as well, for example, to predict employee churn, or to understand information flow across the organisation. All these insights aid the management to curb the problem areas proactively. For example, Sysco (2019), another American multinational firm, involved in marketing and distributing food products, kitchenware, etc., has been able to target immediate retention strategies for its delivery associates using analytics and bring an improvement from 65% to 85% in their retention rates. This directly corresponds to savings in hiring and training costs for the firm. However, although the application of analytics can impart unprecedented insights for effective decision-making, the success of its implementation depends on a number of factors such as availability of data, leadership, and commitment of the management and so on. The case, therefore, highlights how HR analytics can aid in decision-making and provide insights into the relation between HR programmes and revenue generation. This chapter builds an understanding of business analytics in general, and the need for HR analytics and predictive analytics, among the readers of this book.

Introduction

As Alexis Fink, General Manager (Talent) says, "Data-driven HR is a mindset – a philosophy about how we make decisions" (Feffer, 2018).

For years, business firms have been making substantial investments in human resources through a variety of HR practices such as compensation, training and development, and career planning, to name a few. The evolution of HRM from the traditional personnel function, which was a standalone entity functioning in an organisation and treating employees like other resources of the firm, to the present role of being a vertically and horizontally aligned strategic business partner, is marvellous. The basic premise of this change is the need to address the dynamicity of the business environment, which demands an organisation to sustain its competitive advantage despite environmental uncertainties. In the present era, human resources are the only unique resources an organisation can have which guarantee a competitive edge since all the other resources – physical and organisational (resource-based view, RBV) – can be replicated in the firms. However, this also poses a consistent challenge on the firm's ability to maintain its workforce, since competing firms are forever on a lookout to 'poach' away its competitive talent.

Management consultants worldwide agree that when organisations look at their talent as a strategic business objective and work towards strategic integration of HRM in their business, organisational success will be automatically guaranteed.

> In the 2017 Deloitte Human Capital Trends, we found that 39% of business people believe their company has 'very good' or 'good' quality data for people-related decision-making and 31% understand what 'best-in-class' people analytics looks like.
>
> *(Bersin, 2017)*

Organisations today are moving towards a quantitative analytical approach to management, from the qualitative approach. In this context, HR practitioners are also adopting an analytical approach which is data-driven and fact-based approach to addressing business problems. People data is growing rapidly, and organisations are keen to develop and gain insights into people data. Resultantly, firms are eager to invest in the application of workforce analytics and the key for firms is to create an organisation that can routinely define hROI, human return on investment. Successful human resources executives in the 21st century prove their worth not by downsizing their own departments, but rather by telling a success story with each investment in human capital – and validating that story with numbers, or hROI. This quantification of HR data marks the trend towards the use of analytics in organisations for business management.

> Business analytics refers to the use of statistical and analytical tools and techniques to interpret and explore business data (regardless of the data structure) to provide data-driven, factual business insights to management, to assist in decision-making.

Business analytics is often viewed as a subset of business intelligence (BI). BI is an umbrella term encompassing analytics, reporting, and database management, in addition to the applications, infrastructure, tools, and best practices used to gain information, improvise on its extraction, and aid in optimal organisational decision-making. The general term analytics comprises of both business analytics and data analytics, with the difference stemming from the data used to gain insights and the relevance and context of insight for a business situation. Nelson (2017) defines analytics as "the scientific process or discipline of fact-based problem-solving". Davenport and Harris (2007, p. 7) define analytics as "extensive use of data, statistical and quantitative analysis, exploratory and predictive models, and fact-based management to drive decisions and actions". Wilder and Ozgur (2015) define it as "the application of processes and techniques that transform raw data into meaningful information to improve decision making". Finally, INFORMS recommends the definition: "Analytics is the scientific process of transforming data into insight for making better decisions" (Boyd, 2012). Although the term analytics was coined late in the 1990s, the concept of analytics has roots in application of traditional statistical techniques, and ever since the concept of quantification of work was proposed by Taylor (2006) in the scientific theory of management.

The widespread growth and adoption of business analytics in organisations can be attributed to a number of factors. The exponential rate at which data is growing is the primary reason for the parallel growth in business analytics applications. This is because firms have understood that these massive amounts of data contain much hidden information for the decision-makers, which only analytics solution can decipher. Further, the proliferation of a variety of data sources and the massive capabilities of the technological solutions to integrate and analyse such data has also prompted firms to tap into the utility of business analytics. The analytics products today are able to capture and analyse data from wide variety of sources, irrespective of the data structure, such as RFID (radio frequency identification) data, sensor data, social networking data, newsfeed data, data from web crawlers and weblogs, ad clicks, IoT (Internet of Things) data, and so on.

> A number of factors contribute to the adoption of analytics in organisations such as rate of growth of data, the advent of new sources of data and technological solutions, techniques to capture data regardless of its structure, and so on.

EXHIBIT 1.1   CORPORATE EXAMPLES OF ANALYTICS ON EMERGING DATA SOURCES

Analytics applied to RFID data has seen numerous applications by retailers for on-shelf inventory management. This application of analytics provides a way of visualisation of product movement, sales traffic, and number of sales in real time.

Data from sensors are widely used for predictive maintenance in manufacturing firms, tracking customer behaviour, and detection of anomalies. For example, Reliance Power uses predictive analytics applied to sensors placed on power generation machines to determine their condition and whether they need maintenance services.

Insurance companies are now using facial analytics to determine age, gender, and body mass index (BMI) of a user based on the uploaded image of their face. Then various insurance options can be suggested to the customer.

Weblog data of the users is used by organisations to determine browsing patterns of the users and predict and suggest possible web pages based on their preferences. This stream of web analytics is widely in use in the retail and marketing industry for advertising web pages based on the browsing history of the user.

Digital marketing firms use ad analytics to discover which keywords in their digital advertisements appealed most to the viewers, based on their response to their ad. The response is determined by tracking the number of people who visited the webpage, who viewed a complete advertisement, who converted into an actual sale, and so on.

Primarily, the use of business analytics can be categorised based on the outcome of the dataset – into classification, clustering and association (Raj, 2015). Further, the categorisation can also be made based on the capability of the analytics solution – into descriptive (basic narration of analysis and events, mostly to be followed by subsequent analysis), predictive (forecasting of future events based on analysis), and prescriptive (highest analytical capability with narration, prediction and recommendation) solutions.

Primarily, three classes of business analytics exist: descriptive, predictive, and prescriptive analytics.

EXHIBIT 1.2   CORPORATE EXAMPLES OF TYPES OF ANALYTICS

Predictive analytics

- Dow Chemicals mines historical data of approximately 40,000 employees and has been able to forecast rates of promotion, internal transfers and labour count required.
- Experian (2020) predicts employee attrition, based on the computation of employee risk factors using predictive algorithms. The prediction was based on approximately 200 attributes like the performance of the supervisor, commuting distance, etc. The firm has been able to reduce turnover by 2–3% over one year of implementation.

Prescriptive analytics

- Predictive modelling of turnover and retention at Nielsen (2020) prescribes retention strategies by years of tenure of its employees. For example, for the first year of new hires, the model prescribes that establishing critical contact points is crucial for retention. The managers of new hires, therefore, are reminded to contact new hires during their first year.
- Optimal staffing was determined at a business firm by applying analytics to data on a number of employees and a number of business activities in

a business unit. The analytics tool prescribed whether the unit was over-staffed or understaffed, based on the correlation between the two datasets.

Descriptive analytics

- A local transport company implemented descriptive analytics on psycho-metric test results of drivers and found that concentration and reactive stress tolerance levels were related to proneness to accidents. This had important implications for hiring drivers.
- Google (Levenson and Pillans, 2017) uses its employee database to describe the traits of key performing employees in different areas of that organisation and then devise their hiring plans accordingly.

Business analytics finds widespread application in all the areas of business func-tions, be it the functional areas of marketing, human resource management, opera-tions and production, or finance. For example, business analytics has been massively used in the marketing function for customer segmentation, and then use the same for targeted marketing such as personalised product offerings, suggesting matching products, and so on. Similarly, it has been used to analyse ad click data to generate ROI on advertisements and predict the efficiency of the campaign. In addition, the clicks have been used to predict future clicks of the user. Also, web browsing history is used to generate purchase recommendations, while past purchase history of the customers is used to generate product recommendations for customers based on the association between products bought together. The advent of the Internet of Things has created a revolution in the manufacturing industry. By placing sensors at appropriate locations on the machines in the manufacturing plants, organisations can tap into device statistics and predict future breakdowns, aiding the firm to indulge in proactive rather than preventive maintenance. A class of analytics called genetic evolution is also used to power search engines, in which massive datasets of documents are searched and fetched based on keyword matches, in a matter of few seconds. In the business function of finance, analytics finds application in insurance fraud detection, prediction of credit card or loan payment defaulters, and segmen-tation of different sources of capital, to name a few.

Human resource management

> HRM can be defined as the process of acquiring, training, appraising, and com-pensating employees and of attending to their labour relations, health and safety, and fairness concerns.
>
> *(Dessler and Varkkey, 2008, p. 24)*

Human resource management (HRM) is the management of the core assets of a firm, which is the 'people'. They are termed as the resources of a firm, since they, by the virtue of their knowledge, skills and abilities, assume a variety of roles in a firm and provide the firm with a competitive advantage. The modern form of personnel management also termed as human resource management is very recent, dating back to the 1940s. The uncertainties in the business environment led to the complexity of the roles performed by a personnel manager, and these consequently yielded a number of human resource management processes. This variety of processes starts from HR planning, to recruitment and selection, to separation from the company, to manage these resources. A major factor which responsible to bring about this change is the change in perceiving an employee – who is now viewed as a resource rather than a passive force of production and one who has human needs and is a part of the society. This has given rise to social aspects of HRM and the role of manager as a caregiver. Besides this, labour unions have evolved, and society has become more educated and aware of one's needs and rights, rising use of technology in organisational functioning, etc., are some of the other factors which have contributed to the functioning of HRM. However, these additional responsibilities require HRM to interface with many other subjects such as psychology, sociology, economics, management, and philosophy. And at present, since people data is available in large quantities, statistics and analytics too have an interface with HRM.

The definition of HRM encompasses both operative and managerial functions. Operative functions are those in which an individual is assigned a specific task or function and has no authority in the same, while a managerial function is the one in which one exercises both control and authority. Edwin Flippo (1984) has enlisted the following operative and managerial functions: planning, organising, directing, and controlling being the managerial functions, while procurement, development, compensation, maintenance, separation, and integration are the operative functions. Each of this functions gives rise to one or more processes in human resource management. Planning implies deciding what HR initiatives need to be taken in order to achieve the organisational goals; organising or staffing implies arranging the jobs, staff, and physical infrastructure; directing implies executing the plans by motivating, controlling, and commanding the staff; and controlling implies verification of the plan implemented whether it adheres to the decided one. Procurement of human resources involves defining requirements for human resources in the firm, attracting them and then selecting the best out of them. Development implies enhancing the skill sets of the employees to meet job requirements and increase their productivity. Compensation involves remunerating employees in a fair and just manner and at competitive rates. Maintenance deals with tasks undertaken to maintain the able workforce in the firm such as through mentoring, communication, etc. Separation deals with employees leaving the firm either voluntarily, involuntarily, or through retirement.

Functions of HRM encompass both managerial and operational functions, and each function gives rise to one or more processes.

Changing role of HRM – strategic importance of HRM

Most of the organisations globally are becoming people-centric today. Since the only organisational resource which can give them a competitive advantage is human resources, there is an unprecedented pressure on the organisations to seek newer ways to hire, retain, motivate, and empower their employees. Further, simply hiring the employees would not achieve the firm's strategy unless it is integrated with overall business strategy. The call of the hour is the adoption of strategic integration of all functional areas towards overall business strategy and objectives. Successful leading organisations have adopted vertical and horizontal integration of HRM with business strategy. This implies that business strategy should translate into and dictate a corresponding HR strategy, while the management levels and operational levels in HRM derive their functional business objectives from this horizontally integrated strategy. Apart from this strategic integration, many other organisational and environmental changes are also changing the role of HRM in overall business functioning.

The present business environment poses a number of challenges to HRM practices of a firm. It is often rightly said that employees today need to do both smart work and hard work to succeed. Globalisation has led to a higher competition which requires employees who are mobile (for example, those who need to move to other countries for work), think quickly, act quickly, and be more productive even with low job security and income. In addition, firms operating at a global level have a diverse workforce in terms of nationality, ethnicity, and cultural differences, and so on. This workforce diversity requires efficient management by the HRM function, as it causes significant workplace behavioural issues. For example, cultural differences affect an individual's perception and thinking patterns, thereby having an effect on team behaviour. Changes in the nature of work due to globalisation have also affected the change in skills required of an employee. Firms are largely knowledge intensive, and employees work with automated machinery. Besides this, a rising trend is towards the delivery of services whereby employees play a front-facing role where they need to take action on the spot or face loss of a customer. Further, the nature of jobs is also changing, with part-time and contractual jobs on the rise. Therefore, there is an unprecedented pressure on the organisations to seek newer ways to effectively and efficiently manage employees, with the need of the hour being to switch from conventional HRM to sophisticated HRM practices. The key to solving this situation is to adopt IT/IS, and the evolving role of analytics has a significant effect on the efficient management of the HR function. Analytics has utility in all functional areas of a business and provides exceptional insights on the performance of a business function, which are not visible to the naked eye. Besides this, analytics can deal with all sorts of data – text, audio, video, etc. – giving incomparable advantage to the management to analyse employee blogs, customer reviews, call centre conversations, employee messenger conversations in the firm, and so on. All of these have made unique contributions to the understanding of organisational behaviour and the formulation of a strategy for the effective management of employees. For example, IT firms in India are faced with high employee turnover rates annually. Analytics goes beyond exit interviews, and digs into employees' employment records with the organisation – tenure, performance ratings, skill levels, and previous experience – and associates each of these with turnover intent. Resultantly, firms have been able to predict turnover better and strategise retention measures accordingly, lowering their overall turnover rate annually. Therefore, analytics is required for effective management of HR function, as well, since it can describe, predict, and then prescribe organisational behavioural issues arising from the changing role of HRM.

Human resource analytics

> A survey by Tata Consultancy Services found that just 5% of big-data investments go to HR, the group that typically manages people analytics.
>
> *(Leonardi and Contractor, 2018, p. 1)*

It is interesting to note that only 16% of the organisations globally report adoption of HR analytics (Marler and Boudreau, 2017), and therefore, conceivably HR analytics is at early adopters stage. However, HR analytics is gaining prominence, since there exists a relationship between HR analytics and demonstrated business impact. When organisations are able to accurately predict and quantify the value of the contribution of the firm's people, better business outcomes are automatically generated. To thrive in tough market conditions, organisations need to quantify their workforce interventions. Workforce analytics or HR analytics should be able to answer basic questions: are the work, organisational strategy/process, structures, and jobs strategically aligned, and is the human capital of the firm sufficiently able to accomplish the same? The application of HR analytics targets at translating HR actions into tangible ROI. The ultimate approach for organisations is to create predictive analytics in HRM – where firms can model the future, based on people insights developed today. Predictive analytics allows the firm to predict the future, adopting a proactive rather than reactive approach to management, by accumulating people data from a variety of sources, regardless of the nature or structure of data, and then applying statistical and analytical tools and techniques to gain insight, such as the causation of HR problem or the relationship between different HR practices and organisational outcomes. The application of predictive analytics to workforce data enables the organisations to cope with the future uncertainties and not fall into the vicious cycle of hiring and firing. These firms have progressed from looking beyond the historic static reporting towards outcome-based predictive measures.

Adoption of HR analytics is at the early adopter stage, with only 16% of the companies adopting the same in the organisations.

Source: IBM (2011)

Analytical approaches can aid the HR executives to quantify their ROI on human capital and HR practices. In addition, they can aid the management in guiding towards shaping a better future of HRM by meeting business objectives. When companies do not generate and utilise business-focused metrics in HR, they do not effectively translate into business outcomes, thereby confounding the actual contribution of HR towards the same. For example, firms might have quantified the impact of training on an individual's performance, but might not have considered the impact on overall business performance. Firms collect huge amounts of HR data, but relatively few retain that data and quantify it to better the performance of a business. It therefore becomes imperative for the organisations to collect the proper data and use analytics to demonstrate the impact of HR investments on business performance, also predicting future needs for better business alignment. For this purpose, HR in organisations broadly requires six tools to use analytics to better business outcomes (Harris, Craig, and Light, 2011). These tools depict the key requirements for a firm in order to equip it with HR analytical capabilities and implement HR analytical applications.

The foremost requirement or the foundation of any good analytical application is the data. Therefore, a firm should have an employee database which would keep the entire employee data in order and aid in tracking and monitoring their key employee metrics. For example, Google (Levenson and Pillans, 2017) maintains a comprehensive database to monitor employee attitudes, behaviours, on-job performance, and so on, which is utilised by Google to apply analytics to predict the probability of success of employees in different work areas. The second tool is to identify the critical talent management or the key segments of employees who are high performing, high potential and is leaders in their work area. The target here is to understand what constitutes each segment of the employee or to understand the basis for differentiation between the employees, which is the key outcome of a predictive analytics application. The third tool is to treat each segment differently, now that the organisation is aware of the differences in each segment and can work out on what they value most. Therefore, the fourth tool is that the firm should develop investments focused on HR, and the predictive action should further be able to signify in time how the HR actions should vary by employee life cycle. For example, Convergys realised that when it distributed annual increments to its employees every six months, instead of after a year, they were more likely to stay with the firm, than otherwise. The fifth step is the contribution of the predictive models towards workforce planning. Through the use of predictive models, HR analytical applications can depict the future business requirements, match the same with current organisational capabilities, and therefore forecast staffing requirements in case of a mismatch. Through the sixth tool, the firm can further extend this analytical capability to its external stakeholders, viz. to manage the supply chain of employees. The predictive HR models should be able to adapt the supply chains as per the business requirements of the firm in lieu of environmental conditions.

Six tools required to use HR analytics to better the business outcomes are: developing a data and employee database, identification of key employee segments, treating each segment differently, focused HR actions by each segment, using predictive models for workforce planning, and extending analytics to external stakeholders.

Technology is an enabler for HR functions. Human resource information systems (HRIS) has brought about basic changes in HR functions, role, and processes and how HR relates to the overall organisation. HRIS can take many forms – limited to a spreadsheet or ERP (enterprise resource planning) systems – with the basic premise of collecting, storing, and disseminating HRM data. This data then allows and enables HR professionals to employ HR metrics to use for problem-solving and assess the efficiency, efficacy, impact, and service of HR. HRIS also inculcates decision support system (DSS) and BI facilities to assist employees and management in decision-making. The importance of integrating such capabilities and technology transforms the role of HR from back end administrative component to a strategic business partner of the firm. Additionally, high-performing organisations are those which possess appropriate tools and technologies to collect and analyse HR data.

HR activities vary by operational and managerial/strategic level of the firm, which in turn leads to variation in data requirements and hence type of DSS needed at each level. The industry has seen widespread growth in the use of DSS & BI tools in HR; however, limited research has focused on this area, as to how DSS can support decision-making in HRM, and how it can be implemented. Therefore, an important consideration in the design of DSS for HRM functions is that a 'one-size-fits-all' approach would not work; rather, the design needs to differ and fit with the context in which decision is made. While some decisions are straightforward, others are complex in nature. For example, DSS varies by the nature of the decision being routine/ad hoc or by the use of DSS by an individual/group of decision-makers. Another design variation is suggested as model-oriented DSS or data-oriented DSS, whereby data is retrieved and presented to DSS and suggestions or alternatives are provided based upon the application of mathematical models to the data, respectively. Power (2002) further expands this categorisation into five additional types: knowledge-driven, document-driven, communication-based, inter-organisational DSS, and web-based DSS.

HR activities – and therefore, the types of DSS – vary by operational, managerial, or strategic level of the firm.

Management activities have also been categorised along the dimensions of management levels and decision-making structure. There are three management levels – operational, managerial, and strategic, while the decision-making structure involves three classes – unstructured, semi-structured, and structured decisions. DSS assists in decision-making for semi-structured and unstructured decisions. Now to assist in this decision-making, data has to be captured through various forms. Practitioners have defined multiple levels of HR metrics which can be captured and used by HR professionals for decision-making. These metrics quantify HR data and, therefore, DSS can work around this data. These metrics can also be categorised into four levels. The first level of HR metrics reflects the performance of basic administration tasks. The second level is human capital metrics, while the third level is HR effectiveness or HR cost-benefit metrics. The fourth level is the highest level, which is the impact or strategic metrics. The companies that use data to develop metrics and thereafter predictive models based on these metrics will have an edge and a sustained competitive advantage in managing and development of talent. The tasks of the selection of candidates and prediction of turnover involve both insight and support through data, metrics, and analytics. Therefore, they can be viewed as semi-structured decisions which can be implemented at management control and operational level. The initial screening of candidates can be considered to be occurring at the operational level, while turnover prediction will be inculcated at the management control level.

HR metrics can be categorised into four levels:

- Basic administrative metrics
- Human capital metrics
- HR cost-benefit metrics
- Impact/strategic metrics

Although HR analytics promises a bright road ahead for the firms adopting this practice, several factors impede the adoption and sustenance of this approach. The foremost restricting factor is the dearth of skilled HR professionals. The specific analytical competencies required by an HR professional to perform HR analytics involves data analyses – basic and intermediate, multivariate models – basic and advanced, data preparation, root cause analysis, research and survey design, and quantitative data collection and analyses (Marler and Boudreau, 2017). However, HR professionals are not always hired for these skills. Further, HR managers need good collaboration and interpersonal skills to gain access to inter-functional data. At the same time, the belief of top management in data-driven HR results too impacts the adoption of HR analytics. The employee resistance to change and technology also inhibits the generalised adoption of analytics in any business area. Further, the HRIS/IT can act as an enabler or inhibitor of analytics adoption in this field. This is because; the primary purpose of HRIS/IT is capturing and systematic storing of data and removal of data redundancy and discrepancy. However, most of the time, the data collected is inadequate, incomplete, and inaccessible, not integrated, or outdated, which inhibits the implementation of HR analytics. Outdated HR systems, lack of integration among these HR systems and with other organisational systems, unwillingness to extract information, lack of orientation of HR managers towards data usage, and lack of decision-making ability and experience have been reported as the barriers to implementation to HR analytics (IBM, 2011).

Barriers to adoption of HR analytics:

- Dearth of skilled HR professionals
- Lack of support from top management
- Employee resistance to change
- Existing HRIS/IT inhibitions
- Lack of accurate, consistent, and complete data
- Difficult-to-access inter-functional data

Steps in the application of analytics – a holistic approach

Organisations have developed their own models for the application of analytics to their business problems. Although the premise of each model is the same, the difference lies in the different need and business objectives that they attempt to satiate using a particular model. In this section of the chapter, few prominent models of analytics applied at leading organisations will be discussed, followed by a generalised step-by-step approach which will aid readers to understand how analytics can be applied in a business area. The IT organisation Accenture, which is a leading IT firm globally, uses a five-step model called DELTA (data, enterprise, leadership, targets, and analysts) to describe the effective implementation of analytics (Harris et al., 2011). These five steps have been described in detail as follows:

Four different frameworks for the application of analytics discussed:

- DELTA framework (data, enterprise, leadership, targets, and analysts)
- Six-step model by Bell (2012)
- LAMP framework – logic, analytics, measures, and process

1   The foundation of any successful analytical application is the data. The first step of the model suggests that the data should be accessible, consistent, and of high quality. In organisations working with disparate HR IT systems, the

challenge of capturing consistent and reliable data increases manifold, owing to increased redundancies and inconsistency in the data among these systems. Additionally, disparate systems do not support time tracking of data, thereby inhibiting longitudinal analysis or establishment of causal relationships between different HR variables. For the development of metrics which gauge HR performance and its contribution to business objectives, it is important to collect the proper data and then model and predicts the performance using these metrics.

2 The second step is to adopt an enterprise-wide perspective for the application of analytics, which requires integration of data, analytical applications, and processes throughout the enterprise. This requires strategic integration of HR with the business objectives, viz. the vertical and horizontal integration. Vertical integration implies the integration of HR objectives with overall business objectives, while horizontal integration implies that HR functions in sync with the other functional areas in an organisation. This way, the analytical capabilities will yield manifold.

3 The third step is the inculcation of HR leaders who demonstrate and advocate the benefits of analytics to the entire organisation. The adoption of analytics requires massive cultural changes and hence often manifests in employee resistance. However, effective leadership is able to time manage this resistance through behavioural, cultural, and technical interventions. Most often, lack of communication is the key reason behind the failure of adoption of such techniques.

4 A model called LOFT (luck, opportunity, frustration, and threat) is widely used to understand how analytics can be adopted in a firm. Many firms adopt it as a matter of luck, some out of frustration arising due to lack of an alternative and some due to a threat from competing firms which have adopted it and succeeded as a result. But not all firms are as lucky, and therefore, they should constantly be on the lookout for an opportunity to implement analytics. At the same time, organisations should also look for payoffs of the implementation and should not just seize any opportunity on hand. Only when some opportunity is consistent with organisational long-term objectives should it consider its adoption and implementation.

5 The most important part is the building and effective utilisation of HR analytical skills. There is a dearth of analytical talent globally since the field is evolving. Only when an organisation has the right skilled staff will it be able to achieve all the previously mentioned steps. The people in a firm should be well-equipped to capture the data, analyse the data through the application of right analytical models, and use the outcomes to aid in decision-making.

Another model (Bell, 2012) summarises the key steps taken by the organisations to implement workforce analytics in an attempt to make a turnaround from the problematic issues that they were facing affecting the performance of the firm and thereby its revenues, costs and profits. These six key steps are:

1 **Frame the central problem** – The idea here is to understand what problem the firm is facing, and which key issue it needs to address in order to solve the problem. For example, if a call centre finds a drop in its call volume, while that of its competitors is rising, it needs to address the issues of customer satisfaction viz. which it can analyse a number of underlying causations.

2 **Apply a conceptual model to guide the analysis** – A consistent theory or consistent background should be available to address the problems. For example, for a call centre, if metrics do not directly address business performance or metrics are changed frequently, it would not result in performance.

3 **Capture relevant data** – This is the case with the majority of the firms. They all collect data from a wide number of sources, but do not know how to use it and put it in context. Sometimes, disparate systems running in an organisation create discrepancies and inconsistencies in data. Therefore, the firm can either hire specialists who know which data to look for, and from which sources, or first integrate the disparate systems so that the data is consistently centralised and therefore most relevant data can be chalked out.

4 **Apply analytical methods** – It is important to discern that not all problems require complex analytical methods; rather, simple frequency distribution or cross-tabulation may do the work. But when an analytical technique is required for application, the organisation needs to carefully select the optimal method which can address the problem.

5 **Present statistical findings to stakeholders** – A business analyst holds expertise in the application of analytical tools, while a manager best understands the problem he is facing and how the system works, which can aid the analyst to dig deeper into the problem. At the same time, if a new strategy is to be framed in light of the findings, then top executives need to be pulled in. Therefore, clearly, the application of analytics requires collaboration among different stakeholders, and resultantly, the findings need to be shared among the stakeholders.

6 **Define actions to implement the solution** – If the analytical solution supports the notion that a large number of metrics and frequent change in the same was a cause of customer dissatisfaction at the call centre, which ultimately resulted in a decrease in call volume; then metrics need to be reframed and reduced to a smaller number. So, the solution proposed by the analytical application needs to be implemented for success and the action plan needs to be drafted for the same. These six steps enable the creation of predictive workforce analytics.

Another popular framework for implementation of HR analytics is the LAMP framework (Figure 1.1). LAMP is an acronym for logic, analytics, measures, and

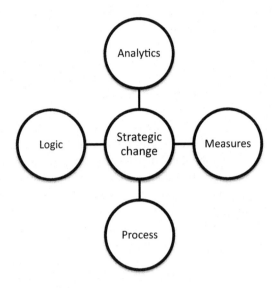

FIGURE 1.1 LAMP framework[1]

process (Cascio and Boudreau, 2011). The framework suggests that these are the key components of driving strategic change in an organisation to reap optimal organisational effectiveness.

Logic implies understanding the story behind the problem. For example, to curb the problem of turnover, look beyond the turnover costs or impact analysis. When an organisation applies the right logical model to the problem at hand, it is able to devise the right measures and drive performance. The HR function in an organisation can have any number of measures following within a specific HR function. However, not all measures are important for resolving the problem at hand, and not all measures also contribute to overall business objectives. Therefore, the framework suggests that those measures which – despite being timely, complete, reliable, and consistent – do not fit the 'context' should be not be used. The logic and metric would only yield something substantial when the right analytical solution is applied to it. When the right conclusion is based on the right data, logic, and analysis, it will automatically yield favourable outcomes. Analytics is used to test the logic with the data at hand to solve the problem. The last part of the framework stresses the importance of change management through participation and involvement. Sometimes, rather than depicting the use of complex analytical models, simple methods of analysis may be used to demonstrate to the user that analytics is efficient in solving the problem at hand. Therefore, using appropriate intervention, education, training, and communication, to name a few, the process of adoption of analytics can be made easier and fruitful for both the employee and the organisation.

Although each of these models has been adopted in different functional areas of management for the application of analytics, a single most important limitation of these models is a lack of focus on the application of analytics. None of these models is able to demonstrate a step-by-step approach to guide the users about the implementation of analytics. These models have stressed more outlining how the implementation of analytics at an organisation for a business problem can be a success. For example, the DELTA framework builds an overview of a supporting framework required for successful implementation of analytics, such as the proper leadership, proper data, appropriate business analysis, and so on. However, even if a firm is equipped with all these elements of the DELTA framework, it may be unable to guide the implementation of analytics to a business problem. Similarly, LAMP framework begins with the assumption that a strategic change is required in an organisation in the context of a business problem it is facing and therefore, a user should apply logic to understand the problem, choose an analytical tool, develop measures to implement that tool, and find processes which need change to overcome the problem. The framework doesn't give emphasis on how to identify a problem and therefore assess whether a strategic change is required or not. In light of these limitations, a different framework is required which overcomes all these limitations and provides a step-by-step guide to the user about the implementation of analytics to a business problem.

This book advocates a step-by-step approach termed as 'holistic approach' (Figure 1.2), loosely based on all the models discussed in the preceding text. This

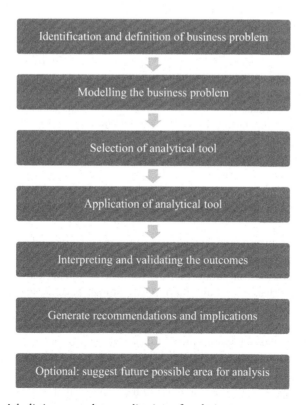

FIGURE 1.2   A holistic approach to application of analytics

approach would aid the reader in grasping and applying the basic concepts of the application of analytics to solve precisely any business problem at hand. The analogy of a doctor and patient has been used to explain the steps in the holistic approach for the application of analytics to a business problem.

1   The first step in the approach states to identify and define the business problem. Many times organisations can easily identify a business problem from their **overall performance metrics.** For example, a consistently high rate of turnover might indicate an underlying organisational issue. This is analogous to the diagnosis of disease by the doctors. The symptoms present in the patient indicate the presence of a disease which can be treated by further diagnosis. However, the treatment would depend on the underlying cause, which can be accurately pointed out through lab tests or scans, etc. Similarly, when a business performance metric fails to meet the set standards, it indicates an underlying problem area.

   Another way for identification of the problem is through **managerial reporting**. A manager in a specific functional area may be experiencing some issues with the concerned stakeholders. For example, a territorial manager might be experiencing a consistent drop in sales of products in a given region of operation, while other regions are working smoothly. Therefore, the decrease in sales is the identification of a problem. Clear definition of a problem implies stating exactly where and what the problem is; why it occurred would follow later. Taking the same example of the decrease in sales, problem definition would involve that sales have decreased over the past one year (may include specifying time frame) for beverages (may include mentioning specific products) in the southern region. This way when analyst would wish to apply analytical method, he would restrict to the application to only past one-year beverages data, for the southern region; and may, later on, include other regions for comparative analysis if the need arises.

CORPORATE SNAPSHOT: PROBLEM IDENTIFICATION

Voluntary turnover metrics in an Indian software firm indicated a steep rise in the number of employees leaving the firm over the past two years. On further investigations, the firm found that the turnover included many key talents of the firm, a clear indication of a problem. Studies have demonstrated that voluntary turnover (leaving an organisation by choice) among employees in an organisation costs it approximately 1.5 times their base pay. This situation clearly builds a background for further analysis to understand why key employees are also leaving the firm. This is also because when timely key employees are retained; however, small the number may be, it saves a huge amount of money when seen in terms of the base pay that they receive.

2   The second step is to model the business problem. This inculcates two steps in the application of business analytics viz. development of a conceptual model for business problem and data collection.

CORPORATE SNAPSHOT: MODEL THE BUSINESS PROBLEM

A sales firm was experiencing difficulties in succession planning of key sale roles, due for retirement in near time. The problem was aggravated by a change in retirement behaviour generally, with a larger workforce adopting part-time or contractual jobs. The firm, therefore, developed a predictive model to forecast who is going to retire. In addition to the conventional factors used for retirement prediction, age and tenure, the firm also included additional factors such as changes in employee role, pay level, rate of change in pay, likelihood of receiving incentives, etc., in its predictive model. This way the firm could effectively manage the retirement cycle of employees.

As will be discussed in subsequent chapters, the development of conceptual models is based on some underlying theoretical frameworks or logic. For example, a decrease in sales might be attributed to adverse employee attitudes or decreased product quality. If the employee attitude is responsible for the same, then the analyst would need to look for ways to collect data on different employee attitudes which have an impact on sales and customer satisfaction. Outlining which attitudes to collect may be ascertained through one's experience, talk with experts or seniors, or theoretical background. The model development may also involve the identification of dependent and independent variables. All these concepts will be discussed in detail in subsequent chapters.

3   A vast variety of analytical tools and techniques are available to a user. In this step, the user first needs to categorise the problem as a classification, clustering, or association problem. Thereafter, the decision can be made regarding the analytical tool.

CORPORATE SNAPSHOT: CHOICE OF THE ANALYTICAL TOOL

A global restaurant chain was seeking newer ways to enhance customer satisfaction. Correlation analysis of historical data of frontline employees and customer satisfaction rates revealed a significant relationship between the two. So the restaurateur decided to improve frontline employee retention to increase the firm's revenue. It built a predictive model on data spanning individual employee details, shift details, restaurant details, and financial and operational performance details, comprising more than 10,000 data points. Since the firm wished to link each of these with overall chain performance, it chose unsupervised learning models such as clustering and logistic regression. Regression is especially useful for hypothesis testing, while unsupervised learning techniques are useful when background about the relationships is not known.

The user should be aware of and consider the assumptions and limitations, including the data requirements for the implementation of the tool, before choosing the same. For example, linear regression only works on linear data. Just as a doctor selects from a range of available treatments depending on the severity of the problem, resources of the patient and the latest technology, the analyst too needs to choose the analytical method. Only when treatment offers an unparalleled advantage does a doctor recommend it to the patient; such should be the case with the analyst. In addition, many other factors play a role in deciding the right analytical tool, such as available budget, time, skill sets of the workforce, need for training, etc.

4   The next step involves the application of an analytical model to the business problem. For this step, the user would often require data preparation and cleansing. For example, the software RStudio works only on variables encoded between the ranges of 0–1. Therefore, the collected data need to be modified accordingly. Besides this, the user should also be aware of the different features of the tool used to view the application and outcomes. Many analytical methods also require setting the parameters, which need to be carefully ascertained.

5   After application of the analytical tool, the user should interpret the outcomes and validate them. A number of techniques are available for validation of results such as lift charts or cross-tabulation for validation of ANN output. Use of such validation techniques adds to the robustness of the analyses. The outcomes should be cross-verified with the conceptual model and then ascertained for future use.

6   The outcomes are of no use until a recommendation or a suggestion can be generated out of the same. A doctor's diagnosis has no value for the ailing until an effective treatment is suggested and put into action. Therefore, following the outcomes of the analytical approach, the analyst can make fact-based and data-driven recommendations for decision-makers to solve a business problem. A specific action plan stating who needs to do what in order to curb the problem needs to be developed. However, this cannot be done in isolation, since all stakeholders must be involved to devise this plan for effective implementation. Further appropriate and timely resistance and change management interventions should also be included in the plan.

CORPORATE SNAPSHOT: INTERPRETATION AND RECOMMENDATION FROM ANALYTICAL OUTCOMES

For the global restaurant chain seeking newer ways to enhance customer satisfaction, the analysis revealed four different clusters of employees working in the restaurants. The firm labelled them as 'socialisers', 'potential leaders', 'entrepreneurial taskmasters' and 'conservative taskmasters', with the latter being the most consistent in job performance. Further, the performance was also strongly dependent on career development opportunities and cultural norms, rather than variable compensation, currently being offered to the employees. Implementations of these findings have resulted in significant improvements in customer satisfaction, speed of service, sales, and attrition rates.

7   Sometimes the solution is able to demonstrate a future area for analyses. For example, assume that analytics suggested that decrease in sales for a retailer in the southern region of operation can be attributed to adverse employee attitudes. However, this was also linked with dissatisfaction with pay among employees working in this region. Therefore, this aspect of the sales peoples in the southern region dissatisfied with pay calls for further investigation. Analogous to a doctor's prescription which recommends not only medicine, dosage and period of treatment, and also future tests if the need arises, this step asks the reader to be on the lookout for such areas which call for future investigations.

Adoption of systems approach/process view

A system is defined by Valacich and George (2017, p. 6) as "An interrelated set of components working within a business unit, and working together for a common purpose". Some essential characteristics of a system are that it contains components which are interrelated, has a specific boundary of operation, serves a definite purpose, operates in a given set of the environment under a certain set of constraints, interfaces with other system components, and has a set of operable inputs and outputs. For example, payroll function has a system which tracks the workdays of employees and computes salary. An important concept in systems is the principle of decomposition; that is, a system can be broken down into smaller components or sub-systems. Now HRM functions can be integrated into one HRIS. Each of these HRM functions can be implemented through various sub-systems. For example, a compensation and benefits system will include performance appraisal, attendance tracking, and benefits administration system. Therefore, each HRM function can be viewed as a system designed to accomplish predetermined objectives. The primary purpose of viewing HRM functions as systems asserts the notions that these systems are designed to achieve predetermined objectives through the implementation of adequate resources, and that these might have sub-systems which perform specialised functions towards the achievement of the goal of a higher system. One very important implication here is that all the systems (and therefore, all HRM functions) are highly interrelated and interdependent. Further, all these systems have defined boundaries under which they operate. When these systems involve a feedback loop, they exercise some degree of control and aid in the effective management of resources. Further, a system would have defined set of inputs flowing in and outputs flowing out, all in sync with the achievement of the objective.

Each HRM function can be viewed as a system designed to accomplish predetermined objectives. A number of processes execute under each system and each process has defined inputs, transformation and outputs. This systems/ process view aids the user to begin the application of analytics to a given business problem.

Now each system and its sub-systems work together to accomplish a goal. In each of these systems and sub-systems, a number of processes are running to achieve the overall system objective. Therefore, a system, sub-system and processes can be seen to form a conceptual hierarchy, and it is not always a necessity that sub-system exists within all systems. For example, a simple HR system of payroll generation would involve the process of first fetching employee work data like absent days and performance rate, then employee record to determine base pay, benefits etc. and then computation of salary and then generating the payroll. This has been depicted in Figure 1.3.

Generally, this process of payroll generation is an operation of TPS (transaction processing system) implemented in a firm. Now scientifically, a process is considered as a transformation of inputs to generate some output. This logic is depicted in Figure 1.4.

The idea behind the process logic is to understand how data is generated and flows in a process to accomplish an overall system objective. Once a user understands this part, then analytics can be applied easily since this understanding aid in modelling of the business problem. Therefore, it is clear that HR functions can be viewed as a system, each of which may have one or more sub-systems, and functioning in a system can be explained by underlying processes.

FIGURE 1.3 Process for payroll generation

FIGURE 1.4   Depiction of process logic

To apply analytics in HR, managers are often confused about where to start. However, this section of the book has imparted a thorough understanding to the reader – that to effectively model an HR business problem, view that problem area as a process and as a part of some overall system. Then apply this process logic to the problem, so that a predictive model can be effectively built on top of this logic. The succeeding chapters will present how this process logic translates to a model of a business problem.

Application of system approach/process view to different HR functions

Following from the previous discussion, this section presents some examples of the application of system approach and process view to different HR functions. Let us first consider the HR function of selection. When we view the selection function of HRM as a system, then its boundaries are limited by the functions of selecting the right candidates and don't involve the function of recruitment. Additionally, the selection system is dependent on the function of recruitment, which provides the necessary inputs such as the number of candidates to be hired, their skill set, the position at which they are hired, and their pay scale, to name a few. Understanding that the recruitment system interfaces with the selection system, one understands that recruitment number, criteria, position, etc., comes from that system, and selection on this basis occurs in the selection system. The output of such a system would be the final list of selected candidates with their positions, pay scale, location, merit, and so on. Typically, the selection system in any organisation involves the sub-systems of receiving candidate applications, screening applications, testing, interviewing, and final selection intimation. How screening of applicants takes place involves a process, and each of these processes has definite inputs, transformations, and outputs. When a reader is able to clearly discern this system and process logic, the definition of problem would be made easier, which in turn would allow for building better conceptual models. Applying the process logic to applicant screening (Table 1.1):

When a reader is able to build such an understanding of systems and processes involved in each business problem, the design of the analytical solution becomes quite easy. For example, here it becomes clear that if an applicant screening system has to be designed, then it needs to accept all the inputs (listed in Table 1.1) for each applying candidates, compare them across benchmarks using simple comparison

TABLE 1.1 Applying process logic to applicant screening

Inputs	Transformation	Output
Candidate demographics	Compare with the existing	Accepted/Rejected
Pass marks/eligibility criteria	criteria in the database	Accepted/Rejected
References		Accepted/Rejected
Skills		Accepted/Rejected

TABLE 1.2 Process logic of offering training programmes to employees

Inputs	Transformation	Output
Candidate demographics	Compare with the existing	Training Programme 1
Current position	criteria in the database	Training Programme 2
Current skills		Training Programme 3
Performance rank		Training Programme n

formulas, and then generate an output whether the candidate is accepted or rejected.

Consider another example of the system of career development. One subsystem in this skill development is training, which further involves a number of functions like programmes offered, evaluation, programme design, etc. Consider the function of offering training programmes to employees. It would be offered based on the current position, skills, and performance ratings of the employees. So, it might involve the following process logic (Table 1.2):

The examples presented here do not involve any high-level design of metrics, data capturing, or application of a complex analytical solution; however, it clearly aids in user understanding that to solve any business problem, identify the systems and processes, and the subsequent inputs, transformation, and outputs. Similarly, the concept can be applied to all the functions of HR and provide a platform for business modelling of the problem, as discussed in subsequent chapters.

Conclusion

In a nutshell, the dynamic business environment calls for adoption and implementation of innovative solutions in the organisation to sustain a competitive edge. HR analytics, despite being in a nascent stage of adoption, has fetched enormous benefits for the adopting firms. Although the demonstration of direct ROI on human capital investments is not possible, design of HR metrics and predictive models based on the same can be inculcated by the firms, since HR investments translate into worker efficiency and productivity and job attitudes, ultimately manifesting itself in work or business outcomes. All the leading firms globally have adopted the HR analytics frameworks. There are many barriers reported for its adoption, namely dearth of skilled professionals, lack of support from top management, lack of availability and access to data, outdated and disparate HR systems, and lack of integration with other organisational systems, to name a few. This book is an attempt to equip managers with the skills to apply predictive analytics in any business area, through the example of building predictive turnover and selection screening system. This chapter explains the different models and frameworks used by the organisations to implement HR analytics, while also explaining the holistic step-by-step approach to the application of analytics. Through the illustration of adoption of a systems approach and process view, the book clearly explains the first step in the step-by-step approach, which is how problem identification and definition can be carried out to apply analytics to solve the problem. The following chapters will practically demonstrate the other steps in the framework through the same example of turnover and retention management.

Glossary

Business analytics refers to the use of statistical and analytical tools and techniques to interpret and explore business data (regardless of the data structure) to provide data-driven, factual business insights to the management to assist in decision-making

Compensation involves remunerating employees in a fair manner at competitive rates

Controlling implies verification of adhering to the plan

Data analytics the scientific process of transforming data into insight for making better decisions

DELTA is a framework developed and used by Accenture to describe the effective implementation of analytics; the acronym stands for data, enterprise, leadership, targets, and analysts

Descriptive analytics a basic narration of analysis and events, mostly to be followed by subsequent analysis

Development implies enhancing the skill sets of the employees to meet job requirements and increase their productivity

Directing implies executing the plans by motivating, controlling, and commanding the staff

Holistic approach to implement analytics lists seven steps to aid a user to understand the application of analytics to a business problem

hROI is defined as human return on investment, which allows the organisation to narrate the success of its HR investments by quantification of HR data through predefined metrics

Human resource management HRM can be defined as the process of acquiring, training, appraising, and compensating employees and of attending to their labour relations, health and safety, and fairness concerns

LAMP is an acronym for logic, analytics, measures, and process; the framework suggests that these four components are the key to drive strategic change in an organisation to reap optimal organisational effectiveness

LOFT is an acronym for luck, opportunity, frustration, and threat, and is a widely used model to understand how analytics can be adopted in a firm

Maintenance deals with tasks undertaken to maintain the able workforce in the firm such as through mentoring, communication, etc.

Managerial function is the one in which one exercises both control and authority

Operative functions are those in which an individual is assigned a specific task or function and has no authority in the same

Organising or staffing implies arranging the jobs, staff, and physical infrastructure

Planning implies deciding what HR initiatives need to be taken in order to achieve the organisational goals

Predictive analytics forecasting of future events based on analysis

Prescriptive analytics highest analytical capability with narration, prediction, and recommendation

Process logic implies that different HR activities can be viewed as a process with definite inputs, transformation, and outputs

Procurement involves defining requirements for human resources in the firm, attracting them, and then selecting the best out of them

Separation deals with employees leaving the firm either voluntarily, involuntarily, or through retirement

Systems approach to HRM implies viewing HRM functions as systems, which are interrelated and interdependent, with predefined boundaries and objectives

Turnover Individual movement across the membership boundary of an organisation

Turnover intent the reflection of the probability that an individual will change his/her job within a certain time period

Review material

1 Explain why firms use HR metrics and are moving forward towards a quantitative approach rather than a qualitative approach.
2 Define analytics and business analytics.
3 List the factors responsible for widespread adoption of business analytics.
4 List different areas of application of business analytics.
5 Define HRM. Explain its evolution from a standalone unit to a strategic business partner.
6 List various functions and activities of HRM.
7 Explain the challenges to HRM practices of a firm.
8 What basic questions can HR analytics answer?
9 List the benefits of the application of HR analytics.
10 List the barriers to implementation of HR analytics in an organisation.
11 Describe the six tools required to use HR analytics in a firm.
12 Explain how DSS varies by level of management and nature of decision.

13 List the four categories of HR metrics.
14 Explain the DELTA framework.
15 List the six steps in the model proposed by Bell for the implementation of analytics.
16 Explain the LAMP framework.
17 Elucidate the seven steps in the holistic approach for implementation of analytics to a business problem.
18 Explain the importance of adoption of system approach and process view for application of analytics.
19 Define turnover and turnover intent.
20 Discuss various factors which affect how turnover varies, such as skill level, experience, and age.
21 How do HR practices affect employee attitudes and hence turnover intent?
22 Explain how a proper screening system can aid in management and reduction of employee turnover intent.

Problem exercises

1 Pick any one function of HRM, and apply the system approach and process view to it. Using the process logic, clearly identify and depict the inputs, transformation, and output for each process under that function.
2 Examine the state of implementation of business analytics in organisations of any one particular industry in your state. Assume that it has to be modelled using business analytics; attempt to define a problem statement for the same. Also, try listing some preliminary factors which contribute to identification and definition of a problem statement.

Case study

How do people analytics impact business outcomes?

People analytics has become mainstream, and organisations globally believe that collecting people data drives better results and organisational growth. A survey by one of the leading firms in India revealed that only 9% of the firms applying analytics are aware of the talent dimensions which have an impact on organisational performance (Leonardi and Contractor, 2018). Most organisations adopt a narrow approach to data analytics, focusing on data about people rather than the interplay among people. 'Relational analytics', an emerging stream in HR analytics, reveals insights based on this interplay, digging into any data which marks communication between the people in the organisation; for example, data exchanges using emails, organisational communicator, file transfers, and so on. Although this data is available in abundance with almost all organisations, very few organisations actually track it and even fewer apply analytics to it, and this data has important implications for workplace performance. In one such case, Leonardi and Contractor labelled this link between relationships among people in an organisation, individual traits and their workplace performance as 'structural signatures', especially relevant in team-based organisations, discerning what constitutes a high performing team, and then use the same for future prediction and modelling. Leonardi and Contractor applied relational analytics to predict about a person – whether he would be an innovator or an influential person; about the team – efficient, or innovative; and about the organisation – siloed or vulnerable. They were termed as six signatures of relational analytics by the authors.

Innovators have 'low constraint', as demonstrated by sociologist Ronald Burt, not restricted to a small group of people. Therefore, relational analytics predicts the individuals with a wide social network, with many connections outside one's own team and department, as innovators. In Figure 1.5, higher intensities of the

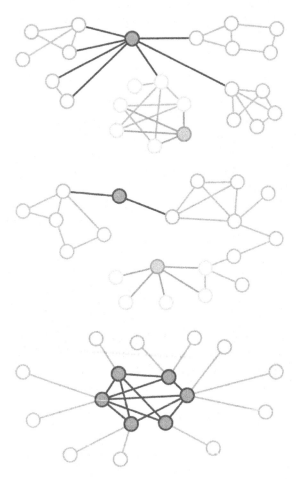

FIGURE 1.5 The six signatures of relational analytics: ideation signature (1.5a), influence signature (1.5b), efficiency signature (1.5c), innovation signature (1.5d), silo signature (1.5e), vulnerability signature (1.5f)

Source: Leonardi and Contractor (2018)

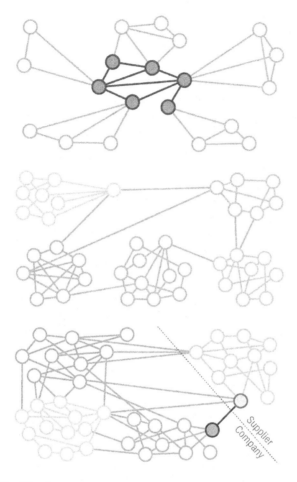

FIGURE 1.5 (Continued)

grey colour in the circle represent innovators, while lighter shades represent idea-tors. When an organisation identifies such individuals and cultivates their signature tendency, they are likely to come up with better business outcomes through the novelty of their ideas and solutions.

Further relational analytics based on the number and diversity of connections, predicts whether individuals are 'influencers', representing the effectiveness of an individual in influencing people's behaviour in the firm. This signature is especially useful when an organisation faces employee resistance and change management.

Similarly, when relational analytics is applied to team structures, teams can have efficiency or innovation signature, depicted in Figure 1.5c and Figure 1.5d, respec-tively, based on two premises of network composition – internal density (strength of interconnections) and external range (overlap among connections outside one's own network). The team members with high internal density and high external range imply access to wider and diverse external resources and efficient team performance. This is labelled as 'efficiency signature'. Such team members consistently depict high performance.

On the flip side, a low internal density and high external range imply that the team would be innovative. The only consideration is the demarcation between how low and how high since a complete disconnect among team members would drop the efficiency to almost zero, while complete connectedness will drop their level of innovativeness. When an organisation is unable to bring diversity through attributes like age, gender, and ethnicity in a team, an attempt should be made to pool the team members from different work areas, which will increase their external range.

Often in organisations, the people working in a given work area or department are deeply connected, while the connections with other departments are low. The ratio of external to internal connections of organisational group members is termed as 'modularity'. It is often suggested that when modularity is in the ratio of 5:1, the group is highly siloed. Silos in an organisation act as inhibitors for healthy communication between organisational members, thereby reducing innovativeness and efficiency of the organisation as a whole. Also, due to a lack of connectedness, they often fail to reach a consensus on overall organisational objectives.

Many times, organisations have employees who do not hold important job titles, but their presence is vital to organisational functioning. This is especially prominent in organisations which have employees dealing with clients, customers, suppliers, or other external stakeholders. As is evident in Figure 1.5f, the supplier indicated by light grey circle connects to four different groups in the organisation through connections to only four individuals who are part of that group. This implies that although the supplier connects to four people, a large number of people in the organisation (approximately 30) rely on these four connections. Therefore, even if one of the employees in these four positions leaves, the communication and connectedness will be highly affected. This is termed as the vulnerability of the organisation. Identification of vulnerable employees in an organisation adds to its robustness and allows it to effectively plan for succession planning when the need arises.

Therefore, when organisations effectively capture and analyse the relational data, they can easily identify and thereby predict – at individual, team, and organisational levels – the composition of six signatures of relational analytics, which impact the business outcomes. This information is easily available in the forms of weblogs, e-trails, chats, email exchanges, etc., and therefore can be tracked and analysed easily. Also, since it is passive data collection, it is far easier and more reliable than data collection techniques like surveys and interviews. Two important considerations while implementing relational analytics in any organisation are to constantly update the data, since relationships, communication, and connectedness keep on changing; and to also inculcate the content of exchange to strengthen the understanding of patterns and a signature.

In a nutshell, adopting a narrow approach to data analysis and focusing on simply the attributes of individuals for predicting work outcomes is a thing of the past. The present organisations must analyse the composition of social networks of individuals, teams, and organisations to discern how to predict the six signatures of relational analytics and then exploit them to improve business outcomes. Such an approach would enable them to realise their goals in an efficient and effective manner, while also promoting productivity and happiness throughout the firm.

Questions

1 Define relational analytics. Discuss its relevance to the organisations.
2 Discuss the sources of data for relational analytics. How do they compare with surveys and interviews?
3 Discuss the signatures of relational analytics for individuals and their effect on work performance.
4 Discuss the application of relational analytics for teams and how they can be used to affect work performance.
5 How can relational analytics be used to analyse organisational structure?

Note

1 All tables and figures prepared by the author unless specified otherwise.

Bibliography

Bell, G. (2012). How understanding workforce data can invigorate your organisation? An interview with Tim Ringo, co-author of calculating success. *Human Resource Management International Digest*, 41–43.

Bersin, J. (2017, December 17). *People analytics: Here with a vengeance.* Retrieved May 2019, from Forbes: https://www.forbes.com/sites/joshbersin/2017/12/16/people-analytics-here-with-a-vengeance/#48dad6332a14

Boyd, A. E. (2012, July/August 6). Profit center: Revisiting 'what is analytics'. *Analytics Magazine*. Retrieved 2018, from http://analytics-magazine.org/profit-center-revisiting what-is-analytics/.INFORMS

Caesars. (2019). *Caesars history.* Retrieved from Caesars Entertainment: https://www.cae sars.com/corporate

Cascio, W., and Boudreau, J. (2011). Making HR measurement strategic. In W. Cascio and J. Boudreau (Eds.), *Investing in people: Financial impact of human resource initiatives* (pp. 10–14). Hoboken, NJ: Pearson Education, Inc.

Concentrix. (2019). *Who is Concentrix?* Retrieved from Concentrix: https://www.concen trix.com/different-by-design/

Dasgupta, S. (2017, February). Trends in top Indian IT companies – from hiring to attrition. *NDTV Profit.* Retrieved 2018, from http://profit.ndtv.com/news/tech-media-telecom/ article-trends-in-top- indian-it-companies-from-hiring-to-attrition-1659231

Davenport, T. H., and Harris, J. G. (2007). *Competing on analytics: The new science of winning.* Boston, MA: Harvard Business School Press.

Davenport, T. H., Harris, J., and Shapiro, J. (2010, October). Competing on talent analytics. *Harvard Business Review.* Vol. 88(10), pp.52-58.

Dessler, G., and Varkkey, B. (2008). *Human resource management* (11th ed.). Manipal: Pearson Education, Inc.

Dow. (2020). *About – changing how the world works.* Retrieved from Dow Chemicals: https://corporate.dow.com/en-us/about.html

Experian. (2020). *Experian at a glance.* Retrieved from Experian: https://www.experian.in/about-us

Feffer, M. (2018). *5 barriers to creating data-driven HR – and how to overcome them.* Retrieved 2019, from TechTarget: https://searchhrsoftware.techtarget.com/feature/5-barriers-to-creating-data-driven-HR-and-how-to-overcome-them

Flippo, E. B. (1984). From mechanics to social responsibility. In E. B. Flippo (Ed.), *Personnel management* (pp. 1–42). Singapore: McGraw-Hill Book Company.

Harris, J. G., Craig, E., and Light, D. A. (2011). Talent and analytics: New approaches, higher ROI. *Journal of Business Strategy*, 4–13.

IBEF. (2018, February). *IT & ITeS industry in India.* IBEF – Indian Brand Equity Foundation. Retrieved 2018, from www.ibef.org/industry/information-technology-india.aspx

IBM. (2011). *Strategic workforce management using predictive analytics.* New York: IBM Software Business Analytics.

Leonardi, P., and Contractor, N. (2018, November). Better people analytics. *Harvard Business Review*, 70–81.

Levenson, A., and Pillans, G. (2017). *Strategic workforce analytics.* London: Corporate Research Forum.

Marler, J. H., and Boudreau, J. W. (2017). An evidence-based review of HR analytics. *The International Journal of Human Resource Management*, 3–26.

Nielsen. (2020). *About US.* Retrieved from N – Nielsen Global Connect: https://www.nielsen.com/us/en/about-us/

Nelson, G. (2017, July 7). Difference between analytics and big data, data science and informatics. *ThotWave Blog.* Retrieved 2018 from www.thotwave.com/blog/2017/ 07/07/difference-between-analytics-and-bigdatadatascience-informatics/

Power, D. J. (2002). *Decision support systems: Concepts and resources for managers.* Westport, CT: Quorum Books.

Raj, S. (2015). Data mining. In S. Raj (Ed.), *Business analytics* (pp. 311–327). New Delhi: Cengage Learning India Pvt. Ltd.

Reliance. (2019). *Company profile – overview.* Retrieved from Reliance Power: https://www.reliancepower.co.in/web/reliance-power/company-overview

Sysco. (2019). *The Sysco story.* Retrieved from Sysco: https://www.sysco.com/About/Company-Profile/The-Sysco-Story.html

Taylor, F. W. (2006). *The principles of scientific management.* New York: Cosimo, Inc.

Valacich, J., and George, J. (2017). The systems development environment. In J. Valacich, J. George, and J. Slater (Eds.), *Modern systems analysis and design* (p. 6). Harlow: Pearson Education Ltd.

Wilder, C. R., and Ozgur, C. O. (2015). Business analytics curriculum for undergraduate majors. *INFORMS Transactions on Education, 15*(2), 180–187.

2
LOOKING FOR DATA

After reading this chapter, users will be able to understand the following key concepts:

- Elucidate the difference between data and information
- Understand different HR data sources available to a business manager
- Infer various obtrusive and unobtrusive techniques of data collection
- Understand the need and means to quantify HR data
- Understand the use of HR scorecards in analytics and quantification of data
- Elucidate role and types of qualitative HR data
- Infer ethical and legal concerns in HR data collection

Opening case

Although career progression is a key priority area for employees of any organisation, they often lack a clear understanding of how to progress along the career ladder. Typically, organisations conduct performance appraisals, based on which employees are promoted along a career path and nominated for skill development programmes specifically designed for the new career role. At IBM, traditionally, employees' skills have been formally assessed through surveys as the skills possessed by an employee were rated by their respective managers. However, these surveys are limited by subjective ratings of the managers and the extent of coverage of all the skills possessed by an employee. Further, performance appraisals were conducted annually. As such, IBM CEO Ginni Rometty was apprehensive about the efficiency of these traditional techniques of performance appraisal and skill assessment. IBM needed a way to redesign these HR functions to indicate to both employee and management – the current skills in demand which employees possess or can be trained for, and an efficient appraisal feedback mechanism for the employees to indicate their areas of improvement.

At IBM, rather than the employee struggling to find a suitable skill development programme, artificial intelligence (AI) and analytics are used to integrate performance appraisal, feedback, and suggestions for an appropriate programme for skill development. IBM's AI can effectively mine the current strengths of an individual based on the identification of patterns in data on tasks that an individual has completed, educational courses that they have taken, and the rankings that they have earned. These data patterns are then associated with adjacent or similar skill sets, and then appropriate recent training programmes are suggested to the user. Further, management updates employees' skills growth quarterly, highlighting the areas for future improvements. Data on these updates, combined with AI skill inference of an employee, is used by a technology called Blue Match at IBM which lists all the job openings in the firm suitable for that employee. Therefore, rather than relying on managerial surveys, IBM looked for alternate data sources for the career development of their employees (Rosenbaum, 2019).

Introduction

Sheri Feinzig, director of the IBM Smarter Workforce Institute, beautifully sums up the sufficiency of data by suggesting that an analyst should never wait for perfect data and stop moving forward, since no dataset is perfect. Further, she stressed that size of data also doesn't matter, and analysts should just focus on the quality of data for which expert advice can be sought. Ensuring that data fundamentals are assessed accurately, an analyst can think of moving forward with that data (Levenson and Pillans, 2017).

Since the beginning of time, business managers have been confronted with the problem of taking business decisions, regardless of the level of management. In the past, they could base these decisions on their judgement and intuition, since the amount of competition was very low and the time to take a decision was huge. However, in contrast, the present business environment poses a lot of uncertainties for the business managers, shrinking the time to take decisions to real-time decision-making. The uncertainties arise owing to enormous competition in the market, increasing customer demands, and decreasing time to market, in addition to the economic ups and downs. Further, the uncertainty is heightened when the manager is unable to judge which data to rely on to make decisions, since decision-making today has moved from intuition-based decisions to fact-based and towards real-time decision-making. Imagine a situation in which an HR manager receives a resignation application from an employee, and the manager has to decide whether to approve or reject the application. The basis for such a decision should not be based on intuition, since the performance of the candidate and his credentials would allow the manager to accurately decide whether the employee is a good fit for the firm at present or not, and therefore, decide whether to accept or reject the application to resign. Therefore, the HR manager needs quick access to data about the employee, his past performance, ratings, postings, projects worked on, and other such credentials. Only then would the manager be able to make a sound decision of approval or rejection of the application. Consider the separation process carried out by Google (Leonardi and Contractor, 2018). When an employee applies for resignation, the company uses employee's past performance data to generate a performance metric for that employee and also computes a likelihood score of success of the employee in future work endeavours. Based on these two metrics, the HR managers at Google decide whether to allow the employee to quit and therefore, accept or reject his resignation. The key implication from this discussion is that for managers to take accurate decisions, they need to collect and interpret relevant data. The process of data collection can be aided through the use of information systems, while the process of interpretation can be aided through analytical systems which analyse the data and generate scenarios for the decision-maker to weigh different decision-making options. In the example of Google's separation process, the data about employee's past performances can be fetched from HRIS (human resource information system), while an analytical algorithm can be used to generate a performance metric and metric suggesting likelihood of his future success. This further clarifies that although managers have to take decisions in real time, they need data to make a sound judgement and in this context, look around to infer which data fits their decision-making needs.

The prominent barriers in data collection for application of workforce analytics are:

- Poor integration of human capital systems internally and with other organisational systems
- Inability to extract relevant information from these systems
- Inexperienced HR professionals
- Questionable quality of data collected
- Unwillingness to use and extract information
- Lack of support from top management

The key to decision-making by business managers lies in making fact-based decisions and to enable the decision-making quickly and in real time; thus, it is required that data be gathered, updated, and stored at a relatively fast pace. Now, HR managers have the most burdening task of 'hiring and retaining' the best-in-class employees for a firm – and they also collect very high volumes of employee data, but lack awareness about effective utilisation of that data. As a study by IBM (2018) reveals, that the HR managers perceive that they face a lot of barriers in using human capital and workforce data to take workforce decisions. The most prominent of these barriers is poor integration of human capital systems, and poor integration of the same with other organisational systems; inability to extract relevant information from these systems owing to inexperienced HR professionals lacking the necessary skills to extract information; and the questionable quality of data collected. Further, unwillingness to use and extract information and lack of support from top management also contributes to the barriers in the use of workforce data to make decisions. This implies that HR managers lack a basic understanding of working around the HR data to make decisions, and this is enhanced when the data collection and storage is irrelevant, siloed and inaccessible. **If an HR manager is equipped with the necessary skills of business analytics, he would be able to identify business problems, model them, and point the data sources and their relevance to solve the business problem at hand.**

This chapter will therefore aid the managers in understanding how to extract relevant information from abundant data lying around them to make workforce decisions. In this context, the chapter in the following sections will shed light on sources and techniques for collection of data through different data sources.

Data versus information

It is very important to build an understanding of the difference between data and information before a user can apply analytics to a business problem. **Data is raw in nature and available in abundance, unorganised, and insignificant in its original form. Unless a context is applied to raw data, it doesn't yield any purpose.** However, when this data is processed to fit into a context or purpose of use by someone or something, the data becomes information. For example, a firm is looking for individuals who can fill vacancies in a managerial position in its sales department, from among salespeople already working with the firm. Now it has been decided by the management that the fulfilment of these vacancies would be based on a given salesman's experience, number of projects, number of product varieties handled, and the number of his sales contacts; all of which available in the firm's information system. However, until there was a requirement to extract all this from the database, it would be termed as 'data' since, in itself, it has no significance. When the management decides to evaluate this data to base its decision of choosing candidates for the fulfilment of vacancies, it becomes information. The difference between data and information is demonstrated in Table 2.1.

Consider a typical bill printed by a point-of-sale (PoS) system at any retail store. The bill contains details such as customer number; date of sale; cashier number; time; item details such as item code, quantity purchased, unit price, and the total amount charged for each item; mode of payment; and so on. All these PoS transactions are structured in a specific format and stored in a transaction table in the store's database as depicted in Table 2.2.

The details in the table are 'data' since in itself it has no significance for any entity. However, when these details are aggregated at the end of each day, to generate accumulated details such as total quantity sold per item, total sales per item, total sales per cashier, total sales per store, and so on, they become 'information', as shown in Table 2.3. For example, total units of Maggi Noodles sold in the number of units is five, with total sales of 300 rupees. This can aid the store manager to decide the number of units to be procured for inventory, revenue per item, and so on.

TABLE 2.1 Difference between data and information

S.No.	Basis	Data	Information
1	Definition	Raw variables holding no significance on their own	Data which fits into specific context/decision-making needs
2	Supports decision-making	Cannot be used in its raw form	Widely used as a basis for decision-making
3	Significance	Insignificant in its original form	Significant for decision-making
4	Representation	May take several forms such as in tabular, graphical, lists, etc.	Expressed as an interpretation, usually narration or description
5	Relatedness to other things	Not related to any other thing	Depicts relatedness/ connectedness among variables

Source: Bellinger, Castro, and Mills (2004)

TABLE 2.2 Raw data in transactions

Transaction #	Item Name	Quantity Sold	Unit Price	Amount Charged
1	Maggi Noodles 450 gm	1	60	60
1	Pril Liquid 140 ml	2	27	54
2	Little Heart Bis 48 gm	5	10	50
3	Maggi Noodles 450 gm	4	60	240
3	Vivel Perfect 20 gm	1	69	69
4	Little Heart Bis 48 gm	10	10	100

Now that the difference between data and information is clear, the second aspect which requires complete clarity is the knowledge of variables involved in any analysis. As in Table 2.3, information depicts total sales, both in the number of units and currency for a particular item available with the store. This quantification of data resulted in two variables: sales in units and sales in currency.

Data collection – sources

Once the business manager understands the business problem, the next step is to look for data to explain and find a solution to that problem. This section discusses some of the pertinent sources of HR data, categorised as internal and external.

Internal data sources

Internal data source implies those data sources which are present within the boundary and control of an organisational system. It is very important to have a strong and integrated IT infrastructure in the organisation to be able to access internal

TABLE 2.3 Extracted information from raw data

Item name	Total sales in units	Total sales in rupees
Maggi Noodles 450 gm	5	300
Little Heart Bis 48 gm	15	150
Pril Liquid 140 ml	2	54
Vivel Perfect 20 gm	1	69
Total sales		**573**
Total units sold	23	

data sources. A business problem in HRM often cannot be solved and explained in isolation, as all the functional areas of a firm work in an interdependent manner. So it is apparent that a problem visible in one functional area may have origin, consequences, or impact on other areas in a firm. Here, infrastructure plays a crucial role in the integration and streamlining of data generated from all functional areas.

Information systems data

The most pertinent of all internal data sources are data generated from **business systems of different functional areas.** Information systems of different functional areas implemented in an organisation serve as the most important and sought-after source in an organisation. But it is relevant as a data source only when it contains periodically updated and reliable data. The interdependence of data different from different functional areas can be well understood through an example. A marketing information system contains data for all the marketing-related functions carried out in a firm, such as pricing, product, placement, and promotion strategies. For any new product development, the firm has to arrange for suitable personnel who have the relevant skills to develop, promote, and market that product. For this, it needs data from the HR information system to chalk out how many employees the firm has with the relevant skill set and if they are assigned to a project or are available for this new product development. In case no employee is available for this development, the firm will need to outsource personnel. For this, it needs data from finance information system to evaluate whether it has the required budget to hire new employees. This example demonstrates the interdependence of functional information system and how the data integrated across these functions can provide a solution to a business problem.

CORPORATE SNAPSHOT: INTERNAL HR DATA SOURCE

A leading multinational shoe retailer Clarks (2020) sought to establish whether there exists a relationship between employee engagement and financial performance of the firm. The retailer sells more than 50 million pairs of shoes each year, enabled through a strong logistics and distribution system. The firm attributes this rate of performance to its employees in the distribution system that ensures the right stock is available at the right place at the right time. It is therefore understandable that to discern how employee engagement at retailer's store drives financial performance, it sought to analyse data from retailer's distribution planning system and included a total of 450 data points on business performance from this system. Several important insights were gained through this analysis, such as that the financial performance of the store was dependent on tenure of the store manager and the team size in a store. Based on these findings derived from the distribution system of the firm, it was able to develop an engagement toolkit for its managers to improve store performance through increased employee engagement.

Data from wearable sensors

Wearable sensors are an outcome of the concept of the Internet of Things. These sensors are devices worn by an individual and are used to collect information about certain variables related to individual performance and movement. Generally, sensors adorned by employees at the workplace are used to track employee movement and productivity, to improve individual performance and drive organisational growth (Bersin, Mariani, and Monahan, 2016). By the use of sensors, their pattern of movement, communication, and travelling, teamwork can be discerned, which can be used to make the work environment more productive. Other possible areas where sensor data can be used are to relocate the employees based on their movement patterns, understand which task types a group of employees prefer, automated temperature adjustments in a room based on how cool or hot employees are feeling in a room, and the possibility of analysing a team without any individual identification or involvement of a team member. The biggest challenge in this form of data collection is convincing the employees to wear devices containing sensors and winning their trust that the data collection will not invade their privacy and security.

CORPORATE SNAPSHOT: SENSOR DATA FOR HR

As an experiment, Deloitte recruited workplace volunteers who would wear badges equipped with sensors to monitor their location, voice, and movement. Analysis of voice-enabled sensors enabled the firm to understand when workers were under stress, and associated this with location of the employee, who they are with, the current event such as a meeting, etc. Based on these findings, Deloitte could deduce that people are happier working in small groups, prefer offices with more windows and light, and expected conference rooms to be large. This way, it could redesign workspaces and notice significant changes in employee productivity.

Data from internal networks – social networking or mobile data

Many big and small organisations run their internal networks allowing the employees to communicate and exchange data on **messengers**, write **blogs**, express their opinions, and connect with the management. This data aids the organisations to understand how employees communicate and interact with each other, which topics they are frequently discussing in their interactions and blogs, and what management-related issues they are experiencing. All of this can be put to good use by the organisations to gain unprecedented insights into organisational behaviour and dynamics. Similarly, the **call log data** collected from official calls made at the workplace or conversations between call centre employees and the clients can be used to understand what makes a call effective and results in positive feedback from the clients. This can be then used to design effective training programmes to teach the employees about how to interact with the clients. Similarly, **employee voice platforms** such as grievance redressal forums or software platforms which allow employees to voice their concerns and grievances can be used to understand the recurring managerial issues that employees are talking about.

CORPORATE SNAPSHOT: INTERNAL NETWORKS DATA FOR HR

Employees working in call centres are dispersed throughout a day so that they can attend a maximum number of calls at their desks, and this inhibits the chances of these employees connecting. However, by analysing their communications on internal networks, it was found that the engagement levels and productivity of these employees were the highest after lunch when they all got a chance to connect. In turn, the firm offered them connecting intervals throughout a day for tea, lunch, etc., where they could communicate with each other, resulting in a significant drop in stress levels and increase in employee productivity.

External data sources

The data sources which are beyond the control of a firm are termed as external data sources. Most often a firm incurs a cost to acquire this data; for example, hiring a firm to conduct surveys or purchasing a published report or buying data from third-party data collection firms. Some of the pertinent external data sources have been discussed.

Business surveys

Many private firms operating multinationally organise surveys and collect data on behalf of a firm. Employee surveys are usually structured to gauge employee perceptions regarding organisational issues. Some of the prominent companies which conduct surveys for organisations worldwide are Gallup, Nielsen, and MacKenzie, to name a few. All of these are headquartered outside India and operate globally. For example, Gallup – based in Washington DC – not only collects data about customer and employees in a country, but also provides analytics and advisory services. Generally, the cost of conducting a survey is based on the number of respondents to be covered in the survey, and for organisations, the cost also varies by the type of respondent, that is, the cost of surveying managers is higher than employees. Further, the cost also varies with the number of locations to be covered.

A survey reveals greater insights about people and organisational dynamics when structured properly, following the design objectives. Therefore, great care needs to be taken while designing a survey, to inculcate the objectives of conducting a survey, while also keeping in mind the needs of the audience. For example, organisational jargon should only be included when conducting an organisation-wide survey. If the survey needs to include respondents beyond the organisation, such as external stakeholders like suppliers or logistics partners, then they might not be aware of organisational jargon. In such a case, the survey needs to exclude jargon.

CORPORATE SNAPSHOT: SURVEYS FOR HR ANALYTICS

At Google (Leonardi and Contractor, 2018), one of the programmes under Project Oxygen was an attempt to flatten the organisation and eliminate hierarchies. The company first needed to determine the employee perception about the need for a manager in the firm. For this, they designed and administered surveys to take feedback from employees about their managers. In addition to this survey data, Google also included managers' performance ratings and productivity metrics, already available in its database. The analysis revealed that when employees perceived their managers to be great in performance and leadership qualities, their team productivity was higher. This implied that there was a need for managers, and therefore, the firm abandoned the idea of removing managerial levels from the firm.

Published research

Research articles or research reports published by independent third-party organisations provide plenty of insights on environmental dynamics. This is often used by the organisations to gain industry perspective of a particular organisational issue. For example, turnover has been a pertinent issue for the IT industry. To determine the magnitude of the problem of turnover being faced by an organisation, the company can compare its turnover rate with industry-wide turnover rates published in research reports. Further, published articles can also provide information to model a problem; that is, to understand the causes and consequences of an organisational issue. For example, Clarks (2020), which is a leading shoe retailer worldwide, attempted to increase employee engagement to improve overall store performance. For this, it correlated various atmospheric factors of the store with employee attitudes and engagement levels. Some of the major findings were that the tenure of team managers and optimum team size directly impacts employee engagement and productivity at the store. Similarly, if management doesn't heed employee perceptions about the music played at the store, it directly impacts employee performance. Similar findings can be used by another retailer to improve its employee engagement and overall store performance. Often, such published research paves way for preliminary inquiry into an organisational problem.

One major factor to be considered while using this as a data source is to determine the authenticity of the research report. Further, the relevance of the research also needs to be considered. For example, the findings from the Clarks case can be applied for preliminary investigations for any retailer with store formats. But for e-tailers like Amazon, the relevance of the Clarks case is questionable as the mode of operation is different for both the firms.

CORPORATE SNAPSHOT: PUBLISHED RESEARCH FOR HR ANALYTICS

Cisco (2020) has used published research on demographic data to determine the location to open new offices. It uses this external data source to find the locations with high availability of key talent, large numbers of educational institutes offering related educational graduation programmes so that the firm can hire new graduates, and where cost and occupancy rate of office space is low; therefore, the number of competing recruiters in the area are also low.

Data from external social networks/web/mobiles

The proliferation of Internet use at the workplace is widely evident and acceptable at many organisations today. Apart from being present and participating in conversations on internal networks of an organisation, employees have been present on external networks, whether professional networks like LinkedIn and Academia, or un-professional like community forums like Twitter, to name one. This has been a cause of concern and an issue of debate for organisations, since it is still not conclusive whether participation on external social networks at the workplace contributes or hinders employee productivity. However, this data can be put to good use by the organisation to understand employee dynamics and interaction dynamics. Social network analysis is a separate stream of HR analytics which attempts to interpret the employee social networks, built through either web, mobile, or social networking sites, both within and outside the organisation. Typically, such an analysis reveals who are the most influencing employees in a firm who act as connectors in and outside a firm. For situations requiring effective change management, such individuals can serve as change agents aiding the organisation to cope with and manage employee resistance during organisational change. Such data often includes messages exchanged by employees through social networks or email, and identifies individuals in the firm with the greatest number of connections and the strength of these connections (how often communication takes place along a particular connection).

Analysis of this data also reveals the internal structure of an organisation. Although HR often depicts organisational structure as a hierarchy, social network analysis has a different story to tell. Most organisations are now drifting from hierarchical siloed organisations towards interdependent and connected firms. Social network analysis provides an insight into the actual roles played and tasks accomplished by people in a firm, and how information and work flows across the organisation. Gaining an understanding of these players in a firm through social network analysis can aid in effective development and retention of these people and their informal networks.

The only concern in using this data is the ethical and legal consequences of tapping emails or private messages of the employees, especially the exchanges which occur on external networks. Employees often perceive it as a breach of trust and security, which directly impacts employee loyalty and commitment to the firm. One way to overcome this issue is to inform and obtain the consent of the employee before using such data. This has been discussed in greater detail in the next section of this chapter.

CORPORATE SNAPSHOT: EXTERNAL NETWORK DATA FOR HR ANALYTICS

Cigna (2019), an American health services firm operating globally, applied social network analytics to identify employees who are the most prominent 'connectors'. Then it surveyed the stakeholders (with which these connectors connected with) to understand their perception of the impact on the firm if these connectors left the firm. Based on these findings, they designed a retention and reward strategy for such employees. The management also admitted that often a firm fails to notice these top connectors as the management generally focuses on its favourites, and therefore, analytics enables them to rethink breaking the conventions.

Data collection – techniques

Edwards Deming believes that without data, you are just another person with an opinion (Deming, 2019). It is highly important to back up your opinions with data. Effective collection of data is one of the most important steps to yield meaningful results after the application of analytics. To avoid ambiguity in the results and outcomes of an analytical solution, it is a must that the data input to the solution is reliable. Therefore, the assessment of an appropriate data collection technique is as important as the identification of the source of data. Although data is available in plenty, how to collect and obtain relevant data is also a technique. The data collection techniques can be broadly categorised into obtrusive/interactive and unobtrusive techniques. Obtrusive techniques include all methods used to collect data through some form of interaction with the individual, especially when the purpose of the interaction is not always clearly communicated, while unobtrusive techniques include all methods whereby the interaction for data collection with the respondents is minimal. All the possible methods of data collection are enlisted in Figure 2.1.

Obtrusive methods of data collection

The first technique in an interactive method is **interviewing**. What an individual can elicit by conducting interviews depends on his abilities and understanding and

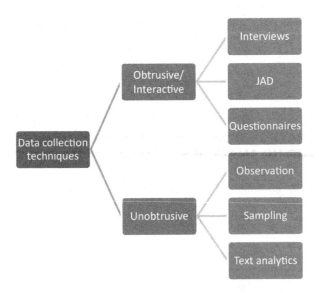

FIGURE 2.1   Data collection techniques

Source: Kendall and Kendall (2018)

communication of the context of an interview to the interviewee. For this, the interviewer needs thorough preparation:

- by reading and gaining as much information about the business problem as possible through background material available like annual reports, fact sheets, existing literature, previous interviews, any available related publications, and source on the Internet;
- then the interviewer needs to chalk out the objectives and goals of the interview and select the appropriate candidates;
- finally, the interviewer needs to choose whether he will follow unstructured or structured interview style, and based on this, he will draft a basic questionnaire to conduct interviews. Further, he also needs to chalk out medium of conducting the interview – face to face, telephonically, or through a virtual connection.

Emphasising on the importance of interviewing or 'asking questions', David Creelman, who heads Creelman Research Group, says that unless one asks many questions to get under the skin of what issue someone is looking to solve, it is not going to serve any purpose. It is important to not just give people the data they ask for – and think they want (Levenson and Pillans, 2017).

It should be kept in mind that if the number of people to be interviewed is smaller, then interviews are a feasible option; else if the number of respondents is large, conducting interviews will be a tedious process, with the potential to introduce bias since those already interviewed may attempt to bias further responses by impressing upon the favourability of their ideas.

The second method is through administering **questionnaires**. This can be done either manually, or through the use of the Internet like Google forms, WhatsApp link, Facebook posts, and so on. When designing a questionnaire, the interviewer chooses open-ended, closed-ended, or use of both types of questions in the questionnaire design. When a limited number of answers to a question are possible, use of close-ended questions is advised, and conversely, when many answers to a question are possible, use of open-ended questions is advised. The sequence or logical arrangement of the questions is also important while designing the questionnaire. Also, it should be kept in mind to not make it too lengthy, complex, and confusing. The wording of the questions should be simple and easily interpretable, and the design should avoid the use of ambiguous words or statements. When questionnaires are used, responses can be quantified through the use of scales and coding, as discussed in the following section.

Through interviews, user stories can also be garnered, which can be experiential like what happened when some business problem occurred, and mostly enlists the personal experience of the individual; explanatory, when individuals are able to state a reason or an explanation for the organisational response to business problem; validating, which is attaching value to organisational response and convincing that it is correct; and prescriptive, when individual makes suggestions of what could have been done instead of the current action.

The final technique is **joint application design (JAD)**. A typical JAD session involves many participants who can articulate their needs and problems well, regardless of the position that they hold, an individual who leads the group, one who acts as a scribe, and one who steers the group in the right direction. Although widely used in system analysis and design, the technique is immensely beneficial, since many participants are interviewed all at once, such that many interview outcomes can be compared one against another at the same time, enabling the presentation of many new solutions for a given problem and supporting joint problem-solving behaviour.

The choice of method would depend on:

- **Availability of appropriate time for data collection** – For example, an interview takes a longer time compared to administering the questionnaire, while questionnaires can be administered to many respondents at once. Also, consider whether there are appropriate resources with the organisation to call participants for a joint interview session such as JAD to brainstorm over the business problem.
- **Possibility of interacting with each respondent** – If the number of respondents is large, then the possibility of reaching out to all or conducting a JAD session is very low, and the only feasible option whereby interaction with respondents is required is the use of questionnaires.
- **When the interaction is the only way to find a solution** – In some situations, it is difficult to gain a complete understanding of our own of the problem; therefore, talks and interactions with actual staff are required to build a complete picture of the problem at hand. In such cases, obtrusive methods come in handy.
- The number of respondents to explain a business problem and find a solution.

SNAPSHOT: REAL-WORLD CORPORATE EXAMPLES FOR DATA COLLECTION TECHNIQUES

A large restaurant chain sought ways to improve business outcomes, owing to poor financial performance. However, it did not have a data backup to find reasons for the same from organisational data. So it hired consultants who decided to conduct a survey. For this, they first listed the key business outcomes which need to be improved and then worked backwards to design a survey, containing questions to measure perspectives on employee engagement which would affect these outcomes. The association between the scores of the surveys and business outcomes were used to assess what drives the performance of the restaurants. These way strategies to improve restaurants' performance were devised.

A multinational shoe retailer was attempting to optimise its benefits packages, by tailoring them to the needs of the employees. For this purpose, they conducted employee interviews asking them which benefits they are willing to trade-off. This helped the firm gain deep insights into what employee value what most in their benefits packages.

A shoe retailer with high levels of employee engagement established through quantitative analysis that a relationship exists between employee engagement and financial performance. Now it sought to uncover which underlying factors lead a particular store to perform better than others. For this, it conducted qualitative analysis in which it invited representatives from store managers and store employees from top-performing stores and conducted brainstorming sessions. In these sessions, the participants were required to list the factors of the store or management, which they think contributed to high performance. An interesting outcome was that frequent transfers of managers among different stores resulted in poor performance.

Source: Vulpen (2018)

Unobtrusive methods

A major limitation of obtrusive methods is the potential to distort the actual information by changing the scenario where the problem is present. When someone tries to obtain perspectives towards a problem that they are facing, the perspective automatically shifts (maybe slightly) since the respondent is now aware that someone is talking about their problem. Therefore, unobtrusive methods prevent such distortion. However, they always need to be paired with interactive methods to yield meaningful outcomes.

The most basic unobtrusive method of data collection is **observation**. By observing the people involved in a business problem, much can be explained. For example, if a manager keenly observes his subordinates at work, he can state their work tendencies and gain an insight into their general attitude towards job, role, tasks, and organisation. If a subordinate is observed to be slow at performing tasks, but is consistent and reports on time, then his overall attitude is positive, although his efficacy might be low. Such insights can be further used to determine job outcomes and organisational outcomes. Observing that an individual is prone to reporting late, or absenteeism at work, might imply his tendency towards quitting the organisation. With some additional data and analysis, this tendency to quit can be predicted.

The second technique is **sampling**. When it is not possible to reach out to all the respondents and a business problem affects the entire organisation, then data is collected from a few respondents who are believed to be representative of the entire population. This is termed as a sample. The advantages of using sampling are that it reduces costs since entire population need not be reached, speeds up the process of data collection, and effectiveness of collected data can be increased through sampling by including those respondents in the sample who matter the most in the business problem. A typical sampling design includes the following elements:

- **Sample population** – This includes identifying all the potential candidates for data collection and typically is specified as 'how many'. For example, the problem in this book addresses the problem of turnover of software engineers in IT firms, working at the first three levels of the firm. Therefore, the population would include all software engineers working at the first three levels in IT companies in the entire country, India. An approximate number is to be typically provided here. This number may be obtained from secondary data sources. In case the data is to be mined out from text documents, then the population would list the data sources and how many documents are available.
- **Sample size** – Since the response from the entire population cannot be elicited and is not also useful, a sample of representative candidates is chosen for data collection. Many formulas are available to compute the sample size, based on the sample population and level of significance. Level of significance or confidence level implies how much error is acceptable in data collection from the sample. For example, if a 5% level is chosen, this implies that the sample may include 5% erroneous samples, but this is acceptable to the analyst. Often, a third attribute considered to determine sample size is variability or heterogeneity in the sample. The more diverse the population a sample has, the larger would be the sample size. Typically for a small population (~200), a census is best for data collection. For larger than this, the sample size needs to be determined. There are two ways to determine the sample size. One way is to look at tables which list appropriate sample size for a given level of significance and total population, while the other way is to use a formula (Israel, 1992). While conducting interviews, a rule of thumb is to interview at least three people at every level of the organisation and at least one from each functional area of the organisation.
- **Type of sample** – Once the sample size is determined; the user has to determine the technique of sample collection. The two broad classes of sample collection are based on probability sampling or non-probability sampling. Further categorisation of these classes is presented in Figure 2.2.

Probability sampling

When all the elements have a certain chance of being included in the sample, it is known as probability sampling. The simplest form of probability sampling is simple random sampling. Typically, using random tables, samples are picked from a population. Random sampling ensures that each element has an equal chance of appearing in the sample. Systematic random sampling implies using a system to

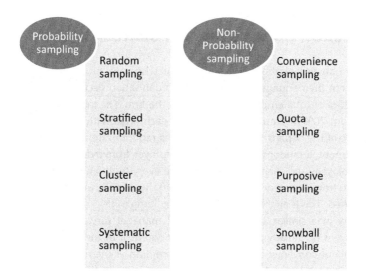

FIGURE 2.2 Methods of sampling

Source: Sekaran and Bougie (2016)

pick up samples randomly. For example, the researcher decides to pick up every 'n-th' element from the population. Stratified random sampling is usually used when heterogeneity in data is high. It involves determining 'stratas', or sub-groups from the population, based on a stratification element. The size of each stratum can be proportional to the size of the strata in the population or disproportional. This way, the sampling design can be a proportional stratified or a disproportional stratified random sampling, respectively. Cluster sampling is used when the population can be divided into sub-groups which are externally homogeneous but internally heterogeneous. It is often carried out in stages – the first stage involves identification of clusters, and the second stage involves choosing a few clusters to pick up samples.

Non-probability sampling

Non-probability sampling technique is based on picking up the samples such that all elements of the population don't have a certain chance of appearing in the final sample. The most basic form is convenience sampling, implying picking up the samples based on one's convenience. Judgement or purposive sampling involves picking up samples based on one's judgement or to fulfil some purpose. Quota-based sampling involves dividing the population into sub-groups and assigning quotas – a fixed number of samples – to be picked from a sub-group. Snowball sampling involves picking the sample from a known set of respondents and then utilising the contacts of these respondents to further pick the sample from. This is appropriate when the sample has to be collected from a particular stream like engineers only, etc.

SNAPSHOT: EXAMPLES OF CORPORATE SAMPLING

Assume an organisation's HR department wishes to survey the employees to discern their engagement levels. The organisation decides to collect data from 20% of total employees working in the firm. For this, it picks up samples from 20% of employees working in each organisation, proportional to the size of the department. This is stratified random sampling. Now for each department, it randomly picks the first employee from a department-wise list of employees and then decides to include every tenth employee on the list, starting from the random pick to include in the sample, until the desired size is reached. This is an example of systematic sampling.

Now in a similar situation, if the HR manager forwards the survey to employees he already knew, who then forwards it to their contacts, it is an example of convenience and snowball sampling. If the manager decides to divide the total sample size (20% of all employees in the firm) into quotas based on department size, it becomes quota sampling.

The third technique is based on **analysis of text documents**. A lot of data in the organisations and about the organisation is available on the Internet, social media, and other networking sites (both internal and external to the firm). Depending on the access available to an individual to these resources, analytics can be applied to understand sentiments and associated keywords to a given business problem.

Unconventional data collection techniques

Since many unconventional data sources have emerged over the years, data about people are also available on these non-traditional platforms. Most of these data lack structure, which is it does not fit into a predefined format and cannot be accessed and stored using conventional techniques. For example, employee conversations on internal messengers or blogs on a company Intranet cannot be stored in a traditional tabular structure or analysed using traditional statistical techniques. For this purpose, newer ways of collection of data have emerged. One of these techniques is **web scraping**, used for targeted data collection from the web, based on specific terms or keywords of interest, through the use of web crawlers (programme script), and then storing it in a more structured dataset at an appropriate location (Vargiu and Urru, 2012). Using web scraping, data can be collected from the web such as online data from websites, social media, and professional networking sites (Platanou, Mäkelä, Beletskiy, and Colicev, 2018), which are also termed as sources of Big Data in HR. When analytical techniques like 'topic modelling' – a popular mining technique which allows discerning the frequency of the presence of particular topics in a text – is applied to the scraped data, it can serve extensive purposes in HRM, such as for mining job postings related to HR (De Mauro,

Greco, Grimaldi, and Ritala, 2017), or for a particular advent like Industry 4.0 (Pejic-Bach, Bertoncel, Meško, and Krstić, 2019), to identify skills in demand or for semantic analysis of résumés (Necula and Strîmbei, 2019). Web scraping can be carried out by writing programming scripts called crawlers which extract relevant data from the web. The popular languages used to write these scripts are R and Python. An example of web scraping will be discussed in subsequent chapters.

Quantification of data

While there are plenty of books on research methods, detailing out on quantification of data, and development of scales for measurement of a given construct, this book will simply discuss practical and feasible ways in which a business problem analyst can rapidly operationalise a variable and quantify the data for analysis. It is imperative to specify here that dimensionality of constructs under study, issues of scaling, and scale development are beyond the scope of this book, to keep the application of analytics as feasible and easy for the managers as possible.

First and foremost, to quantify any data/variable/object in business management, one needs to visualise some of its attributes or characteristics which can be assigned some number, symbol and possibly be measured. For example, if one wishes to quantify job satisfaction, then first he needs to identify associated attributes or traits of job satisfaction which can be numbered. The attributes of job satisfaction may include satisfaction from the supervisor, from subordinates, from salary, from employee benefits, from career growth opportunities, and so on. **Wherever direct quantification of the variable is not possible, its associated attributes need to be quantified. And sometimes, the business problem requires digging into the attributes of the variable at hand; in that case, the quantification of associated attributes also becomes necessary.** Further, it needs to be understood that some variables can be directly quantified, while others are subjective. Whenever subjective variables need quantification, then the techniques of scaling and rating and ranking of data needs to be done which serves our purpose. Therefore, quantification of variables involves the following:

1 Deciding whether a variable can be directly quantified or otherwise.
2 Identifying associated attributes/characteristics of the variable.
3 Deciding whether attributes are objective or subjective.
4 For subjective variables, deciding how to scale for quantification – nominal, ordinal, interval, or ratio scales.
5 Further, deciding whether a rating scale or ranking scale technique be used for data collection.

Types of scales

The way the data is 'scaled', the depth of information that can be obtained varies. Scaling the data provides a means to categorise the respondents based on the scaled variable and therefore aid in analysis. Let us take a simple example of cricket players who are numbered from 1–11 and each team has its identifying team name such as India or England. Therefore, assigning simple numbers and team names to the players aids in categorising the players into Team India or Team England, and thereby would aid in the comparison of the final scores, as well. Aggregating the scores of all players from Team India and Team England provides a basis for comparison among the scores and deciding the winner of the match. Similarly, the HR data in organisations also needs to be scaled.

Nominal scale

The preceding example of cricket players in a team is an example of a nominal scale. Here categories of respondents are created by simply assigning numbers to the players. When we assign categories or labels or numbers to the data for identification, we create a nominal scale. This scale only allows categorisation, calculation of frequency count, and percentages within categories. It is unable to inform beyond this. In business management problems, this scale is useful when some sort of categorisation is required in the problem.

SNAPSHOT: REAL-WORLD EXAMPLE

For the problem of turnover intention in the text analyses, the turnover intention has to be gauged from three different categories of employees; therefore, assigning employee category to data items is an example of a nominal scale. Similarly, assigning categories of marital status also implies the use of a nominal scale.

Ordinal scale

When the numbering or categories assigned to data items are rank ordered, it is called an ordinal scale. For example, from a bunch of retention benefits offered to the employees, they are asked to indicate the ten most preferred mix of benefits. For this, they rank the benefits listed in the order of 1–10, 1 for most preferred and 10 being least preferred. This is an example of the ordinal scale. In addition to the creation of categories, ordinal scales provide information on the amount of difference between different categories. However, the extent of the differences is not explained by this scale.

SNAPSHOT: REAL-WORLD EXAMPLE

Gauging employee perception at a firm to discern which is the most preferred retention benefit and least preferred retention benefit can be answered using an ordinal scale. But the extent to which the preference differs cannot be answered.

Interval scale

As the name suggests, here the data items are placed between appropriate intervals on a scale. With this, the scale aids in measuring the extent of differences between categories. It also allows performing certain other mathematical operations such as computation of means and standard deviation.

SNAPSHOT: REAL-WORLD EXAMPLE

For example, for each retention benefit, employees are asked to indicate to what extent they agree that they have a preference for that benefit. Responses are to be indicated on an interval scale – strongly agree, agree, neutral, disagree, or strongly disagree – and a score from 5–1, respectively, is assigned to each response.

Now, how many strongly prefer, how many prefer, how many are unconcerned, how may don't prefer, and how many strongly don't prefer a retention benefit can be interpreted by using this scale. However, when we compare the category responses across this scale for the magnitude of difference, it doesn't indicate anything substantial. For example, the difference between 5 and 4 on the scale is the same as between 4 and 3 or between 3 and 2, and so on. So because there is no point of origin, the magnitude of differences across the scale remains the same and represents nothing substantial. However, this scale has high mathematical value, since measures of dispersion, standard deviation, and variance, in addition to measures of central tendency, can be computed using this scale.

Ratio scale

All the limitations of previous scales are overcome in this scale. This scale assumes an origin point 0, thereby aiding in measuring the magnitude of differences, the proportion of differences, and the order. These scales lend themselves to many statistical analysis techniques.

SNAPSHOT: REAL-WORLD EXAMPLE

For example, when we ask the respondents to indicate their age on pre-labelled categories, as shown in what follows, it is an example of a ratio scale:

Please indicate your age:

Below 30 years 30–50 years   50 and above

Similarly, when the respondent is asked for a definite number, is also an example of a ratio scale. For example: number of years of experience in present organisation _____; number of projects worked on _____.

Rating and ranking scales

A rating scale asks the respondent to rate different survey items on the same scale. The most commonly used rating scale is a Likert scale, which allows the respondents to rate a given item on 5–7 balanced responses (depending on whether a 5-point or 7-point scale is chosen), whereby often mid-point of the scale represents 0. The sum or average of the responses to different items on a rating scale represents the total score of a particular construct. A ranking scale, on the other hand, asks the respondents to rate all the survey items on the same scale, according to his/her preference. The rank for each item is interpreted individually, and usually indicates the importance of an item towards complete construct.

SNAPSHOT: REAL-WORLD EXAMPLE OF THE RANKING SCALE

A ranking scale for the same would be: On a scale of 1–5, rank the following items according to your perception of their importance towards overall job satisfaction: salary ___; supervisor attitude ___; organisational benefits ___; career advancement opportunities ___; job position ____.

SNAPSHOT: REAL-WORLD EXAMPLE OF A RATING SCALE

To measure job satisfaction of employees, a scale needs to incorporate various attributes of a job which can have an impact on employee satisfaction such as: satisfaction arising from salary, employee benefits, job position, supervisor support, subordinates, career advancement, and so on. Each of these attributes is subjective, so a rating scale can be used to quantify each attribute, such that the sum or average of these represents the overall job satisfaction. For example, using a 5-point scale, some of the items on the scale may include:

How satisfied are you with your salary?: ___totally dissatisfied; ___somewhat dissatisfied; ___doesn't matter; ___somewhat satisfied; ___ totally satisfied.

How satisfied are you with your supervisor's attitude?: __totally dissatisfied; __somewhat dissatisfied; __doesn't matter; __somewhat satisfied; __totally satisfied.

How satisfied are you with your organisational benefits?: __totally dissatisfied; __somewhat dissatisfied; __doesn't matter; __somewhat satisfied; __totally satisfied.

Assuming a score of 1 is assigned to totally dissatisfied and a score of 5 is assigned to totally satisfied, the sum total or average of responses across all these items represents the respondent's overall job satisfaction.

HR metrics, KPIs (key performance indicators), and HR scorecard

Metrics are the traditional tool to quantify a firm's data. HR metrics are quantitative measurements indicative of the performance of an HR function. The organisations must identify and track those metrics which play a vital role in organisational functioning and have a direct impact on its overall performance and productivity. These metrics are key metrics or key performance indicators (KPIs) of the firm and they indicate whether or not HR function is contributing to overall organisational strategy. These KPIs vary by the type of industry and from one organisation to another. For example, the HR metric 'cost per hire' is very important for organisations which hire often such as marketing or advertising firms, whereas it plays little role in academic institutes. Some of the widely used metrics are absenteeism, turnover rate, employee engagement score, net promoter score, training effectiveness, and so on.

SNAPSHOT: CORPORATE EXAMPLE OF USE OF METRICS

One prominent use of talent analytics is the use of human capital facts. These facts are metrics with the ability to express a single version of truth regarding individual-level and enterprise-level performance. They may include headcount, turnover, etc. For the application of analytics, it needs to be deciphered how many data points would be required to obtain this single version of the truth. For example, Jet Blue Airways uses only one metric to measure employee engagement, which is the 'crew member net promoter score'. For the collection of data for this metric, the firm simply asks the crew member annually on the date of their hiring how likely they are to recommend the company to others. This metric not only gauges the engagement levels, but is also predictive of the intention of the employee to stay with the firm.

It a tedious task to identify KPIs in HRM, since it is very difficult to measure direct outcomes of people's efforts which have an organisational impact. Hence, firms translate the organisational strategy to HR goals and then determine the KPI for the same. For example, if an organisational strategy is to drive organisational growth through innovation, then the HR goal would be to identify innovative employees present in the firm or hire new ones with high innovation potential. In either case, the KPI would be the quantification of employee innovative behaviour, which can be done through a rating scale. Tracking this KPI among employees periodically would aid the HR function to determine whether or not HR goal is aligned with organisational strategy of innovating.

Another technique used to identify KPIs is the use of a balanced scorecard. Originally, the concept of the balanced scorecard was developed by Kaplan and Norton (2000). They provided a tool through which the firm's management could translate organisational vision and strategy into four quantifiable and operational perspectives, viz. the financial, customer, learning and growth, and internal business process. The tool allows the management to translate the strategy into actionable objectives for each perspective, such that for each objective, the measure (means to quantify the same), target, and actual achievement of the objective can be recorded. Many organisations and management functions have since adapted this tool as per their needs and strategy.

SNAPSHOT: CORPORATE EXAMPLE OF HR SCORECARD AND KPIS

The revenues of a shipbuilding company were dwindling owing to low-cost outsourcing of cargo ships. Since it wasn't possible to compete on cost-differentiation strategy, it was decided to strategise on product differentiation since its current clients were willing to pay a higher price for its specialised high-tech cargo vessels. The implication was to hire high-skilled innovative people (learning and growth perspective) while keeping the cost of hiring low (financial perspective). Further, the firm identified that it had to improve its production process to reduce lead time and become the most attractive employer (process perspective). The next step was to identify the KPI and the target for each of these perspectives.

To establish a measure for its strategy of innovation, it decided to market five new innovative products every 95 days. For hiring high-skilled innovative people, it decided to annually determine the quality of hire by gauging managerial satisfaction score on a scale of 0–1 and set the target at 0.85. Further, the target to reduce hiring cost was set at US$3.5 million per year, while to operationalise its status as a 'most attractive employer', it decided to gauge time to hire in number of days (targeted at 25) and the industry index of top employers benchmark (targeted at top 20%); and for reduction in process lead time, it targeted product acceptance ratio at 90%.

Source: (Vulpen, 2017)

Similarly, for different functions of HRM, an HR scorecard can be developed. Similar to the Robert and Kaplan approach, for the development of HR scorecard, organisational strategy first needs to be translated into HR operational perspectives, and then measures and targets can be defined. These measures, also termed as indicators, can be categorised as leading or lagging. Leading indicators can be used for predictive analytics, as they often precede an event. For example, employee absenteeism is a leading indicator of employee turnover intention. Lagging indicators can be used for descriptive analytics as it relates to past events. For example, employee sickness rate is a lagging indicator of labour cost. It completely depends on the context of the situation whether a given indicator would be leading or lagging. A scorecard can be developed for assessing the maturity of the HRD function of an organisation (Rao, 2014). There are four dimensions which indicate the maturity level of an HRD function – HRD systems, HRD competencies, HRD culture, and HRD business linkages. Therefore, typically an HRD audit would be conducted to assess the maturity level of each of these dimensions, and then scores would be assigned for the same. This way, the firm can quantify HRD maturity level in a firm.

Qualitative data

Just as quantitative data narrate a story based on numbers, qualitative data use words (Currence, 2019). Business analytics techniques have paved the way for inferring qualitative data, as well, such as text conversation between employees on messengers, audio conversations between employees and customers in tele-calling, or blogs and opinions of the employee shared on a firm's internal networks. Qualitative data refers to the non-numerical data which can be collected using the same techniques of data collection. Often, qualitative data collection can serve as a prelude to application of quantitative data analytics. However, with the emergence of advanced analytical tools and techniques such as those based on natural language processing (NLP), text mining, sentiment analysis, topic modelling, etc., qualitative data is evolving as an interesting source for analytics as it can provide unprecedented insights to the firms.

Both numbers and words are important to gain organisational insights, as often words explain the story behind the numbers. There are several important techniques for qualitative data collection similar to the ones previously listed. They may include interviews, brainstorming, and surveys. Exit interviews have been used extensively by the organisations across industries to interview the employees who have applied for separation from the firm. It is usually a reactive interview, since the employee has already decided to leave the firm, and is generally conducted a day or two before the employee is about to leave. This method of data collection allows the employees to express their views rather freely since they will be leaving the firm soon. Data collected through exit interviews provide important insights to the firm about the reasons behind leaving. Surveys are used by the firms to gather information on employee perspective on a particular issue or organisational intervention, or to gauge employee attitudes and work outcomes. For example, a survey can be used to determine how effective a training programme is perceived to be by the employees. Anonymous surveys, such as the ones organised by the global giant Gallup, allow the employees to express their opinions freely, and since they are administered on a large scale, the ability to generalise based on these findings is higher. Brainstorming as a qualitative data collection technique allows the involvement of a diverse workforce, and therefore, generation of new ideas for a particular problem can happen during the session.

SNAPSHOT: CORPORATE EXAMPLE OF QUALITATIVE DATA COLLECTION

A retailing firm regularly surveyed the employees working in its stores regarding their perception about store atmospherics. The firm determined that most of the employee discussions were about the music played in the store. The analysis also revealed that these employees were more engaged than others and also complained about the lack of attention from management. The management quickly realised that it had recently switched to low licensing cost music to be played in the stores, and reverted its decision. The analysis of the next set of surveys demonstrated the benefits of this decision, as the employees were indeed talking about the music, but were thankful to the management for being attentive.

A huge amount of unstructured and text data is being generated in HR departments. For example, an employee voice platform such as one for redress of grievances has lots of text, audio, and maybe videos, as well. The firms can use this data to analyse the patterns among the voices, such as which issues are most talked about on these platforms, and the source of their origin, such as which departments or area of work they mostly refer to. Further techniques like topic modelling can identify which pertinent topics appear in these voices – which are the most common themes. Similarly, queries at HR helpdesks can also be mined to identify patterns and trends in the same, thereby driving improvements in handling the queries and saving costs (Green, 2018). Such types of qualitative data analysis can yield insights which would have not been normally possible through traditional or structured data collection techniques.

Ethical and legal concerns

Since people data is highly sensitive data, it is a key concern for the organisations to carefully evaluate the ethical and legal concerns of this data. People analytics, which attempts to decipher people interactions, needs access to the conversations between the employees of an organisation. However, this has to be communicated to the employees if their conversations on official platforms for interaction are being tracked for analytics. Many firms run their internal networks where people can exchange emails, write blogs, and exchange conversations through messengers; however, tapping into this data without notifying the employees would be a sign of intrusion. Organisations are now using wearable sensors to monitor employee activity in the firm as a means to improve employee health and well-being at the workplace. However, despite the reported advantages of using this technique, one of the major barriers to its adoption is a breach of privacy of employees and disclosure of confidential employee information (Schall, Sesek, and Cavuoto, 2018).

To overcome these ethical concerns, an organisation needs to inform the employees through policies, clearly describing the means and devices for tracking such employee information (Jacobsa et al., 2019). However, it completely depends on the legal framework of the country of operation as to what can be included in organisational policies, as the legal policies differ from one country to another (Levenson and Pillans, 2017). For example, in the US, data generated by employees at the workplace is the property of the firm. In India, the laws governed by Information Technology Act, 2000 (Prakash and Dwivedi, 2018) allow employers to collect and monitor sensitive employee data as long as they inform the employees of their policies. They need to explicitly mention the type of data being collected, the purpose of collection, the duration for which it will be used, and whether it would be shared with a third-party user. Some countries even mandate the involvement of employees to choose the means suitable for data collection and monitoring. Studies have proven that such forms of employee involvement benefit organisational outcomes (Jacobsa et al., 2019), for example, when the use of wearable devices for tracking employee movement to improve employee safety and well-being at the firm is chosen by the employees themselves, rate of adoption of these devices is high. When an organisation seeks employee consent before resorting to such practices and involves them in implementation, it brings two-sided benefits to both the parties. One, organisations need to evaluate the need and purpose of this form of data collection, and second, employees feel empowered through involvement and understanding the benefits of such implementation, and employees' loyalty increases. Although it might be challenging for firms to address all employee queries for data collection, they need to strike a trade-off between ensuring transparency with employees and driving business performance.

Conclusion

The quote by Edward Demings still stays relevant, that "Without data, you are just another person with an opinion" (Vulpen, 2017). The point is all the more pertinent for organisations looking to gain greater insights into people and organisational dynamics. However, the question which persists for managers is where to locate the data. The manager, when faced with a business problem, needs to identify the sources which can explain the causes and consequences of the problem, such that it can aid in gaining an insight into the solution. This chapter, therefore, aids the manager to determine which source of HR data can be utilised, how to collect data from that source, and, if need be, how the data can be quantified. This chapter, therefore, provides comprehensive detail of the different sources of HR data present within and outside a firm which can be tapped by a manager to apply HR analytics. Also, the chapter discussed various obtrusive and unobtrusive, and conventional and unconventional, techniques through which HR data can be collected from these sources. Finally, the chapter presents some means used to quantify HR data, namely the use of scales, metrics, KPIs, and scorecards. The chapter lists real-world corporate examples to demonstrate the use of each concept presented in the chapter.

Glossary

Convenience sampling implying picking up the samples based on one's convenience

Data raw variables holding no significance on their own

External data sources data sources which are beyond the control of a firm like business surveys, published research, external social networks, web or mobiles, etc.

HR scorecard a tool through which the firm's management can translate organisational vision and strategy into quantifiable and operational perspectives through the identification of measures or indicators and setting targets

Information data which fits into specific context/decision-making needs

Internal data sources data sources which are present within the boundary and control of an organisational system, such as information system data, sensors, etc.

Interval scale the data items are placed between appropriate intervals on a scale; with this, the scale aids in measuring the extent of differences between categories

JAD joint application design is a session which involves many participants who can articulate their needs and problems well

KPI Key performance indicators are those metrics which play a vital role in organisational functioning, are derived from organisational strategy, and have a direct impact on its overall performance and productivity

Metrics the traditional tool to quantify a firm's data; HR metrics are quantitative measurements indicative of the performance of an HR function

Nominal scale when categories or labels or numbers are assigned to the data for identification; this scale only allows categorisation, calculation of frequency count, and percentages within categories

Non-probability sampling technique is based on picking up the samples, such that all elements of the population don't have a certain chance of appearing in the final sample

Obtrusive data collection techniques when the purpose of collection is known or explained to the respondent, including interviews, JADs, and questionnaires

Ordinal scale when the numbering or categories assigned to data items are rank-ordered

Population all the potential candidates for data collection

Probability sampling   when all the elements have a certain chance of being included in the sample

Purposive sampling   involves picking up samples based on one's judgement or to fulfil some purpose

Qualitative data   non-numerical data which can be collected using the same techniques of data collection; often, qualitative data collection can serve as a prelude to application of quantitative data analytics

Quota sampling   involves dividing the population into sub-groups and assigning quotas fixed numbers of samples – to be picked from a sub-group

Random sampling   ensures each element has an equal chance of appearing in the sample

Rating/Ranking scale   A rating scale asks the respondent to rate different survey items on the same scale; a ranking scale, on the other hand, asks the respondents to rate all the survey items on the same scale, according to his/her preference

Ratio scale   This scale assumes an origin point zero, thereby aiding in measuring the magnitude of differences, the proportion of differences, and the order

Sampling   involves collecting the data from a few respondents who are believed to be representative of the entire population

Scaling   data scaling provides a means to categorise the respondents based on a scaled variable, and therefore aid in analysis

Snowball sampling   involves picking the sample from a known set of respondents and then utilising the contacts of these respondents to further sample

Stratified random sampling   usually used when heterogeneity in data is high; involves determining 'stratas' or sub-groups from the population, based on a stratification element, such that the size of each stratum can be proportional to the size of the strata in the population or disproportional

Systematic random sampling   implies using a system to pick up samples randomly; for example, the researcher decides to pick up every 'n-th' element from the population

Unobtrusive data collection   techniques when the purpose of collection is unknown or hidden from the respondent, including observation, sampling, text analytics, etc.

Wearable sensors   devices worn by an individual and used to collect information about certain variables related to individual performance and movement

Web scraping   used for targeted data collection from the web, based on specific terms or keywords of interest, through the use of web crawlers (programme script), and then storing it in a more structured dataset at an appropriate location

Review material

1 Explain the need for HR managers to base decisions on data.
2 List the barriers in data collection for HR analytics.

3 Compare data and information with relevant examples.
4 List obtrusive techniques of data collection.
5 List the ways in which HR manager would decide which obtrusive data collection would be useful.
6 List unobtrusive techniques of data collection.
7 Define sampling, sample population, and sample size.
8 Differentiate between probability and non-probability sampling.
9 List different probability sampling techniques.
10 List different non-probability sampling techniques.
11 Elucidate the steps involved in quantification of variables.
12 List and explain the types of scales.
13 Explain KPIs and their relevance in application of analytics.
14 Discuss HR scorecard in detail.
15 What is the importance of qualitative data in HR analytics?
16 Elucidate various types qualitative data used in HR analytics.
17 Discuss different internal sources of HR data.
18 Discuss different external sources of HR data.
19 What do you understand is meant by ethical and legal concerns in HR data collection?

Problem exercises

1 Assume that you as a HR manager of the firm are equipped with the task of identifying the optimal profile for successful employees. Which data sources would you use for this purpose? Justify your answer(s).
2 Suppose your firm has recently started operating out of India, and you are in charge of managing the Indian workforce. You decide to implement social networking analytics to determine how social network dynamics differ by countries. Would it be ethical and legal for you to do such an analysis? Why or why not?

Case study

Margdarshan – building HR as a strategic business partner

Sampann Corporations (name has been changed to protect the privacy of those interviewed) is a leading textile firm operating out of India. Its major areas of operation include spinning, knitting, and processing yarns of thread, fabric, and manufacturing textile products like towels and garments. The textile industry in India is highly people-intensive and faces stiff competition in terms of procurement of a skilled workforce. Sampann has been able to hold on to its workforce better than competing players in the market; however, the management often felt that it has a hard time acquiring workforce from the market, despite its long history of operating in the textile industry in India. Besides, the HR function at the firm was not able to justify its existence, such that the management often questioned its role in contributing to organisational productivity and performance. Faced with these challenges, the HR executive at Sampann, Mr Arpit Sharma, decided to work around HR data to demonstrate how HR function contributed to the firm's performance. However, the firm had no consistent data backup available for analysis.

Mr Sharma, therefore, decided to design a HR scorecard called 'Margdarshan' which would gauge the performance of HR through KPIs and thereby sufficiently exhibit how HR contributes to firm's performance. Since the biggest challenge was to make Sampann a preferred employer of choice, Mr. Sharma crafted this as HR strategy and designed strategic objectives for the HR function, such that it could contribute to overall business growth. Then to develop measures for each of these objectives, Mr. Sharma identified enablers, drivers, and deliverables, based on which he designed a 'return card', depicting all the HR metrics and their contribution to overall organisational growth. The quantification of data was unprecedented in the firm, and the results were magnanimous. Through quantified outcomes, business management was able to visualise the strong role of HR function, and also identify areas of improvement through which Sampann could establish itself as employer of choice in the market.

Some of the objectives derived from HR strategy were: 'developing a feeling of belongingness and sense of pride in each employee', 'create and establish open channels of communication', 'creating environment of learning and growth', 'enhance teamwork and good employee relationship', 'ensuring employee well-being and safety', and 'introduction of systems and standardisation across business functions'. To develop these objectives, informal discussions were held with the workforce of the organisations to understand their perspective on what was lacking in the organisation to make it an attractive employer. Besides this, brainstorming sessions with other HR executives and managers also lead to the emergence of these themes as HR objectives to attain the previously mentioned strategy. The next step was to understand how to measure these objectives. For this, it was at first imperative to know how these are facilitated in the organisation – that is, through which instruments or systems it could be operationalised. For example, to develop a sense of belongingness among employees, it was necessary to monitor their satisfaction levels. Further, it was required to have a system to timely address their grievances, adopt and implement preventive dispute practices, and establish forums where employee discussions with management can be held and solutions can be worked around on issues faced by the employees. These were termed as enablers by Mr Sharma. Identification of these enablers made the task of identification of drivers easier. Drivers were the actual metrics or quantified values which gauged the implementation of an objective. For example, for the enabler of grievance redressal, the drivers identified were 'number of upward complaints' (those not resolved at the lowest level of redressal), percentage reduction in upward complaints (this year over previous year), average complaint handling time, and average response time to complaints. Similarly, for the enabler of satisfaction among employees, the drivers were number of satisfaction surveys conducted annually, the average number of

MARGDARSHAN at Sampann

*HR Deliverable "**staff/worker satisfaction**" increased **% of staff falling in satisfaction curve** by ________________ and **% of workers falling in satisfaction curve** by ________________, which in turn reduced the **attrition** by ________________, resulting in increased **productivity** by ________________*

*HR Deliverable **Fair communication** decreased the **average period taken for responding the staff/worker complaints** by ____________days increased **% of staff falling in satisfaction curve** by ________________ and **% of workers falling in satisfaction curve** by ________________, resulting in **decreased attrition** of workers by ________________ and decreased attrition of staff by ________________*

FIGURE 2.3 'Margdarshan' scorecard at Sampann

respondents in each survey, number of satisfied employees, percentage reduction in dissatisfied employee (this year/ over previous year), number of activities conducted for welfare, and employee entertainment.

Similarly, for all other objectives, enablers and drivers were identified. This way HR data could be quantified. Now to generate a scorecard called 'Margdarshan' by Mr Sharma (Figure 2.3), each of these drivers were categorised into deliverables, which is under a particular heading under which HR performance could be reported. For example, all the enablers of satisfaction were grouped under the deliverable of 'employee satisfaction', all enablers of grievance redressal were grouped under the deliverable 'communication', and so on. This categorisation facilitated the recording and reporting of HR performance data.

The tool has been able to provide unprecedented insights into the firm's management and also demonstrate the contribution of the HR function to overall business performance. By monitoring the reduction in complaint responding and handling time, the firm was able to investigate and depict how it affected employee satisfaction levels, and therefore develop means through which an improvement in complaint redressal can be made. In turn, it enabled the development of fair communication among organisation and employees, thereby increasing its attractiveness as an employer of choice. Quantification of HR data and use of surveys and scorecards allowed Mr Sharma to demonstrate and justify the existence and contribution of the HR function to overall firm performance.

Questions

1 Discuss the process adopted by the HR manager at Sampann to develop HR scorecard.

2 How was HR data quantified in this case, and what was the purpose of quantification?
3 From your understanding from the text, identify enablers and a few drivers for the objective of ensuring employee well-being and safety.
4 Which other external data source would you suggest using in this case for achievement of the HR strategy of becoming an employer of choice?

Bibliography

Bellinger, G., Castro, D., and Mills, A. (2004). *Data, information, knowledge, and wisdom.* Retrieved from academia.edu.

Bersin, J., Mariani, J., and Monahan, K. (2016, May 24). *Will IoT technology bring us the quantified employee?* Retrieved August 2019, from Deloitte Insights: https://www2.deloitte.com/us/en/insights/focus/internet-of-things/people-analytics-iot-human-resources.html

Chow, C. (2018, February). *How to measure internal communications: Analysis and insights.* Retrieved from Social Chorus: https://socialchorus.com/blog/how-to-measure-internal-communications-analysis-and-insights/

Cisco. (2020). *Location analytics: A new platform for engaging users.* Retrieved from Cisco Meraki: https://meraki.cisco.com/solutions/location_analytics#:~:text=A%20new%20platform%20for%20engaging,no%20additional%20cost%20or%20complexity

Cigna. (2019). *Cigna Company Profile.* Retrieved from Cigna: https://www.cigna.com/about-us/company-profile/

Clarks. (2020). *Clarks – retail analytics.* Retrieved from SPScommerce: https://www.spscommerce.com/resources/clarks-case-study/

Currence, J. (2019, May 23). *Three key tools for collecting qualitative data.* Retrieved September 21, 2019, from SHRM: www.shrm.org/resourcesandtools/hr-topics/behavioral-competencies/pages/three-key-tools-for-collecting-qualitative-data.aspx

De Mauro, A., Greco, M., Grimaldi, M., and Ritala, P. (2017). Human resources for big data professions: A systematic classification of job roles and required skill sets. *Information Processing and Management*, 1–11.

Deming, E. W. (2019, June). *Thought for the day.* Retrieved 2019, from The Tribune: www.tribuneindia.com/news/thought-for-the-day/without-data-you-are-just-another-person-with-an-opinion – w-edwards-deming/787471.html

Green, D. (2018, November 22). *Using employee text analytics to drive business outcomes.* Retrieved October 2019, from my HR Future: www.myhrfuture.com/blog/2018/11/21/using-text-analytics-with-people-data

IBM. (2018). *IBM global human capital study.* Human Capital Management for Government. New York: IBM.

Israel, G. D. (1992, November). *Determining sample size.* Fact Sheet PEOD-6. Gainesville, FL: Institute of Food and Agricultural Sciences, University of Florida.

Jacobsa, J. V., Hettinger, L. J., Huang, Y.-H., Jeffries, S., Lesch, M. F., Simmons, L. A.,. . Willetts, J. L. (2019). Employee acceptance of wearable technology in the workplace. *Applied Ergonomics*, 148–156.

Kaplan, R. S., and Norton, D. P. (2000). Using the balanced scorecard as a strategic management system. *Harvard Business Review*, 1–13.

Kendall, K., and Kendall, J. (2018). Information gathering methods. In K. Kendall and J. Kendall (Eds.), *System analysis and design* (pp. 103–154). Hoboken, NJ: Pearson Education, Inc.

Leonardi, P., and Contractor, N. (2018, November). Better people analytics. *Harvard Business Review*. Vol.88(10), pp.52-58

Levenson, A., and Pillans, G. (2017). *Strategic workforce analytics*. London, UK: Corporate Research Forum.

Mazor, A. H. (2019). *Talent acquisition analytics*. Retrieved from Deloitte: https://www2. deloitte.com/us/en/pages/human-capital/articles/talent-acquisition-analytics.html

Miller, R. (2015, February 24). *New firm combines wearables and data to improve decision making*. Retrieved July 2019, from Tech Crunch: http://techcrunch.com/2015/02/24/new-firm-combines-wearables-and-data-to-improve-decision-making/

Necula, S.-C., and Strîmbei, C. (2019). People analytics of semantic web human resource résumés for sustainable talent acquisition. *Sustainability, 11*(13), 2–18.

Pejic-Bach, M., Bertoncel, T., Meško, M., and Krstić, Ž. (2019). Text mining of industry 4.0 job advertisements. *International Journal of Information Management, 50*, 416–431.

Platanou, K., Mäkelä, K., Beletskiy, A., and Colicev, A. (2018). Using online data and network-based text analysis in HRM research. *Journal of Organizational Effectiveness: People and Performance*, 81–97.

Prakash, A., and Dwivedi, S. (2018, July 22). *Here's what employers must know about employee privacy rights*. Retrieved July 6, 2019, from People Matters: www.peoplematters.in/article/technology/heres-what-employers-must-know-about-employee-privacy-rights-18814

Ranosa, R. (2018, November). *How this global airline used analytics to improve hiring*. Retrieved from HR Tech News: https://www.hrtechnologynews.com/news/talent-acquisition/how-this-global-airline-used-analytics-to-improve-hiring/116491

Rao, T. (2014). *HRD audit: Evaluating the human resource functions for business improvement*. New Delhi: Sage Publications India Pvt. Ltd.

Rosenbaum, E. (2019, April 3). *IBM artificial intelligence can predict with 95% accuracy which workers are about to quit their jobs*. Retrieved August 20, 2019, from CNBC: www.cnbc.com/2019/04/03/ibm-ai-can-predict-with-95-percent-accuracy-which-employees-will-quit.html

Schall, M. C., Sesek, R., and Cavuoto, L. A. (2018). Barriers to the adoption of wearable sensors in the workplace: A survey of occupational safety and health professionals. *Human Factors The Journal of the Human Factors and Ergonomics Society, 60*(3), 351–362.

Sekaran, U., and Bougie, R. (2016). Experimental designs. In U. Sekaran and R. Bougie (Eds.), *Research methods for business: A skill building approach* (pp. 242–256). West Sussex, UK: John Wiley & Sons Ltd.

Vargiu, E., and Urru, M. (2012). Exploiting web scraping in a collaborative filtering- based approach to web advertising. *Artificial Intelligence Research*, 44–54.

Vulpen, E. v. (2017). *Human resources KPIs: An in-depth explanation with metrics & examples*. Retrieved June 2019, from AIHR Analytics: www.analyticsinhr.com/blog/human-resources-key-performance-indicators-hr-kpis/

Vulpen, E. v. (2018). *15 HR analytics case studies with business impact*. Retrieved October 2019, from AIHR Analytics: www.analyticsinhr.com/blog/hr-analytics-case-studies/

3

MODELLING THE BUSINESS PROBLEM

After reading this chapter, users will be able to understand the following key concepts:

- Define a model and its need to analyse a business problem
- Define the influence diagram and how they lend to the primary development of models
- Understand the components of a business model of a business problem
- Understand different variables used in modelling of business problem
- Understand how systems approach/process logic can be used for the development of a business model
- Understand the need and role of building a theoretical foundation for the development of models
- Explain what is meant by organisational jargon
- Understand the role of understanding organisational jargon for developing predictive models

Opening case

Drug abuse is a major problem in the US, and it is even more difficult to build models which can predict with high accuracy levels who is going to indulge in drug abuse. As a data scientist at a leading healthcare Cosley recalls, there is a distinction between opioid abusers and non-abusers who take opioids. The target of a predictive model is to identify these non-abusers with high potential of converting into abusers. This is possible when the predictive model can distinguish between the characteristics of both categories of drug users, and then associate the two categories to predict how likely a non-abuser is to convert into an abuser.

The analytics team of Cosley, therefore, had discussions with healthcare providers to understand the behaviour of these drug users. They discovered that although frequent doctor visits were predictive of drug abuse, some other major behavioural traits were the appearance of certain specific symptoms and diseases associated with doctor visits, visits to more than one doctor, and residing in a particular region as identified by ZIP (postal) code. Based on such observations, the analytics team of Cosley designed a predictive system with 742 variables, adding to the computational intensity of the model such as that with Big Data analytical models. The team discovered that adding such a wide number of variables increased the prediction accuracy to 85%, aiding them to identify in advance the users who are at high risk of turning into drug abusers. This led the team to adopt preventive care when they could design educational campaigns, or directly ask the patient's healthcare provider to intervene, and distribute amnesty boxes, wherever required, to collect excess medications being dispersed.

This case implies the need to accurately design a predictive model to increase prediction accuracy. This chapter, therefore, focuses on key concepts in developing a predictive model for HRM.

Introduction

To find a solution to a problem, managers cannot rely solely on their intuition and judgement. They need to back their decisions with appropriate data and then make fact-based decisions. But the question is: how will a manager deduce facts from data? The previous chapters gave an insight into the concept of HR analytics and the various steps involved in the application of analytics to a business problem. Although the manager may gain access to relevant data to solve a business problem, he would still not be able to make fact-based decisions unless he builds a mathematical or statistical model of that problem, and then applys this model on the data to find facts to make decisions. The process of decision-making also specifies listing different decision alternatives and then using particular criteria to make a decision. These criteria might be simple and logical such as choosing that alternative, which is profitable, or the one which maximises employee benefits or minimises organisational losses, and so on. But for the generation of decision alternatives, a formalisation of a model of the business problem is a necessity. Therefore, it is imperative for someone applying analytics to be familiar with the fundamentals of modelling a business problem. Unless the design is not appropriate, there is no point in applying analytical tools, since design issues cannot be fixed by analytical techniques (Light, Singer, and Willett, 1990).

A model is formally defined as:

> A model is an abstraction or representation of a real system, idea or object.
>
> *(Evans, 2016, p. 18)*

By this definition, a model may be as simple as a graphical illustration of the most important features or characteristics of a concept under study; or may be as complex as involving design of a mathematical or statistical representation. For example, simply depicting the annual placements of the students occurring from a particular university through the help of a line chart is a model. Further, fitting a mathematical function to this line chart or curve such as $P = a.b^{eT}$ is also a model establishing a mathematical relationship between the number of placements (P) and time of year (T), where a and b are constants. Generally, for the application of business analytics, models are built to establish relationships between business outcomes so that different decision alternatives can be generated and predictions can be made by the managers.

Models can often supplement or support managerial intuition and judgement. For example, an HR manager's intuition might say to hire new employees for a new project, rather than train the existing ones, but how many to hire would be answered by a mathematical model.

SNAPSHOT: CORPORATE EXAMPLE OF THE NEED FOR MODELLING BUSINESS PROBLEM

A firm witnessing high employee turnover, despite offering the best compensation and benefits package to its employees, could not find out a reason for the turnover. Then it started searching for other factors like organisational climate, supervisor relationship, etc., to determine the cause of the turnover. It correlated all organisational and employee data available with the firm, and discovered that those quitting the firm had not been promoted from a long time, most of them had been working under a few common supervisors, and relatively few organisational interventions had occurred in those organisational areas where turnover was highest. The mathematical fitting of correlation identified some areas of concern which intuition or judgement would never have.

Typically, before proceeding to build a mathematical model, some managers may use graphical illustration techniques such as an **influence diagram** (Evans, 2016) to gain an understanding of various features of business problems and how they affect each other. In other words, how major elements of a business problem are related to one another can be illustrated visually using these influence diagrams (Figure 3.1).

Consider a simple business problem of low sales at retail stores of the organisation. Now the low sales can be attributed to either high product pricing or poor performance of store employees. Assuming product pricing to be consistent for a long while, such that it does not affect sales, the only cause which requires further investigation is employee performance. The manager now needs to dig further to identify the elements which can have an impact on employee performance. For example, store ambience, training for client handling, rapport with the store manager, etc., can be some underlying causes.

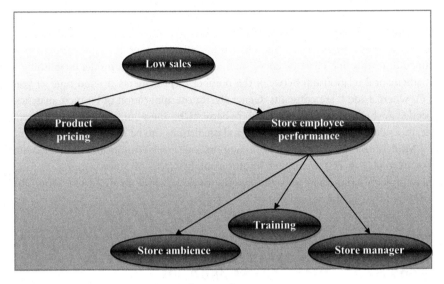

FIGURE 3.1 Corporate snapshot: influence diagrams

Source: Evans (2016)

A business model of any given business problem involves the following components:

1 Identifying research variables
2 Developing a theoretical foundation
3 Developing a conceptual model of the relationship between the variables and explaining the reasons for the established relationships

---

As is clear from this example, the use of the influence diagram aids in understanding the major elements of a business problem and how they are related to each other. From this, it becomes easy to develop a mathematical model, if a manager has all the relevant data about these major elements. These diagrams also provide a basis for preliminary investigation of the relationship between these elements. Only those elements need to be included in the models which have a strong relation. The identification of these elements or major features of a problem comes from managerial experience and theoretical foundations. Further, to build a mathematical model, two fundamental requirements are data and variables. The following sections of the chapter, therefore, present concepts related to various variables used in building a model, and the use of theory in the identification of major elements of a variable.

Modelling the business problem[1]

Business managers are not statisticians, and therefore the firms often hire analysts to fulfil this role. However, the present business environment demands the integration of the role of a business analyst with the role of a business manager, so that preliminary investigation and solution to any business problem can occur at the level of a business manager itself. This reinforces the need for a manager to equip himself with the knowledge of business analytics. Any analytical or statistical algorithm will yield only what is fed into it, implying that the way a business problem is structured by a manager will guide the application of analytics and future interpretation of results yielded by the application. So, it is imperative for the business managers to understand the basic structure of any business problem, to enable accurate modelling and consequent analysis.

Each of these steps is discussed in greater detail in the coming sections of the chapter. Raw data itself cannot narrate a story; it needs to be modelled to be exposed to some sort of analysis and then generate information. For this purpose, managers must first need to differentiate between data and information, since data are all around them and they need to extract it to fit into their decision-making needs. Second, they need to identify various variables from the data which would aid in the extraction of information through the application of business analytics.

Variables in modelling of a business problem

As the name suggests, a variable is anything whose value varies. For example, the total sales variable in the previous example varies by each item, each day, and each store. Therefore, sales, whether in the number of units or currency, is a variable. Any research problem involves the following basic type of variables (Sekaran and Bougie, 2010) (Bajpai, 2011).

Dependent variables

The analyst or researcher is interested in analysing something, and this variable – which is of prime interest for the analyst or researcher – is called a dependent variable. The reason it is termed as dependent is that it depends on something else to explain the variability in its occurrence. For example, sales vary by type of item, day of the week, and store. So how many sales will occur is dependent on the type of item, day, and store. Therefore, a sale is a dependent variable. Whenever a manager or an analyst models a business problem, then the variable which lends itself to the primary investigation, for which some underlying factors or causes need to be discerned, will be the dependent variable. Take another example, where a human resource manager notices that employees' absenteeism is highest on Monday and lowest on Friday, and is also related to employee department. So, the dependent variable, in this case, is absenteeism.

CORPORATE SNAPSHOT: DEPENDENT VARIABLE

A transportation firm sought to improve its hires who are new drivers, to reduce the cost of road traffic accidents. For this purpose, they sought to redesign their hiring assessment for drivers. Therefore, they built a predictive model which could predict the likelihood of a driver getting into a road accident based on his psychometric traits. Clearly, in this example, although the prime objective is to improve the quality of hires and reduce the cost of road accidents, the dependent variable used is the likelihood of involving in an accident.

Now, a business problem may also involve more than two dependent variables. Sometimes, managers realise that although absenteeism results from low job satisfaction and organisational commitment among employees, job satisfaction and organisational commitment themselves can be attributed to environmental and individual factors. So here, multiple variables are involved for analysis, giving rise to a multivariate analysis problem.

Independent variables

Independent variables are always defined in the context of the dependent variable involved in the study. Those variables, which affect the dependent variable, are termed as independent variables. Whenever a change in value occurs for the dependent variable, it can be accounted for by the independent variable. Four conditions have been established to justify an independent variable. First, both independent and dependent variable must co-vary, either positively or negatively. For example, sales of beverages and temperature in a region co-vary, since a change in temperature always brings about a change in sales of beverages. Second, there should be a time relationship such that the occurrence of independent variable always precedes the change in the dependent variable. For example, if the sales of beverages rise without a change in temperature, then certainly, change in sales cannot be attributed to change in temperature. Third, when explaining the effect of change of one independent variable, others should be controlled for. Fourth, a theoretical framework which logically establishes the relationship between the two should always exist. For example, change in income and obesity has no logical backup; hence, this relationship is not acceptable.

CORPORATE SNAPSHOT: INDEPENDENT VARIABLE

In the same example of transportation firm seeking to improve its quality of new hires to reduce the cost of road traffic accidents, the firm predicted the likelihood of a driver getting into a road accident based on his psychometric traits. The traits used were concentration, motor speed, reaction speed, stress tolerance, tracking deviation, etc. Each of these is an independent variable for this example.

Moderator variables

Any variable which can moderate or modify the relationship significantly, between the independent and dependent variable is termed as a moderator variable. This implies that whenever the moderator variable comes into the picture, the original relationship is changed. They are of huge importance in research studies, since if the presence of such variables is ignored, the implications of the model of the business problem becomes largely irrelevant once they come into the picture. Consider a simple example of the relationship between sales of a product and its price. The higher the price, the lower the sales, and the lower the price, the higher the sales. However, the relationship is significantly changed when a discount offer is introduced. The higher the discounts, even if the price is higher, sales are expected to rise significantly. Therefore, as Figure 3.2 depicts, sales being the dependent variable and the price being the independent variable, discounts can be identified as a moderator variable.

It should be well established here that the context of the research problem will indicate whether to include a given variable as an independent variable or moderator variable, and whether there is a need for moderator variable in the present study or not.

CORPORATE SNAPSHOT: MODERATOR VARIABLE

It has been empirically demonstrated that employee engagement is directly linked to business performance. However, an international oil company assessed that the relationship is significantly altered by the state of safety practices adopted in the company. When the firm improved and communicated those safety standards to the employees, it witnessed a significant improvement in employee engagement and business performance. Therefore, while modelling such a situation, the status of safety practices can be used as a moderator variable.

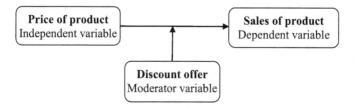

FIGURE 3.2 Dependent, independent, and moderator variables

Consider another situation where preliminary analysis reveals to the manager that turnover intention is high when employees exhibit low levels of both job satisfaction and job fit. However, the manager also finds that this is only the case with operational workers, while at managerial positions, the turnover intention remains the same irrespective of perceived job satisfaction for all employees. Only when employees at managerial positions perceive low job fit is their turnover intention affected. This implies that in the case of operational workers, we have two independent variables – job satisfaction and job fit – while in the case of managerial workers, the dependent variable is the same, turnover intention; the independent variable is job satisfaction, while job fit becomes the moderator variable. That is, only when the perceived job fit of managerial workers is affected is the relationship between their perceived job satisfaction and turnover intention altered. While in the first case, there is no need to include a moderator variable, the second situation of managerial workers clearly demands the inclusion of a moderator variable for modelling of a business problem. Typically, moderator variables are rarely used in actual business modelling, since they require thorough theoretical support, as well.

Mediator variables

As the name suggests, a variable which mediates or intervenes in the relationship between dependent and independent variable is termed as a mediator variable. The primary objective of a mediator variable is that there exists no direct relationship between the dependent variable and the independent variable, and therefore the relationship can be well explained through a mediating variable (Figure 3.3). If a researcher removes the mediating variable, the relationship might also vanish. For example, a rise in income leading to obesity has no direct reasonable explanation; however, when a mediating variable 'higher access to food sources' is added in this relationship, the relationship makes sense. Therefore, access to food sources is a mediator variable.

Clearly, in this example, social capital affects self-efficacy through the mediating role of psychological well-being, and social capital cannot directly impact self-efficacy. Now, here also, it depends on the context of the research problem at hand, whether the relationship between dependent and independent variables needs a mediating variable. In many situations, the relationship has sufficient theoretical background, for which an intervening variable is not required.

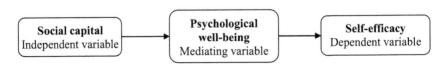

FIGURE 3.3 Dependent, independent, and mediator variables

Control/Extraneous variables

While mediator and moderator variable are used to understand the influence or relationship between two dependent and independent variables, the third category of variables is also included in research design. These variables are called 'control', 'controlled', or 'extraneous' variables. The basic premise of including a variable as a control in a research model is to control for its effect on the dependent variable, by holding these factors constant. The researcher is not interested in the effect of this variable on external outcomes; rather, he wishes to constrain the research model by specifically introducing a variable which acts a control. Consider, for example, that use motives influence actual product use. Suppose a researcher is interested in investigating how use motives affect actual use behaviour. In such a case, 'habit' will be used a control variable, since it constrains the relationship between motivation and actual use; that is, an individual is not motivated to use a product, but is using it out of habit.

Application of process logic to an HR function lists inputs, transformation and output. Each of these inputs will serve as an independent variable, while output will serve as the dependent variable. Both the transformation and outcome will suggest which analytical tool would be most useful for a particular application.

It should be noted here that if mediating, moderator, and control variables are significant in any given research model, they need to be subjected to separate analysis and investigation, which is a different area of analysis, beyond the scope of this book. However, tools like SmartPLS based on partial least squares modelling are an excellent tool for preliminary analysis of such relationships. Readers of the book interested in further reading on these topics might find the links and books provided at the end of this chapter useful.

The role of systems/process approach in problem modelling

The variables identified by the business manager will serve as the basis for the application of analytics. Since the manager applied the process approach to the business problem, he can now clearly infer that the input in a process will act as an independent variable in the predictive model, while the output will act as a dependent variable. Understanding what transformation they have to undergo is crucial to any problem modelling, and here the experience and intuition of the business manager serve the most important role. However, when both experience and intuition fail, existing literature serves the purpose. Therefore, managers need to discern how the independent variables should be treated to achieve the desired output state of the dependent variable, and this 'how' is the transformation that they undergo. Now let us understand this through examples.

Recalling the application of process/systems approach to different HR systems, let us understand how these can be used to develop a model. One major sub-system of recruitment is the process of applicant screening, for which we could infer that after application of process logic, inputs to this process are candidate demographics, pass marks, skill levels, and valid references, while the outcome can take either of two values: accepted or rejected. The transformation that occurs is simply comparing the input values to benchmark values in the database. Clearly, in the predictive model, each of these inputs will be the independent variable. The 'outcome' is the dependent variable (single variable) which can take two values, accept or reject. It is very important to understand that how each of these independent variables affects the dependent variable can be deduced from the manager's experience and theoretical background.

Let us recall the second example of the application of process logic to the function of offering training to the employees. From this example, as well, the independent variables would be the inputs to the process – candidate demographics, current position, current skills, and performance rank; while the dependent variable would be the different training programmes offered by the firm. The purpose of the analytical model will still be the same: to compare the input values of independent variables to existing criteria data for each training programme in the database and then suggest a suitable programme. Similarly, the process logic and identification of dependent and independent variables allows effective and hassle-free development of the predictive analytical model.

> Predictive models can be categorised as supervised or unsupervised learning models. Systems approach and process logic apply to supervised learning predictive models.

The predictive models can be broadly categorised as supervised or unsupervised learning models. **A supervised learning model is a model in which the values of the target or dependent variable are known beforehand, such that an algorithm can be applied to map input values to output values, to obtain the function for mapping, and to aid in future predictions of target variables.** In mathematical notation, if x ◊ represents the input values and Y ◊ represents the output values, then supervised model involves mapping $Y = f(x)$ to deduce the function $f(x)$ for mapping, such that future predictions of Y can be made based on values of x. The model is termed as supervised since the algorithm can iteratively predict Y based on x, and compare the predicted values with actual output values to correct the algorithm used for prediction. It is perceived as analogous to supervising classroom learning. Generally, the most common supervised learning problems are regression and classification. Regression establishes a relationship between the dependent and independent variables, while classification categorises the output variable based on certain features. **An unsupervised learning model is a model in which the outcome or dependent variable and its values are unknown, such that the model aims to elucidate the underlying structure in the data.** This algorithm works on its own to identify how data points are related to one another; therefore, no supervision is possible. Most common unsupervised learning problems are clustering and association. While clustering uncovers how different groups or clusters are present in a dataset, association investigates how different data items are related to one another, such that if one occurs, the other also occurs. Association is most useful in building rules.

Typically, the systems approach and process logic are applicable in supervised learning problems, since dependent and independent variables can be identified. However, when such clarity is not available from a business problem, unsupervised models need to be built. This is a separate area of analysis discussed in subsequent chapters covering topics on clustering and association.

Building up of theoretical framework aids the manager/analyst/reader in the following tasks of modelling of business problem:

1   Providing a conceptual basis for identification and definition of variables to be used in business problem modelling
2   Aiding in providing representation of the relationship between the variables
3   Providing a conceptual basis for the relationship between these variables

---

Building a theoretical foundation

All analytical algorithms, tools, and techniques will work around the variables discussed in the preceding section. If a manager, in light of the identified business problem, successfully identifies the relevant variable, he will accomplish application, analysis, and interpretation of analytics to solve the business problem at hand. Now that we have understood the concept of data and information and different types of research variables, let us attempt to understand the next component of modelling of a business problem practically. **Basically, by modelling a business problem, it is implied to structure the variables in such a manner that the relationship and interplay between these variables can be interpreted through the application of appropriate algorithms.** Similar to a statistical model, where the relationship between variables is structured through mathematical equations, a business model also tries to formulate and establish some sort of relationship between the variables. Depending on the analytical tool chosen by the business manager, the relationship can be defined; however, the basic concepts remain the same.

Each sort of model requires effective identification of dependent, independent, control, and other research variables if they apply in the given situation. Whenever a manager encounters a business problem, he needs to discern what would be the ultimate impact of the problem, how it can be quantified, what has caused the impact, and how these causes can be quantified. The quantified impact is the dependent variable, and the quantified cause becomes an independent variable in any business problem model. For example, a sales manager encounters a problem of slow business growth in a given sales region; the ultimate impact would be on number and volume of sales (that is, both in currency and in number of units). Therefore, the volume of sales becomes the dependent variable. The sales manager's insight reveals that low sales can be attributed to salesman attributes (like low contacts, absenteeism, etc.), highly competitive products, quality, etc. Therefore, these variables form the independent variable. However, quality can also be taken as a control variable. Now let us assume that the manager is interested in analysing cause-effect relationship to determine which independent variables have the highest influence on declining sales, and therefore, decided to apply regression. For this purpose, he would have to model the relationship as a mathematical equation. So, the basis is the accurate identification of dependent and independent variables, and the model would develop on the tool chosen (discussed in greater detail in the next chapter).

Now how can a user interpret and decide which would be the independent, moderator, or mediator variables? For this, the reader needs to be aware of building a theoretical context around the problem which would aid in the identification of the different types of variables in a business problem. The theoretical framework will aid the reader and the business manager to provide a basis for both identification of variables to be used in modelling of the business problem, and justification of the relationship between identified variables and dependent variable. Therefore, the building up of theoretical framework aids the manager/analyst/reader in the following tasks of modelling of business problem:

1 Provide a conceptual basis for identification and definition of variables to be used in business problem modelling
2 Provide representation of the relationship between the variables
3 Provide a conceptual basis for the relationship between these variables

Further, once the theoretical foundation has been laid down, the reader can – based on the analytical tool to be used – develop hypotheses, or generate testable models. Conceptual basis and identification of variables will aid in providing clarity to the manager involved in problem modelling and further aid in the identification of scale items and source for the data collection on those variables. A conceptual model and representation of the relationship between variables are based on adequate theoretical foundations. In a way, this lets the user build a structure around the literature he has gathered on the business problem in context. The theoretical framework allows the reader to examine whether the relationships should be modelled as positive or negative relationships, and then analytical tools can affirm whether the theory is validated by current study or not. Now the question is: what is the source of building the theoretical framework? Managers can often find the theoretical foundations in the literature available from previous researchers carried in the organisations, in theories of different managerial concepts available in the literature, and from findings of previous interviews or surveys conducted in the organisation on problems similar to the one currently undertaken.

Typically, these theoretical insights can be fetched from managerial wisdom itself. Active involvement of senior leaders and management executives of the firm involved in applying analytics reveals the basis for developing a hypothesis, identifying the target or independent variables. Analysts can search for theory based on the insights gained from such discussions and wisdom to build a background for their predictive model.

The role of understanding organisational jargon for developing predictive models

Organisational jargon refers to the common terms used in organisational conversation, not formally defined but frequently exchanged across the firm. Two major challenges in implementing an analytical approach to business problems are first, determining and justifying the need for an analytical tool, and second, the ability to narrate the results of implementation such that it can be acted upon. In both parts, organisational jargon and organisational language plays a key role. Management information systems, when implemented properly in place, can deliver 80% of the facts for decision-making; they just need to be presented correctly (Van der Togt and Rasmussen, 2017). For the remaining 20% of insights, sophisticated analytical tools are required. Still, in such scenarios, management and employees alike have to be convinced of the application of analytical tools, for which the importance of insights generated from such applications need to be communicated across the organisation. Further, once the results are generated from an analytical solution, they need to be spread across the firm in such a manner that the affected stakeholders can act upon them. In all these cases, the terminology and language used should be common and consistent between different parts of the organisation and analytical tool used. For example, if the analytical model suggests reducing the number of headcounts to improve a firm's performance, there should be clarity on which employees are being referred to in these headcounts since the analytical model has been fed data on those particular employees only. Assume that reasons for turnover have been discerned using an analytical model for the top executives in an IT firm. The model has revealed an insight that the headcount should be minimum at the top level while maximising key talent. Two ambiguities would result from such insight without an agreed-upon workable common language. First, does the headcount at the top level include just executives, or also other employees working at the top level of the firm? Second, what is meant by key talent? Clarity on such issues can be gained only through an understanding of organisational jargon. If these ambiguities are not resolved before the implementation of an analytical tool, then the results and outcomes will not be relevant and actionable. One of the major reasons for the failure of adoption and application of analytical tools is a lack of understanding of how to act upon outcomes of analytical application and clarity in understanding of the results of these applications.

Conclusion

Business managers are flooded with data and information, and face enormous pressure to make fact-based decisions in real time. Although information systems often generate almost 80% of the facts for decision-making by their design objective, managers many times need to investigate deeper and generate insights beyond this 80%. For this purpose, they need to develop sophisticated analytical models around the available data and then communicate the results of the application of the model so that actions can be taken in the firm. This chapter, therefore, presents a discussion on the concepts involved in developing a predictive analytical model. The reader is acquainted with a definition of a model and the purpose a model serves in analysing a business problem. Further, a preliminary investigation tool called an influence diagram is presented, and how it lends itself to the primary development of models is also discussed with relevant business examples. The components of a business model of a business problem and different variables used in modelling of business problem are also discussed. Many examples from corporate have been included in the text wherever appropriate. Readers are also familiarised with development of models from the application of systems approach/process logic to HR functions. Further, a detailed explanation on the need and role of building a theoretical foundation for the development of models has been presented, followed by the role of understanding organisational jargon for the same. Briefly, readers are also acquainted with the difference between supervised and unsupervised learning models. This chapter lays the foundation among the readers to understand how advanced analytical techniques are applied to actual business problems.

Glossary

Components of a business model   include research variables, theoretical foundation, and conceptual model, establishing the relation between the variables

Control variable   The basic premise of including a variable as a control in a research model is to control for its effect on the dependent variable, by holding these factors constant

Dependent variable   the variable which lends itself to the primary investigation, for which some underlying factors or causes need to be discerned and which depends on something else to explain the variability in its occurrence

Independent variable   always defined in the context of the dependent variable involved in the study; those variables, which affect the dependent variable are termed as independent variables

Influence diagrams a visual representation of how major elements of a business problem are related to one another

Mediator variable a variable which mediates or intervenes in the relationship between dependent and independent variable; the primary objective of a mediator variable is that there exists no direct relationship between the dependent variable and independent variable, and therefore through a mediating variable, the relationship can be well explained

Model an abstraction or representation of a real system, idea, or object

Moderator variable any variable which can moderate or modify the relationship significantly between the independent and dependent variable

Organisational jargon refers to the common terms used in organisational conversation, not formally defined but frequently exchanged across the firm

Role of the theoretical framework provides a conceptual basis for identification and establishment of the relationship between research variables

Supervised model While developing and training a predictive model, if outputs are also known for all inputs in the dataset, such that output generated by the analytical technique can be compared with actual output, is known as supervised learning

Unsupervised model If while developing a model, clear identification of the dependent variable cannot be done or value of output is not available in the dataset, it is known as unsupervised learning

Review material

1 Define a model.
2 Define influence diagram.
3 State the need for modelling a business problem.
4 State the role of an influence diagram in developing a model for a business problem.
5 List the components of a business model of a business problem.
6 Define dependent variables.
7 Define independent variables.
8 List the four conditions to justify the existence of an independent variable.
9 Define moderator variable.
10 Define mediator variable.
11 Differentiate between moderator and mediator variable.
12 Define control and extraneous variables.
13 Explain how the application of process logic to an HR function aids in the development of an analytical model.
14 Distinguish between supervised and unsupervised learning models.
15 Explain the role of theoretical framework in developing a predictive model.
16 What is the relation between process logic and theoretical background while developing an analytical model?
17 Define organisational jargon.
18 Illustrate the role of understanding jargon for developing predictive models.

Problem exercises

1 Imagine you as a student have to develop a predictive model which can predict which students will get placed in the current year. Discuss with placement co-ordinators in your batch and concerned staff to understand how the process of placement works.

    a Apply systems approach and process logic to your understanding of the process, indicating inputs, transformation, and output.

    b Identify various research variables that you will use to build a predictive model for this problem.

2 Form groups of six students each in the class. Split each group into two and ask both of these sub-groups to visit a few retail stores around their vicinity.

    a Record the performance of each of these stores in terms of revenue, unit sales, employee satisfaction levels, store manager rating, store ambience rating, and other metrics as pre-discussed among the group members. (You might need to use a survey to measure satisfaction, manager rating, and ambience rating from employees of each store).

    b Now each of the sub-groups should develop a predictive model based on its findings, with store performance (in revenue or sales) as the dependent variable and all others as independent variables. Now discuss the problems encountered in recording the observations. How difficult or easy it was to convince the employees to share data? Was there ambiguity in terms used in conversations or the survey? List these terms and how they were resolved.

    c Now summarise the necessity of common language while developing a model.

Case study

Can store performance be predicted from the talent value chain?

Analytics has now become mainstream, with each functional area and each sort of organisation adopting it. Although in the nascent stages of evolution, people analytics was adopted by a leading organisation, now the scenario has completely changed. The organisations are now applying people analytics to generate unprecedented insights especially discover surprising ways to manage and understand talent. An illustrative case is that of a leading global restaurateur (Arellano, DiLeonardo, and Felix, 2017) which used analytics to demonstrate how effective management of frontline staff at its restaurants drives overall business performance. This was a deviation from the traditional applications of people analytics, and therefore, modelling this business problem was quite different and tedious. However, the results were exciting as the application of this model yielded dramatic improvements in customer satisfaction, overall service delivery and business out-comes such as a 5% increase in sales in the testing phase of the deployment of the model itself.

The firm had already worked on conventional techniques to boost performance such as franchising outlets in certain locations while maintaining corporate-owned restaurants at some locations, but results were poor. Adding to the pile of these problems, the company witnessed a higher rate of employee turnover than its com-petitors. The firm, therefore, decided to take an alternate route, believing that if it makes efforts to bridge employee turnover gaps and retain its employees, it would be able to boost performance. So, now the firm had to look for data to explain employee turnover and then define ways to curb this turnover. Business analysts and senior leaders of the firm participated in extensive discussions and decided on three dependent or target variables – revenue growth per store, average customer satisfaction, and average speed of service (per shift of the employees). So, the model that would evolve from this process would contain the previously mentioned three target variables and data related to frontline staff (employees), becoming the inde-pendent variables, such that the model would explain how these independent vari-ables affect the target variables.

Next, the firm needed to identify these independent variables related to front-line staff. For this, it searched its internal data and was able to include many data variables in the model from internal data. However, the firm realised that internal data variables need to be supplemented with external data, as well, since some data points in internal data were missing and certain variables which played a crucial role in explaining the current business problem were never collected and stored as internal data. The latter (lack of data availability) was noticeable in three areas – selection and onboarding (specifically defining who and for what traits gets hired), data on management of daily activities (including managing people and environ-ment), and data on behaviour and interactions (to explain employee behaviour in the restaurants).

Experts and thought leaders within and outside the firm suggested that person-ality is a significant factor in explaining individual differences and therefore may also explain the differences in restaurant performance arising from frontline staff variations. This led to the inclusion of personality traits and cognitive skills as inde-pendent variables in the model. For the collection of data on the same, the firm ran a series of online games among restaurant employees to gauge their personality and cognitive skills. Further, the analysts suggested that the management of employees and the environment also has a significant effect on employee performance, which may consequently impact the store performance. Analysts supported this notion with theoretical analysis and suggested that a culture of conducting employee engagement surveys should be adopted in the firms to assess how favourable is employee perception towards management and restaurant environment. For data collection on this, the firm administered McKinsey & Company's Organizational Health Index (OHI), which includes 37 management practices contributing to overall firm performance. Gauging this survey data would allow the firm to assess how management practices and leadership affects frontline employees. Further, employee behaviour was tracked using sensors, along with their physical movement in the restaurant, tone and duration of their conversations, and collaboration. Based on past experiences, projects, and researches, external variables which were included in the model were: demographics, commute distance, and previous retail experience of the frontline employees.

The data on all these variables, including the financial performance of the store, comprised the final dataset of the model, totalling more than 10,000 data points. On a theoretical basis, and based on years of experience of senior leaders in the firm, more than 100 hypotheses were drafted, establishing the relationship between the target and independent variables. Here since the target and independent variables were predefined, along with the hypotheses, and the firm implemented logistic regression (supervised learning technique). This analysis was also supplemented with unsupervised learning technique. The results were surprising and myth-busters for the senior leaders, defying their basis of hypothesis in many cases. For example, unsupervised learning revealed that based on personality, frontline employees can be categorised into four archetypes – 'potential leaders', 'socialisers', 'conservative taskmasters', and 'entrepreneurial taskmasters'. Contrary to the hypothesis, that hiring for friendliness (socialisers) would drive store success, hiring for focused and distraction-minimising employees was supported by data analysis. Further, variable incentives poorly impacted performance, while career development options and cultural norms had a positive effect on worker outcomes. In addition to this, rather than the tenure of the manager, managerial attitude including empowering, inspiring, recognising, and building team culture affected frontline employees in their outcomes and performance. An interesting insight was that although longer employee shifts had been adopted to ease commuting and managerial responsibilities, it was, in turn, decreasing productivity.

Based on these findings, the firm decided to change its way of functioning as a pilot in one market of its operation. It was currently operating in four US markets. The company witnessed phenomenal results – customer satisfaction rose by more than 100 percent, speed of service also improved while turnover lowered substantially, contributing to a 5% increase in sales. Therefore, hiring for and management of an appropriate combination of people skills drives business success, especially in the retail sector. Further, sole reliance on management intuition or wisdom might not always be true, owing to environmental dynamics. However, combining managerial wisdom with analytics often provides insights not apparent through logic and most useful to drive business success.

Questions

1 Explain how the global restaurateur identified and defined its business problem.
2 List the dependent and independent variables used in the case to build a predictive model.
3 How did the firm decide on target variables?

4 Discuss the steps adopted by the firm to identify independent variables and data collection for the same.

5 Based on outcomes of modelling discussed in the case, explain how analytics combined with managerial wisdom provides the most useful business insights.

Note

1 Remember that this is step 2 of the holistic approach outlined in beginning of the book for adoption and implementation of analytics.

Bibliography

Arellano, C., DiLeonardo, A., and Felix, I. (2017, July 27). *Using people analytics to drive business performance: A case study*. Retrieved from McKinsey& Company: https://www.mckinsey.com/business-functions/mckinsey-analytics/our-insights/using-people-analytics-to-drive-business-performance-a-case-study

Bajpai, N. (2011). *Business research methods*. Noida: Dorling Kindersley (India) Pvt. Ltd.

Evans, J. R. (2016). Introduction to business analytics. In J. R. Evans (Ed.), *Business analytics: Methods, models and decisions* (pp. 1–35). Harlow, England: Pearson Education, Inc.

Light, R., Singer, J., and Willett, J. (1990). *By design: Planning research on higher education*. Cambridge, MA: Harvard University Press.

Marr, B. (2017, June 16). *How big data helps to tackle the No 1 cause of accidental death in the U.S.* Retrieved September 2019, from Forbes: https://www.forbes.com/sites/bernardmarr/2017/01/16/how-big-data-helps-to-tackle-the-no-1-cause-of-accidental-death-in-the-u-s/#7c3a2cc139ca

McKinsey. (2019). *Organizational health index*. Retrieved from McKinsey & Company: https://www.mckinsey.com/solutions/orgsolutions/overview/organizational-health-index

Sekaran, U., and Bougie, R. (2010). The research process: Theoretical framework and hypothesis development. In U. Sekaran and R. Bougie (Eds.), *Research methods for business: A skill building approach* (pp. 67–99). New Delhi: Wiley India (P) Ltd.

Van der Togt, J., and Rasmussen, T. H. (2017). Toward evidence-based HR. *Journal of Organizational Effectiveness: People and Performance*, 127–132.

4

PREDICTIVE ANALYTICS TOOLS AND TECHNIQUES

After reading this chapter, users will be able to understand the following key concepts:

- Understand the broad classification of various predictive analytical tools and techniques
- Learn about reasons for the popularity of R and its interface
- Understand some popular predictive analytical tools used in HRM and how they work
- Understand different HR analytics software available in the market

Opening case

A global healthcare services firm was experiencing significant turnover among its registered nurses. Despite exit interviews conducted by the firm, it was unable to locate the real reasons for turnover. Therefore, the firm outsourced the entire process of managing turnover to a third-party analytics company. The company, on its behalf, conducted exit interviews, which were non-biased and non-judgemental. This increased the response rate to exit interviews to 80%, while earlier it was staggering at approximately 30%. Thereafter, they implemented text analytics on exit interviews and identified the overall sentiment of the nurses towards the firm. The sentiment analysis revealed that all the registered nurses who were quitting the firm had a negative sentiment towards the firm. This was a serious situation, since not only the firm was suffering losses from current turnover, but it would also suffer in the future due to reduced inflow of applicants owing to bad word of mouth spreading from the dissatisfied nurses. Therefore, the firm needed to understand the reason for leaving and look for ways to improve. So, the analytics company applied topic modelling to the exit interview data and identified three common and major themes which were recurring and prevalent in most of the interviews. These three areas were: supervisor performance, onboarding experience, and coaching. The firm, therefore, took initiatives to create awareness among supervisors to exhibit superior performance since it directly affects the line staff. It also brought about changes in the orientation programme and provided enhanced training and coaching programmes at its premises. Within a year of bringing about the changes, the firm witnessed an unprecedented decline in turnover, dipping lower than the previous three-year record. The turnover costs of the firm fell by US$12 million. It also increased the morale and commitment of the nurses to the firm (HealthFirst, 2018).

Introduction

Since analytics is an evolving field, numerous techniques are available, only adding to the confusion of an analyst to decide which tool would be the best for application. A general answer can be to identify what business outcomes are required and what value addition these business outcomes would create, and then select a tool which would aid in generating these business outcomes. A lead workforce intelligence consultant at KPMG suggests that most companies do not attach HR analytics to specific business outcomes, putting it in danger of hanging in a bubble. Such companies need to ask questions such as: "If an analytical tool can reduce attrition from 5% to 4%, what value will that add to the business, and is it worth it?" (Levenson and Pillans, 2017). Asking the right questions and then analysing the business worth and value contribution of such questions would enable the firms to choose proper analytical tools and also add business value through HR analytics.

Classification of predictive analytical tools

By the time the user develops an understanding of the business problem and develops a predictive model for the same, he gets a lot of insight into what needs to be done with the data. One of the most basic classifications of predictive analytical tools is supervised and unsupervised learning methods. The basic distinction between the two is the availability of values of target or dependent variable (variable to be predicted). When values of the target variable are known beforehand, then the analytical tool can learn how to compute the target variable by comparing the computed value with actual observed values. This is termed as supervised learning – learning in the presence of a supervisor such that errors are corrected immediately.

Two most common classes of predictive analytics techniques that emerge on this basis are classification and clustering. When class labels are already known, and the tool simply fits the incoming data into these class labels based on some criteria, it will be termed as supervised classification. For example, employees being classified as good performers or bad performers is an example of a supervised classification technique. When labels are not known, and data has to be grouped or assigned into specific groups, usually based on the similarity between data items, it is unsupervised learning termed as clustering. For example, employee satisfaction concerning a newly launched HR policy has no particular label and therefore is a clustering technique. Other techniques include pattern matching and association, whereby analytical technique explores how data items are related to one another. A relatively emerging technique is data visualisation. Further classification can also be made based on the type of data at hand.

Popular predictive analytical tools in HRM-artificial neural networks (ANNs)

When the relationship between independent and dependent variables is complex, tools such as general linear models or artificial neural networks (ANNs) are used. ANNs are used to model any type of complex functional relationships and do not require to pre-specify the relationship between covariates and response variables. Typically, ANNs have been widely used in the field of management for the tasks of classification. A normal human being has 10^{11} neurons and there are 10^4 synapses per neuron. A typical composition of a biological neural network is shown in Figure 4.1. Each neuron receives signals from synapses and for a period of latent summation, which is a brief interval; it sums all the inputs it has received at neurons to which it will then respond. There are two sorts of impulses: excitatory and inhibitory. When excitatory impulses exceed inhibitory impulses by threshold value which is 40mV., the neuron is said to fire, resulting in some form of human activity.

The same processing of a biological neural network is modelled using ANN and general topology of the modelled neural network is depicted in Figure 4.2.

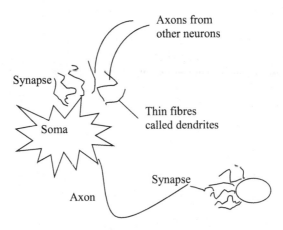

FIGURE 4.1 Composition of one biological neuron

Source: Zurada (1994)

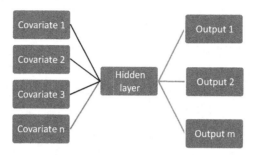

FIGURE 4.2 Topology of an artificial neural network

An ANN has multiple layers – one layer is the input layer, the second layer is composed of one or more hidden layers, and the third layer is that of output or response variables. The input layer can contain one or more covariates, while the output layer contains one or more outputs. The hidden layer can have more than one sub-layer. The output in ANN is computed as the weighted average of the inputs. More weight of input means more contribution of that variable towards the output. The observed data is used to train the network, and ANN learns the functional relationship by adjusting weights for each input in multiple iterations, at least until error stage is reached. Many models have been defined to compute the weighted average and decide on the number of iterations.

One of the most widely used neural network algorithms is multilayer perceptron. Here the output is a simple non-linear function of the sum of inputs. Weight of input describes its importance in determining output. If weight is negative, it inhibits the output rather than activating it. Multilayer perceptron (MLP) (Gunther and Fritsch, 2010; Zurada, 1994) is like a directed graph which has nodes and directed edges. A representation of the MLP typology is shown in Figure 4.3.

Each node represents one neuron, and covariates are represented by single neuron each. Similarly, in the output layer, response variables are represented by one neuron each. The hidden layer is termed so because it cannot be observed in nature; this is also referred to as the 'black box' nature of ANN. Another neuron termed as constant neuron represents an intercept similar to intercept in regression, which represents variation not directly arising from any covariate. The connection (directed edge in the graph) between two neurons is called a synapse. Theoretically, any number of covariates and output variables are possible to be included in ANN.

Two functions are operating in this network: integration function and activation function. A weight is attached to each synapse between the input and hidden layer and hidden to the output layer. The data passes as signals through the networks the weights are adjusted till the desired minimum error is reached. Integration function combines all input signals while the activation function transforms the aggregated input into an output. The simplest MLP (multilayer perceptron) has n

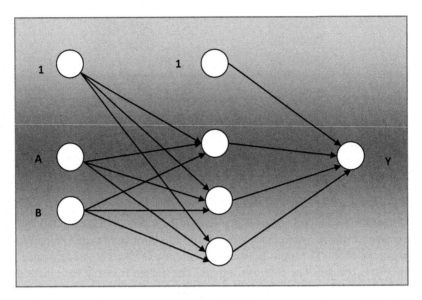

FIGURE 4.3 ANN with two input neurons, three hidden neurons in one hidden layer, and one output neuron

Source: Gunther and Fritsch (2010)

input variables, one output neuron, and no hidden layer. The output is computed as follows:

$$o(x) = f\left(w_0 + \sum_{i=1}^{n} w_i x_i\right) = f(w_0 + \mathbf{w}^T \mathbf{x})$$

In the preceding equation, w_0 depicts the intercept, $\mathbf{x}$ represents a set of all covariates and w_i represents a set of all synaptic weights. This is simply an extension of GLM which has link function f^{-1}. It is seen that this is simply equivalent to regression parameters computed by GLM. When the hidden layer is included which has J hidden neuron, then the function computed becomes as under:

$$o(x) = f\left(w_0 + \sum_{j=1}^{J} w_j . f\left(w_{0j} + \sum_{j=1}^{n} w_{ij} x_i\right)\right)$$
$$= f\left(w_0 + \sum_{j=1}^{J} w_j . f(w_{0j} + \mathbf{w}_j^T \mathbf{x})\right)$$

In this case, again, w_0 depicts the intercept for output neuron, while w_{0j} represents intercept of jth hidden neuron, x represents a set of all covariates, and w_j represents a set of all synaptic weights leading to jth hidden neuron. So, the integration function simply computes the weighted average. It is shown in MLP that when a piecewise continuous function is to be modelled, one hidden layer is sufficient (Hornik, Stichcombe, and White, 1989). The activation is generally a bounded non-decreasing non-linear and differentiable function. The commonly used functions are logistic function or hyperbolic tangent function. A typical activation is:

$$f(x) = \frac{2}{1 + e^{-\alpha x}} - 1$$

$$f(x) = sgn(x) = \begin{cases} -1, & x < 0 \\ 1, & x \geq 0 \end{cases}$$

The first equation simply represents a squashed signed function with different curves which vary with different values of α. As $\alpha \rightarrow \infty$, function f(x) becomes sgn(x). The first equation is termed as bipolar continuous function, while the second equation is called a bipolar binary function. They are also said to display sigmoidal characteristics. The activation function should be chosen according to the inputs fed to the algorithm. For example, if the input is binary, use a logistic function.

An algorithm in neural network assigns weights and then after computing, the weighted output compares it to the actual output provided in training data. Then corrections are made in weights and comparison is made again until least error state is reached. This process is called supervised learning. The following steps are utilised in a neural network for weight training or supervised learning:

- Initially, all weights are set to random values which are drawn from a normal population or set to user-specified values.
- Now the algorithm in the neural network computes the output from the given set of inputs and these weights. If the training is incomplete, the output will differ from the observed output.
- The network therefore computes and error function E which can be the sum of squared errors (SSE) or if the output is binary, then cross-entropy is computed. Here, o denotes the computed output and y denotes the observed output while ih denotes the input-output pair.

$$E = \frac{1}{2} \sum_{l=1}^{L} \sum_{h=1}^{H} (o_{lh} - y_{lh})$$

- The weights are adjusted according to the rules of the algorithm which generally is the minimisation of the error function. The process stops once the criteria are fulfilled.

This process specifies a traditional backpropagation algorithm. Another algorithm, a resilient backpropagation algorithm, is a slight variation of backpropagation. In this, gradient or derivative or error function is computed, and an attempt is made to reach the local minima of the error function. Correction to weights is applied by moving in the opposite direction to that of local minima. If the partial derivative turns out to negative, the weight is increased; otherwise, weight is decreased. The quantity which is added or subtracted for weight adjustment is termed as learning rate η_k. In traditional backpropagation algorithms, the learning rate is fixed, while in resilient algorithms, learning rate and a sign of partial derivative are used for weight adjustment, which ensures balanced learning for the whole network. The weight adjustment in traditional backpropagation algorithm is done as per the following rules:

$$w_k^{(t+1)} = w_k^{(t)} - \eta . \frac{\partial E^{(t)}}{\partial w_k^{(t)}}$$

The weight adjustment in the resilient backpropagation algorithm is done as per the rules mentioned as follows:

$$w_k^{(t+1)} = w_k^{(t)} - \eta_k^{(t)} . sign\left(\frac{\partial E^{(t)}}{\partial w_k^{(t)}} \right)$$

Here, t represents the step of iteration while k represents the weights.

Another variation is resilient back propagation with weight backtracking, which allows the algorithm to move to one previous stage in case a minimum is missed. A pseudocode (Reidmiller and Braun, 1993, pp. 25–27) for the same is presented as follows:

```
for all weights {
    if (grad.old * grad > 0){
        delta := min (delta * eta.plus, delta.max)
        weights = weights - sign(grad) * delta
        grad.old := grad
    }
    Else if (grad.old * grad < 0){
weights = weights + sign(grad.old) * delta
delta := max (delta * eta.minus, delta.min)
        grad.old := 0
    }
    Else if (grad.old * grad = 0){
weights = weights - sign(grad) * delta
        grad.old := grad
    }
}
```

A glimpse of the preceding algorithm provides the reader with an understanding of how ANN tries to classify and predict the data. Theoretically, the pseudocode works by first computing the gradient of the error term by finding the difference between observed values of the target variable with values computed using the algorithm. Then the product of gradient with gradient computed in the previous iteration of the algorithm is computed. When the observed value (O) is greater than the computed value (C), then since the error is positive, the gradient will also be positive. If the previous gradient was also positive, then by the algorithm, $w_k^{(t+1)}$ will be increased by $\eta_k^{(t)}$ from previous value $w_k^{(t)}$. If still after this correction, the gradient is positive such that O > C, then since their product will also be greater than zero, the algorithm will keep on applying the correction to the weight until a minimum error gradient pre-specified in the algorithm is reached. This indicates that the algorithm is converging. On the other hand, if the product is negative, and if O < C, the weight is increased and iterations continue until minimum error gradient is not reached. It is worth mentioning here that the minimum and maximum values for the gradient are pre-specified in the algorithm as 'threshold' values.

ANN has found widespread application in modelling complex functional relationships between covariates and response variables. Additionally, since it is not necessary to pre-specify the type of relationship between these variables, it makes ANN a highly attractive analytical tool. It has higher accuracy than conventional analytical tools used for classification such as regression, etc. Further, it can work on Big Data, as well.

Decision trees

Analogous to the trees in nature, decision trees present the structure of decision-making in a tree-like manner. It is a graphical depiction of how various alternatives can lead to a particular decision. An example of a decision tree depicting the risk of being diabetic depending on body mass index (BMI), heredity, and daily exercise routine of an individual has been shown in Figure 4.4.

Unlike a natural tree, the root is shown at the top, while branching is done with the help of conditions until terminal nodes representing decision is not reached. The condition nodes are also called as the internal nodes, based on which branching or splitting of a tree is done. This visual depiction demonstrates the importance of each feature, the first splitting or decision-making feature is BMI, followed by heredity and exercise routine. It also helps in establishing relationships between different features used for decision-making. Since this decision tree is classifying whether an individual is a low risk or high risk for diabetes, it is termed as **a classification tree**. When the target variable represented by leaf nodes in a tree can be labelled into particular classes, and then decision trees are applied on such data, it is known as classification tree. On the other hand, a **regression tree** is the one which predicts continuous values, rather than classes. Typically, the algorithm used to apply decision trees in various statistical packages is known as **CART** (classification and regression tree).

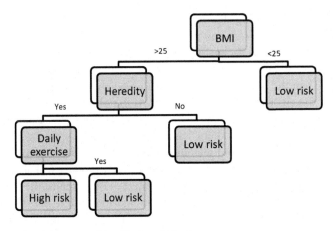

FIGURE 4.4   Decision tree: risk of being diabetic

Let us acquaint ourselves a bit with the working of a decision tree algorithm. The first thing that happens in the tree is to split the dataset based on the most important feature. However, to identify the most important feature, the tree first takes all the features in the dataset and generates splits of the tree. So, if there are three features, three primary candidates for the first split will be generated by the algorithm. Now, the chosen split is the one which minimises the cost of splitting. For the example presented in the text to predict the risk of being diabetic, the feature which costs least for splitting is BMI. As the split generates groupings of data based on categories of features, further splitting involves identifying the most important feature in each sub-group formed in the first split. In this manner, this algorithm is recursive, as it keeps on generating sub-groups based on least-cost criteria.

The functions used to compute the least cost in the decision tree either attempts to reduce the error in predicting target class or standard deviation. The formula of least cost based on latter is a Gini index score, often used for classification tree while the former is generally used for regression trees. For a regression tree, for each data point, the formula used to compute the value of cost function is:

$$\text{Cost function for Regression tree} = \text{Average } [y - (predicted\,value)^2]$$

The mean of all these values is then computed, by summing and dividing by the number of data points. For each candidate split, this computed value of cost function is compared, and the algorithm picks that split which has a minimum value of this function. The formula for Gini index, G is given by:

$$G = \text{Sum } [pk \star (1 - pk)]$$

Here, pk is the proportion of occurrence of the same class in a particular group. That is, if a decision tree has only one class, then $pk = 1$, called perfect class purity.

In a similar class, the decision tree may have two classes, one with all the inputs, the other with none, each carrying *pk* equals to 1 and 0, respectively.

The next question is how does the algorithm decide when to stop splitting? Sometimes, a tree may have a large number of nodes and branches, which may become complex to interpret. This is called *overfitting of data*. So, some criterion needs to be supplied to the algorithm to enable it to learn when to stop further split of data. There are three main techniques adopted in an algorithm for this purpose. The first method is specifying the acceptable *minimum number of training inputs to be used for each leaf*. If to reach any leaf in the tree, the minimum specified number of training data points were not used, that leaf is not included in the tree. The second method is specifying the *maximum depth*. With this, the user is restricting the maximum total length of the path to reach from the root node to the terminal node. The third and most widely used method is *pruning*, which also enhanced the performance of a decision tree. Analogous to the pruning of a natural tree, pruning of a decision tree involves removing the leaf nodes containing features with low importance. Pruning can be done based on either reducing error or cost complexity. Error-reducing pruning attempts to remove nodes starting from leaves of the tree, such that the overall accuracy of the tree doesn't reduce. In highly complex trees, cost complexity pruning attempts to remove those nodes which are attached to a complete sub-group, in a manner that a learning parameter alpha remains largely unaffected. This can also be termed as weakest link pruning.

K-nearest neighbour (KNN)

The term K-nearest neighbour, abbreviated as KNN, is a supervised learning algorithm, which is applied for classification and regression. To understand how KNN works, the user needs to keep in mind that the target variable to be predicted has class labels. Therefore, when a training dataset is presented to KNN algorithm, it learns all features of the data for a given class label of the target variable. It is one of the simplest methods of classification and prediction, as it uses this learning to classify an unlabeled observation into existing classes. It predicts the class of a given dataset by comparing its closeness with its k nearest neighbours. The class with the highest vote is deemed to be the class of input data. For example, a food item can be distinguished as a main course or dessert, based on two main factors – nutritional value and sweetness. Although the actual distinction may involve a large number of other variables, here it has been assumed that simply these two factors are the deciding criteria. Generally speaking, main course meals are higher in nutritional value and lower in sweetness. Now, consider that it is required to categorise ice cream as a main course or dessert item. To decide this, KNN considers the nearest neighbours of (food items similar to) ice cream based on nutritional value and price of the same. In this example, shakes, mousse cakes, pastries, and custard are four nearest neighbours of ice cream, which are low on food value and high on sugar content. Therefore, ice cream is also categorised as dessert. Therefore, it is simple to grasp the idea of working of KNN. So each time, a new data item is presented to KNN, it computes the similarity between the existing data items and input data item, based on features or characteristics of the data items.

There are two important considerations in this algorithm. First, the technique used to compute the similarity between data items, and second, the number of neighbouring items to be considered while categorising the input. There are primarily three methods used to compute the similarity between data items – Euclidean distance, Manhattan distance, and Minkowski distance. However, the most widely used measure is the Euclidean distance.

Euclidean distance

As per Euclidean distance, the distance between two data points in two-dimensional space can be computed using the formula:

$$d = \sqrt{(x1 - y1)^2 + (x2 - y2)^2}$$

where $x1$, $x2$, $y1$, and $y2$ are the x and y coordinates of the two points in a two-dimensional space. This formula has a basis in the Pythagorean theorem and can be extended to three-dimensional space, as well. In general, the formula to compute the distance between any two points can simply be written as:

$$d = \sqrt{\sum_{i=n}(x_i - y_i)^2}$$

Manhattan distance

When the two points among which the distance is to be computed follows a grid-like path, it becomes Manhattan distance. It is known as the absolute sum of the difference between the two data points.

$$d = \sum_{i=1}^{n}|x_i - y_i|^1$$

So if the x and y are vectors in two-dimensional space (for simplicity, assume a function with a finite number of values in both x and y axes), then Manhattan distance is computed as:

$$d = (x_1 - y_1) + (x_2 - y_2) + (x_3 - y_3) + \ldots + (x_n - y_n)$$

Minkowski distance

Minkowski distance is a general distance metric, such that both Euclidean distance and Manhattan distance is a special case of the same. It is important to note that computation of Minkowski distance applies to normed functions, which are always real-valued and positive, such that it is zero only when the function itself is zero. A simple formula used to compute Minkowski distance is:

$$d = \left(\sum_{i=1}^{n} |x_i - y_i|^p \right)^{\frac{1}{p}}$$

When p = 1, it becomes Manhattan distance, and when p = 2, it becomes Euclidean distance. The distance computed by this formula will always be a linear straight line.

The KNN algorithm computes the conditional probability of a data point belonging to a particular class, using the distance computed using a given metric supplied in the function, and then assesses how similar the data item is to a given class. Now the second consideration can be discussed; that is, the number of data points to be considered while computing the distance. It is not possible to compute the distance for all data points in a given class, especially when the number of data points is large, so KNN computes the distance for a small number of data points (referred to as K), which can be either supplied by the user while coding the function for KNN so that using hit and trial, the optimal value of K is determined. Otherwise, the user can supply a grid of values of K in the function for which the algorithm is repeatedly re-run, and the optimal value of K is thereby determined.

It is important to mention here that the value of K cannot exceed the number of data points in the dataset. Now the optimal value of K can be determined by the optimality assessment metrics produced by the algorithm. Using a technique called cross-validation, whereby the dataset is divided into training, validation, and test data, the KNN algorithm is run for a range of different values of K and the prediction accuracy of the model is tested to determine the optimal value of K. The accuracy metrics commonly used in KNN are RMSE (root mean square error); R Squared (coefficient of determination), which is a measure of the variance in model fit, that is, how well the predicted values fit the original values; accuracy determined by mean absolute error in observed and predicted values; and ROC (receiver operating curve). ROC curve is plotting the confusion metric for different K values, and the area under the ROC curve is used to assess how well the model can classify. Therefore, the KNN algorithm performance is evaluated using any of the previously described metrics, and the optimal value of K is determined by the optimal value of the performance metric. For example, assume KNN is being used for a classification problem for values of K ranging from 1–50 and using RMSE, the model performance comes highest for K = 29. Then the optimal value of K would be 29, and for classification prediction for future data inputs, the algorithm will compute the distance from 29 nearest neighbours. Whenever the algorithm finds the data input belonging to a class based on least distance computed from the neighbour of that class, it will generate a vote for that class. This process is repeated for 29 nearest neighbours and the class which gets the highest number of votes is the predicted class. This is also termed as computation of conditional probability; that is, the probability of the data point belonging to a particular class, given the probability of belonging to other classes, as well. This algorithm is practically demonstrated in R in Chapter 7, and all the concepts discussed in this chapter have been practically illustrated.

The biggest limitation of KNN is the computation time required for testing and prediction, which increases manifold with an increase in the number of items in the dataset. Also, the KNN algorithm exhibits poor performance when the dataset has several features for classification, which confuses the algorithm to compute the nearest and farthest neighbour. Despite the drawbacks, owing to advancements in computation speed of machine learning models, KNN is widely used for recommendation engines like Amazon's 'recommendations'. KNN also finds extensive use in speech detection services like voice assistants and the typical 'auto-suggest text' feature in search bars, whereby prediction of remaining text is made by the software based on the content typed in by the user. In HRM, it can be used for initial applicant screening in the selection process.

K-means clustering

The most widely used clustering method is K-means clustering. It is important to mention that readers must not confuse K-means clustering with K-nearest neighbour algorithms. While the former is unsupervised, the latter is widely implemented for classification based on class labels already present in the dataset and is a supervised learning technique. However, both have one thing in common: the use of distance metrics. While KNN uses distance metric to find class similarity, K-means uses distance metrics to identify different groups or clusters present in the data which have higher similarities among them. K-means clustering is an unsupervised learning technique used to divide a given number of observations into K groups, which are homogenous and share similar features.

A pertinent term in K-means clustering is 'centroid', which implies the centre of each cluster or group of observation. The distance of each observation is computed from the centroid, and allocation to a particular cluster, is done based on least distance. After allocations, the mean of the number of observations is computed for each cluster and represents the centroid for that cluster. The target is to minimise the centroid to the least value, such that the in-cluster variances are minimal. It is an iterative algorithm, such that for each iteration, allocations are varied in clusters, centroids are computed, until an optimal number of clusters and an optimal number of allocations are reached. There are two ways to stop the iterations in the algorithm – one, by specifying the number of iterations, and two, when no more significant changes are detected in values of the cluster. The metric normally used to compute the distance from a centroid for a given data point is squared Euclidean distance.

There are broadly two mechanisms in which standard algorithm executes. K data points are randomly picked from the dataset and specified as centroids. K-means clustering then builds the clusters by computing the distances of each data point from these centroids. After all data points are exhausted in the dataset, the mean value of each cluster is computed, which becomes the new centroid of that cluster. The process is iterated until optimal conditions are reached. In another technique, the data points are randomly allocated to K clusters, and the mean of each cluster representing its centroid is computed.

Similarly to KNN, optimality checks have to be carried out to determine the optimal value of K. However, this also poses the biggest limitation to the working of the model. K-means clustering algorithm attempts to build spherical clusters with the almost same size and therefore, it may at times produce 'wrong' classifications. It has been seen that its performance is rather unpredictable, since it works well on some datasets while not working on other datasets. At the same time, the algorithm can work well with large datasets in small time frames. Resultantly, it finds application in market segmentation, astronomy, etc. Sometimes, the analysts may also utilise this technique to generate an initial set of clusters, which can be refined later by application of advanced techniques. One of the most popular applications of this algorithm is in 'feature learning', which has been implemented in natural language processing models, as well. Using training data, K-means is used to produce clusters, and for each cluster, the features are then analysed and labelled. The inputs from test dataset are then used to predict which cluster a data point belongs to, and then its features are specified.

Text analytics

Text analytics is a machine learning technique working on the principles of natural language processing (NLP) to extract meaning from text data present in an unstructured format. It implies mining textual data to elicit sentiments, keywords used, and the structure of the text. With enhanced capabilities for storage and processing of diverse data, text analytics has now become commonplace. Since textual data is not structured, it cannot be stored in conventional relational databases with tabular structure. However, advents of storage platforms like non-relational databases (MongoDB, for example) have facilitated this storage of textual data, aiding firms to now look for tools which aid in the analysis of this data. Text analytics has roots in NLP, and works by breaking the sentences into most basic components – phrases, punctuation, breaks, etc., and then tokenising it to impart meaning. The outcome of text analytics involves identification of syntax, semantics and content of the text data, all of which are added to the knowledge base for future analysis. The key steps involved in text analytics are :

1   **Identify the language of the text** – Many software and analytical algorithms come with the inbuilt capacity to identify the language used in the text. It is completely dependent on the algorithm of how many languages it supports. Further analysis cannot be carried out unless language has been identified.

2   **Tokenisation** – The text contains many different units like words, punctuations, hyperlinks, etc. Tokenisation involves breaking down the text into these individual units, and the simplest form of the algorithm will simply remove the punctuation and retain all the words. So, if a text contains three lines with six words each, tokenisation will simply generate (6 × 3) 18 words. Defining a token completely depends on the language of the text. For example, for the English language, tokens are white spaces and punctuation. Simple rule-based algorithms will be able to identify these tokens in the text and eliminate it, retaining the remaining text for further analysis. However, simple rule-based tokenisation cannot work on all languages. For example, Chinese doesn't include white spaces; in that case, tokenisation cannot work.

3   **Sentence formation** – This part of text analytics sets to identify the boundaries of the text; that is, imparting the meaning to the text where it ends and the next one begins. For English, common punctuation marks like period and question mark indicate the end of a sentence. However, exceptions exist like a period may be used to abbreviate the title of a person like 'Mr.', 'Dr.', and so on. These boundaries not only vary by language, but also by the mode of writing. Social media platforms like Twitter have a trend of breaking the sentences by hash '#' symbol. So in the case of Twitter data, tokenised data will contain hashes to aid in the identification of the presence of different sentences in the text.

4   **PoS tagging** – As everyone is familiar, each language has a notation for word usage. For example, the English language specifies whether a word is a noun, pronoun, verb, adjective, etc., to determine its contribution to speech. Therefore, PoS tagging (part of speech tagging) is the process of identification of notation for each token to determine its contribution to overall speech.

5   **Light Parsing** – Light parsing, also called chunking or phrasing, involves combining PoS tagged tokens into phrases to form tagged phrases like noun phrases, verb phrases, etc.

6   **Syntax analysis** – Syntax analysis is used to develop a syntax parse tree for the text, to depict syntactical usage in the same. It imparts a structure to all the analysis listed previously. Use of syntax can completely change the meaning of a word. Therefore, syntax analysis attempts to determine the context in which words have been used in the sentence.

7   **Lexical chaining** – Lexical chaining is also a prominent area of application for topic modelling of text. Lexical chaining involves relating different sentences by their meaning and strength of relationship to an overall topic. The placement of different sentences in the document doesn't matter; if they imply the same and relate to the same topic, they will be lexically chained together.

All of these steps have been put to good organisational use. Feature extraction is an area of application of text analytics which identifies the prevalent themes, intentions, and sentiments in the text, and thereby aids in sentiment analysis. In HRM, sentiment analysis finds widespread usage in replacing annual engagement surveys. Organisations now use artificial intelligence to track employee sentiments through their conversations on organisational platforms. Topic modelling is another area of text analytics useful for identifying the major prevalent themes in the text. This, too, can be used in a variety of ways by the firms. Applying analytics on exit interviews, organisations can infer through topic modelling, which are the prevalent and recurring topics in the interview. This might prove highly useful for understanding the causes of turnover in the firms. Text analytics also finds application in document categorisation and retrieval. This can be used for automated screening of job applications. The text of incoming résumés can be analysed to identify if they fulfil all the eligibility criteria for a job and therefore, get shortlisted for the further selection process. Web scraping can also be done to collect résumés for job openings in the firm and then categorise and sort them as per their match with different jobs in the firm, without any manual intervention.

Different HR analytics software available in the market

The most popular analytical tools available in the market applies to the field of HRM, as well. A list of the most popular tools below, followed by a brief outlook of the popular software platforms and analytics consultancy firms in the market.

R

R is one of the most powerful and popular open-source software for statistical analysis and computing. It can run on multiple operating systems such as Windows, Unix, and Mac OS. Its popularity is owing to many reasons:

1   It is an open-source platform.
2   It can run on multiple operating systems.
3   It has wide support community and number of free video demonstrations, making it quick and easy to learn.
4   It has a repository of packages which provide automated algorithms for different statistical and analytical functions, requiring minimal coding effort from the user.
5   Rattle is a GUI built on R, which further simplifies the user interaction with R.
6   The open-source community of R developers continually contribute updated packages and techniques to further enhance the ease of applying analytics by the users of R.
7   For each package, a wide number of practice datasets are also available.

A typical R interface is as shown in what follows. It is divided into four sections. On the top left is the scripting page, where the user can type R script or code for

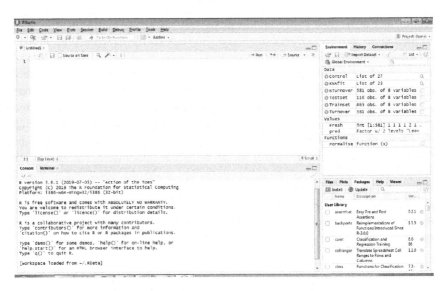

FIGURE 4.5   RStudio interface

execution and even save it for later use. On the top right is the Global Environment tab. It depicts all the active datasets and all global variables in the current state of R. On the bottom left is the Console window, which shows the code and outcome of the execution of R script. The bottom right part offers Help, Files, Plots, Packages, and Viewer functions. A summary regarding any package and current available packages can be viewed from this tab. This tab also features the ability to view Plots, copy them, or extract them in a pdf file. All the remaining functions are intuitive to understand.

In this book, the interface RStudio version 3.6.1 for Windows (32 bit) has been used. For the reader's machine, the suitable version can be downloaded from the link:

1   To download RStudio – https://cran.r-project.org/
2   To download R tools – https://cran.r-project.org/bin/windows/Rtools/

To work on any statistical analysis technique in R or any dataset, it first has to be installed and imported, respectively. R works by 'R packages', all of which are available on the Internet and open access. For example, a package called CART (classification and regression tree) contains the automated functions to implement popular classification and regression algorithms like KNN. It also contains the code to implement confusion matrix in the form of a function, such that the user simply needs to provide appropriate values of arguments in the confusion matrix function, and the rest will be executed automatically. By clicking on Packages in the bottom right corner, the list of available packages can be discerned. To be able to use a package in the current session of R, it has to be checked from that tab, or the user may install the package by typing in the code

```
install.packages ("package name")
```

This code will direct the software to automatically search the package online and retrieve and install it. Please note that R is highly case sensitive language. Therefore, it is advised to use the codes in the same manner as specified in this text.

To work on any dataset, it needs to be imported in the current session. Remember that for each R session, the dataset has to be fetched again. Also, to avoid keying in the dataset name repeatedly for writing the script, users can simply attach the dataset to the global environment, using the code

```
attach("dataset name")
```

Anything which appears in the global environment tab will be available for use in the current session of R. It is generally advisable to normalise the dataset or scale it for use in any statistical analysis, since this eliminates any errors due to extreme values. Further, using Pareto's rule, the dataset should be split into training and test data (the usual proportion is 80:20). A technique called cross-validation used to assess performance a statistical model splits the dataset into test, training, and validation datasets. All of these, and important packages, have been practically illustrated in R in subsequent chapters.

Python

Similar to R, Python is another high-level programming language. It is also gaining popularity in the present analytical scenario. However, the users generally find Python to be a bit more difficult, only owing to lack of extensive documentation and support for the language online, as is the case with R. Both the languages have good capabilities, and there are just minor differences. Putting it in simple terms, R does not have object-oriented capacity like Python, while Python does not currently support the wide range of statistical packages and distributions as in R. Another reason why Python seems difficult to the end-user is that it does not support extensive packages like R enabling automation or very lesser coding for implementing statistical functions. However, this limitation can be attributed to the language being relatively newer than R. All the available packages with Python are contained and can be viewed from PyPi index. It is generally assumed that for standalone applications, like individual analysis or implementation on single servers, R is the language of choice, while if the application requires integration like with websites, then Python is the language of choice. Like R, Python is an open-source language.

SAS

Another popular platform for analytics which has been a market leader for a long while now is SAS, which can also work on multiple operating systems. The only limitation is that it is a paid service and not free for use. However, lately, SAS has come up with University Edition, which is a free version of SAS with limited capabilities. SAS has found applications in all streams of analytics for all types and scales of business. The firm has been proactively developing solutions for any form of analytics that emerges in the market. In 2018, it was also pronounced as a leader in the field of AI solutions. With an unbeatable presence in the market for many decades, the firm has been able to collect diverse data from disparate sources, and that is also one of the reasons why SAS solutions are robust and practical.

PowerBI

Microsoft, which is a dominant market leader for computers and operating systems, has also developed a powerful solution for analytics, 'PowerBI'. This product is part of a bigger Microsoft platform called 'Power Platform', which enables firms to make informed, powerful, and real-time decisions, starting right with the framework to collect such data which enables these decisions. Microsoft products have been labelled as magic quadrant leaders by Gartner Group. The advantage of using PowerBI is that since the Microsoft Office suite is widely in use, the product starts data analytics by labelling the data in the suite itself, which facilitates data analysis. It is an open-source cloud-based intelligence service suite. For 1 GB of data storage, the product offers unlimited use and access to all the capabilities.

Tableau

Tableau is an immensely popular data visualisation tool. It has also been placed among leaders like Microsoft in the magic quadrant leader by Gartner Group. The product is based in California (US). The power of Tableau lies in mainly two things: its extensive data visualisation support facilitating building up of simple charts to complex dashboards with embedded graphics available a click away, and the ease with which a non-technical user can also build up a stand-alone data visual in the platform. The product also offers to supplement the visuals with real-time data updates and integration of data from across diverse platforms. The Tableau suite contains five tools that are divided into two categories: developer and sharing tools. Creation of data visuals is done in developer tools, namely Tableau Desktop and public. The sharing of these visuals is done using sharing tools, namely Tableau online, server, and reader. It can connect with any data platform ranging from simple Excel or pdf to complex databases like Amazon Web Services or the Microsoft Azure platform. One of the most significant uses of Tableau is for visualisation of Big Data such as depicting cross-country interaction strength on Facebook for all the countries across the globe where Facebook is utilised.

Conclusion

Applications of predictive analytics to diverse areas of HRM are growing exponentially. This can be attributed to several factors like availability of wider and low-cost storage platforms, increases in data diversity, ability to tap into this data, and development in different types of techniques available to analyse this data. Despite the growing disparity in data, the application of analytics is proliferating, owing to almost parallel advancements in the techniques to analyse this data. In this context, this chapter therefore presents a discussion of major analytical tools and algorithms specifically used in the context of predictive analytics. The chapter discusses ANN, KNN, decision trees, K-means clustering and text analytics. All of these can be deployed on commercial software available for analysis, requiring the client firm to simply make the data available. No upskilling of the current workforce or hiring anew needs to be carried out when commercial platforms are used. However, commercial platforms are sometimes quite expensive, and they also do not allow integration of data and develop a solution completely customised for the firm. So, the decision-maker needs to develop a solution of his own. This chapter, therefore, also discusses the major tools and platforms available in the market for implementation of these analytical algorithms.

Glossary

Activation function   transforms the aggregated input into output, such as the use of the sigmoid function to convert the output into binary classes

Artificial neural network   ANN is a mimic of biological neural networks used to model any type of complex functional relationships and do not require to pre-specify the relation between covariates and response variables

Classification tree   When the target variable represented by leaf nodes in a tree can be labelled into particular classes, and then decision trees are applied on such data, it is known as classification tree

Condition nodes   in decision trees are also called internal nodes, based on which branching or splitting of the tree is done

Decision trees   present the structure of decision-making in a tree-like manner, a graphical depiction of how various alternatives can lead to a particular decision

Integration function   in ANN combines all input signals to compute the weighted average to be used as the output of the network

K-nearest neighbour   abbreviated as KNN, is a supervised learning algorithm which is applied for classification and regression; it predicts the class of a given dataset by comparing its closeness with its K-nearest neighbours, and the class with the highest vote is deemed to be the class of input data

Lexical chaining   involves relating different sentences by their meaning and strength of relationship to an overall topic

Light parsing   also called chunking or phrasing, it involves combining PoS tagged tokens into phrases to form tagged phrases like noun phrases, verb phrases, etc.

Multiple layers in ANNs one layer is the input layer, the second layer is composed of one or more hidden layers, and the third layer is that of output or response variables

PoS tagging (part of speech tagging) is the process of identification of notation for each token to determine its contribution to overall speech

Pruning of a decision tree involves removing the leaf nodes containing features with low importance, which can be done based on either reducing error or cost complexity

Resilient backpropagation algorithm Gradient or derivative or error function is computed, and an attempt is made to reach the local minima of the error function; correction to weights is applied by moving in the opposite direction to that of local minima

Regression tree predicts continuous values, rather than classes

Supervised learning When values of the target variable are known beforehand, then the analytical tool can learn how to compute the target variable by comparing the computed value with actual observed values; this is termed as supervised learning, learning in the presence of a supervisor such as errors are corrected immediately

Text analytics a machine learning technique working on the principles of natural language processing (NLP) to extract meaning from text data present in an unstructured format. It implies mining textual data to elicit sentiments, keywords used, and the structure of the text

Tokenisation involves breaking down the text into these individual units, and the simplest form of the algorithm will simply remove the punctuation and retain all these tokens

Unsupervised learning/clustering When labels are not known, and data has to be grouped or assigned into specific groups, usually based on the similarity between data items, it is unsupervised learning termed as clustering.

Review material

1 Discuss supervised and unsupervised learning.
2 List the various types of predictive algorithms.
3 Define ANN.
4 Explain briefly how biological neural network works.
5 List the three layers in ANN.
6 How is output computed in ANN?
7 Name and explain the most widely used neural network algorithm.
8 List and explain the two functions used in ANN.
9 List the commonly used activation functions.
10 List the steps used in building an ANN model for supervised learning.
11 Discuss how resilient backpropagation algorithm is different from the conventional backpropagation algorithm.

12 Explain how resilient backpropagation with weight backtracking works using pseudocode.
13 Define decision trees.
14 List the nodes in decision trees.
15 Distinguish between the two types of decision trees.
16 Name the R package used for implementing decision trees in R.
17 Briefly explain how the decision tree algorithm works.
18 Explain the functions used to compute the least cost in decision trees.
19 How does the decision tree algorithm decide when to stop splitting?
20 Define pruning.
21 Define KNN.
22 List the three methods used in KNN to determine the similarity between neighbouring items.
23 Write the formulas for Euclidean distance, Minkowski distance, and Manhattan distance.
24 How is the optimal value of K determined?
25 List the commonly used accuracy metrics for KNN.
26 What is a major limitation of KNN?
27 List some areas of application of KNN.
28 How is K-means clustering different from and similar to KNN?
29 Define centroid.
30 Explain the basic functioning of K-means clustering.
31 List the two ways in iterations can be stopped in K-means clustering.
32 Discuss the limitations of K-means clustering.
33 Explain an application of K-means clustering.
34 Define text analytics.
35 List and explain the key steps involved in text analytics.
36 List some common applications of text analytics and their role in HRM.
37 List some popular analytical tools.
38 Discuss some reasons for the popularity of R.
39 Explain a typical R interface.
40 List some differences between R and Python.
41 What is one major advantage of using PowerBI?
42 What are the two key reasons for the success of Tableau?
43 List the five tools in the Tableau suite.

Problem exercises

1 Search the Internet to find commercial software specialising in HR analytics/people analytics/workforce analytics. Also, attempt to find their pricing schemes. Tabulate and report your findings.
2 Given a function with the coordinates $\{(2,3), (3,4), (6,7), (10,3)\}$, find Euclidean distance, Minkowski distance, and Manhattan distance for the dataset.

Bibliography

Anderson, B. (2020, August). *Gartner announces the 2020 Magic Quadrant for Unified Endpoint Management.* Retrieved from Microsoft: https://www.microsoft.com/security/blog/2020/08/20/gartner-announces-microsoft-leader-2020-magic-quadrant-unified-endpoint-management-uem/#:~:text=Gartner%20announces%20the%202020%20Magic%20Quadrant%20for%20Unified%20Endpoint%20Management,-Brad%20Anderson

Gunther, F., and Fritsch, S. (2010). neuralnet: Training of neural networks. *The R Journal,* 30–38.

HealthFirst. (2018). *Outsourcing exit interviews at health first cut turnover costs by over $1 million.* Retrieved 2019, from People Element: https://peopleelement.com/health-first-case-study/

Hornik, K., Stichcombe, M., and White, H. (1989). Multi-layer feedforward networks are universal approximators. *Neural Networks,* 359–366.

Levenson, A., and Pillans, G. (2017). *Strategic workforce analytics.* London, UK: Corporate Research Forum.

Luellen, E. (2019, April 21). *An updated text analytics primer: Key factors in a text analytics strategy.* Retrieved 2019, from Towards Data Science: https://towardsdatascience.com/a-text-analytics-primer-key-factors-in-a-text-analytics-strategy-d24dc84a5576

Maurer, R. (2019, August 20). *Employee sentiment analysis shows HR all the feels.* Retrieved 2019, from SHRM: www.shrm.org/resourcesandtools/hr-topics/technology/pages/employee-sentiment-analysis-shows-hr-all-the-feels.aspx

Mohler, T. (2018, September 5). *The seven basic functions of text analytics.* Retrieved May 2019, from Lexalytics: www.lexalytics.com/lexablog/text-analytics-functions-explained

Reidmiller, M., and Braun, H. (1993). A direct method for faster back propagation learning: The rprop algorithm. *Proceedings of the IEEE International Conference on Neural Networks,* 24–28.

Sen, S., and Sengupta, R. (2018, December). *How natural language processing can revolutionize human resources.* Retrieved 2019, from AIHR Analytics: www.analyticsinhr.com/blog/natural-language-processing-revolutionize-human-resources

Smith, D. (2019, October 22). *SAS is No. 1 in advanced and predictive analytics market share, says analyst report.* Retrieved from SAS: https://www.sas.com/en_gb/news/press-releases/2019/october/sas-is-no-1-in-advanced-and-predictive-analytics-market-share.html#:~:text=SAS%20led%20with%20a%2027.7,in%20the%20category%20each%20year

Zurada, J. (1994) *Introduction to artificial neural systems.* New Delhi: Jaico Publishing House.

5

EVALUATION OF ANALYTICAL OUTCOMES

After reading this chapter, users will be able to understand the following key concepts:

* Understand the need for validating analytical outcomes
* Learn about the technique and need to split the dataset into training and test data
* Understand the purpose and implementation of cross-validation
* Learn about performance evaluation indices for clustering
* Understand various techniques used to validate classification algorithms
* Understand the concept and implementation of a confusion matrix
* Understand the different basis for selecting a particular predictive analytical tool

Opening case

A firm set out to build a mobile app which allowed the users to recall memories through the videos, images, and other data stored on their mobile device, in the form of shareable graphics. However, a key consideration was that the app design should be simple enough to allow a naïve user to utilise the app features and build their shareable graphic like a GIF. The firm realised that it needed to inculcate augmented reality which could, for example, identify people in the background of an image or video and then use that for segmentation of this visual data on the device, which could later be used for creating an experience of memories for the user. Initial development of the app started at the firm itself with their in-house team; however, they failed in their efforts miserably due to a large number of bugs and crashes of the app, eliminating the possibility of marketing such a product. Therefore, they hired the services of an analytics services firm which specialised in the development of such analytical solutions. Further, the firm required that the device does not use a backend server or cloud storage, since it poses additional concerns for the end-user like security, and also increases the processing time and price. So, they decided to develop the app on the mobile device itself. Also, the firm receives actionable user feedback and keeps on incorporating it in the design by adding new features (Kodra, 2019).

Introduction

The preceding case is an illustration of how the choice of analytical tool and platform required implementing that tool varies with the application at hand. An important perspective is that unless the proper questions are asked, proper answers cannot be obtained despite having relevant data in hand (Fankhauser, 2018). The real value of the application of the analytical tool lies in the accuracy of the output that it has generated. If the tool is not able to deliver the results that it was designed for and answer the questions or solve the business problem at hand, the tool is of little use for the decision-maker. Therefore, validation and evaluation of the tool to judge its accuracy and determine performance is a key feature of the implementation of the analytical tool. Further, a wide variety of such tools and techniques are available in the market. A user is often confounded with the situation where several tools offer a solution for a given problem. It is imperative in this context to understand how to choose among these different platforms. There are many deciding factors which influence the choice of the proper tool. Additionally, the user can apply different tools for the same situation and then compare to make out which is the best option for that business problem. This chapter, therefore, discusses different techniques used to enhance and evaluate the performance of analytical algorithms and a possible framework depicting the decision criteria to choose among the tools and the platform required to implement it.

The need to validate analytical outcomes

Validation of analytical outcomes serves two major purposes – one, evaluating the optimality of the results fetched, and two, ensuring that the outcomes provide the results in consensus with the purpose for which predictive model was developed. For the latter, the idea is to inculcate the outcomes in the design of the model. This means ensuring a backward approach, by asking the right questions as per the need of the decision-maker and then determining from the model design if those needs are being fulfilled. Interpretation and validation of analytical outcomes require that the definitions used to build a data model are agreed upon by multiple partners involved in utilising the outcomes of that data. As discussed in Chapter 4, organisational jargon and organisational consensus on the use of terms used for building that model play a key role while validating and interpreting the outcomes. Ultimately, it's about the managers and decision-makers who will be utilising the output of the model. The output from the models should be data-driven, such that the metrics provide valuable insight for the decision-maker. If the tool is unable to depict a valuable metric, a score, a quantified performance output, it is of little use for the decision-makers. The former requires technical know-how for implementation, since the user needs to determine whether the model designed is delivering the optimal outcomes or not. In this context, there exist a few generalised techniques, and some techniques which vary by the predictive analytical model. The chapter first presents the general techniques applicable to all the models and then provide a discussion of techniques specifically meant for the models discussed in this book in previous chapters.

A third purpose of validating the outcomes may also include evaluating if the tool used for implementation is the right one or not. For example, if the predictive model is expected to classify the outcomes and then predict, many tools would serve this purpose. How does a user ensure that the tool that he has chosen is the appropriate one? A tool like clustering may be high on accuracy but may yield the number of classes lesser than the ones that exist in the data. Another tool like decision trees generates the appropriate classes (supervised learning), but does not inculcate all features present in the data for branching. These considerations also have to be kept in mind by the user, while validating the analytical outcomes. Therefore, validation is not restricted to the evaluation of the performance of the predictive model designed by the user, but also ensuring that the right techniques have been chosen to build the model and the right metrics are used to assess the performance. Often, for the third type of validation, analysts compare the performance of different models for the same scenario. For example, for a classification and prediction problem, the analyst can build a KNN, ANN, and decision tree model within the same set of code and evaluate how the performance varies across different models.

Techniques of validating analytical outcomes

Validation of the performance of the model will vary with the type of technique, which will be discussed in detail in the next section. Validating whether the outcomes are consist with the objective for which the model was designed is intuitive, and requires efficient judgemental analysis by the developers and users of the system. They can determine this by posing the right set of questions to the software and then determining whether or not they are fetching satisfactory results. Now to improve the performance accuracy, techniques like splitting the data and cross-validation of data are carried out as general measures for all analytical outcomes.

Splitting the dataset into test and train

It is a general rule of thumb to split the dataset into training and test data, and the most widely used rule for splitting is Pareto's rule which divides the dataset by 4:1, reserving 80% for training and 20% for testing. Simply, the accuracy of the model can be used to assess how well the model did at, for example, classifying the dataset compared to the actual target classes present in the dataset. When both training and test data is the same, then the model is bound to give 100 percent accuracy. A common problem in using out-of-sample data is the problem of overfitting (Cawley and Talbot, 2010). This means that the model is generating accurate classifications, but not taking into account all the features present in the dataset. Overfitting also implies that the model has accounted for all the features in the dataset to such an extent that now generalisation from the model for other data samples becomes difficult. Therefore, the target of building a model is not ensuring complete fit to the dataset, since the data also contains bias and random noise. Overfitting also becomes a problem when the model chosen is not appropriate, or the number of features in the model is very high or the dataset is too small for the possibility of generalisations. The splitting of the dataset into training and test overcomes the problem of overfitting. Rather than using an out-of-sample data, test data would be a more accurate predictor of model performance. It is the most widely used method since it is both complex and flexible method. However, when out-of-sample data is used to evaluate the accuracy, the estimates may vary owing to high variance. For this purpose, another technique called cross-validation is used.

Splitting the dataset can be carried out manually if the number of rows in the dataset is known in advance. Manually computing the 80% and 20% of the total number of rows will provide the training and test dataset. For example, if the dataset contains 581 rows, the code to manually split the data in R is given by:

```
trainset ← Dataset[1:465,]
testset ← Dataset[466:581,]
```

To overcome manual computation, sample() function in R can be used by typing the code:

```
New ← sample (2, nrow(Dataset), replace=TRUE,
    prob = c(0.8, 0.2))
Traindata ← Dataset [New==1,]
Testdata ← Dataset [New==2,]
```

In the first line of code, a dataset 'New' is created which simply have the numbers 1 and 2, randomly assigned to a row, such that 80% of the total rows have number 1 and 20% have number 2. The total number of rows in New is equal to the total number of rows in the original dataset. Then by picking up similar rows from original dataset as in 'New' containing only 1s are assigned to 'Traindata' dataset, while remaining goes to 'Testdata'. If the user wishes to ensure that each time the code is executed, test and train datasets have the same data rows, then set.

seed() function can be used. Simply before assigning the data to test and train, use set.seed(1234) or any other random number.

Cross-validation

This is one of the most widely used techniques for out-of-sample or independent sample testing of the model performance. Typically, a model is trained using training data and tested using test data, both of which are derived from the same source dataset. Cross-validation generates an independent sample of data points, similar to the data contained in the source dataset. Then it checks the model accuracy in predicting this data since it wasn't used in training the model and then indicates possible issues in the model like selection bias and overfitting.

In cross-validation, a dataset is divided into test, train, and validation data. Here, train data is used to train the model, test data used to test the model, and validation data to validate model outcomes. Typically, multiple rounds of cross-validation (k-fold) are performed using different data partitions generated from the dataset. The results of the validation are averaged over all rounds of cross-validation reflected as a measure of prediction accuracy. A k-fold cross-validation implies dividing the dataset into k subsamples, training the model on k-1 samples and validating with k-th sample and repeating the process k times. This process ensures that each subsample is used at least once for validating the outcomes. Although k is unfixed and varies by user choice, a general value used is tenfold cross-validation.

Techniques used to assess cross-validation outcomes are dependent on the type of model on which cross-validation is applied. It is simply a means to enhance the model accuracy. Therefore, accuracy parameters specific to that model reflect how effective cross-validation was. For example, for classification analytical tools, misclassification error, RMSE, MAE, etc., can be used a metric to gauge cross-validation effectiveness. Typically, cross-validation is also applied to repeatedly compute the model output for a range of values of model parameters, to determine the optimal parameter value.

To implement cross-validation in R, trainControl() function is used which has the format:

```
trainControl(method="cv", number = 10)
```

This code will implement tenfold cross-validation (cv). If the user wishes to repeat tenfold cross-validation, then another argument can be supplied in the same function:

```
trainControl(method="cv", number = 10, repeats=3)
```

This code will now repeat tenfold cross-validation three times.

How validation technique varies by analytical tool

For different tools, the techniques used to assess the analytical outcomes also vary. For the type of outcome provided by the tool and the objective for which the tool is implemented, the technique used for performance assessment will also vary. This section, therefore, presents some specific methods of evaluating the performance outcome for a specific model.

Validating the results of K-means clustering

The basic objective of clustering is to partition the data into clusters such that each cluster has the minimum variation among the group of data points belonging to that cluster, and the variation among different clusters is maximum, ensuring that the objects contained in the cluster are highly differentiated from each other. Distance metrics can be used to evaluate the performance of clustering since it is based on distance measures, the homogeneity within and heterogeneity across clusters can be evaluated. Based on this objective, three internal measures are available known as clustering indices.

Compactness

Compactness is a measure of the homogeneity of a cluster that is an assessment of the similarity of the data points belonging to a particular cluster. The indices used to compute compactness are distance metrics, namely cluster–wise average or median distances between observations within a cluster. The lower the value, the better the clustering.

Separation

Separation is a measure of the heterogeneity of a cluster that is the assessment of the distinctness of the clusters from each other. The indices used to measure separation are distances between centroids and pairwise minimum distances of observations belonging to different clusters.

Connectivity

Connectivity is a measure of the predictive effectiveness of clustering, in the sense that how effectively the tool can place a data item in the same cluster as their nearest neighbour. It reflects whether the optimal value of K is chosen from the clusters or not. A value close to zero is preferable for connectivity. The range of values extend from zero to infinity, and the target of the model is to minimise it to the maximum extent possible.

Generally, most of the clustering indices used in analytical algorithms combine compactness and separation and provide one generalised index, given by the equation:

$$Index = \frac{(\alpha \times Separation)}{(\beta \times Compactness)}$$

Where α and β are weights.

Two of the most widely used indices are silhouette width and the Dunn index. The silhouette() function is available in R in 'cluster' package. Silhouette width varies between −1 and 1, where 1 indicates good cluster match, zero indicates a borderline match, and −1 indicates the wrong match.

Dunn index is available in cluster.stats() function in 'fpc' package, and also in NbClust() function in 'NbClust' package (Charrad, Ghazzali, Boiteau, and Niknafs, 2014).

Additionally, external validation of the cluster can also be done by comparing the computed clusters against a reference. This can also be implemented using cluster.stats() function. This function returns a 'corrected Rand index' which is a measure of how similar partitions are in reference and computed cluster datasets.

Validating the results of classification algorithms

Confusion matrix

The most commonly used tool for validating a classification algorithm (Santafe, Inza, and Lozano, 2015) like ANN and KNN which predict the classes, and not the probability of belonging to a class for a dataset, is the confusion matrix. A confusion matrix is an N × N matrix used to depict the accuracy of the prediction algorithm, where N is the number of classes in the dataset used for training and prediction. This matrix contains the classes in the data and cross-tabulation of how many times a particular class was accurately predicted and how many times wrongly predicted as the other class by the analytical algorithm. For a two-class prediction and classification, the confusion matrix would look like Table 5.1:

TABLE 5.1 Confusion matrix

	Class 1	Class 2	
Class 1	A	b	Class 1 predictions = a/(a + b)
Class 2	C	d	Class 2 predictions = d/(c + d)
	Sensitivity = a/(a + c)	Specificity = d/(b + d)	Accuracy = (a + d)/ (a + b + c + d)

Here, a was the number of times the algorithm was able to accurately predict class 1 as class 1, while b was the number of times class 1 was predicted as class 2. Similarly, d was the number of times algorithm was able to accurately predict class 2 as class 2, while c was the number of times class 2 was predicted as class 1. The five metrics derived from the confusion matrix have been depicted in the table.

1   Accuracy is the proportion of accurate total predictions made by algorithm viz. the total number of predictions.
2   Sensitivity is the proportion of actual positive cases predicted (total class 1 actual predictions viz total class 1 observations).
3   Specificity is the proportion of accurate negative cases predicted (total class 2 actual predictions viz. total class 2 observations).
4   Precision is the proportion of class 1 predictions.
5   Negative prediction value is the proportion of class 2 predictions.

The confusion matrix is available as function confusionMatrix() in the caret package of R. Along with building the confusion matrix and listing the five metrics previously discussed, it also displays NoInformation rate, which depicts the proportion of largest class present in the dataset. Likewise, it also displays the test results (P-value) of running a hypothesis to determine if the prediction accuracy with all classes included in the dataset is higher than the prediction accuracy for only the largest class.

The code for classification matrix in R can also be typed in manually:

```
results <- data.frame (actual=Testdata$TargetColumn,
    prediction=nn.results$net.result)
results
roundedresults <- sapply (results, round, digits=0)
roundedresultsdf=data.frame(roundedresults)
attach(roundedresultsdf)
tab <-table(actual, prediction)
table(actual, prediction)
```

Misclassification error is the error made by predictive algorithms in wrongly predicting a data item as belonging to a target class, where its actual class is different than the one predicted. For the tabulation of the confusion matrix in Table 5.1, the code to compute misclassification error is:

```
#misclassification error
1-sum(diag(tab))/sum(tab)
```

Lift charts

Lift chart is used when the model computes probabilities of classes. It is a very effective technique to determine how well the model can distinguish between different classes in the dataset. It compares the model performance with an ideal lift chart where the accurate numbers of predictions are equal to the number of observations in the dataset, and also a random lift chart where the percentage of respondents is always 100%. Lift chart displays the change in the accurate number of predictions for each decile of the population, against the cumulative population till that decile. This chart depicts the graph in two axes – x-axis represents the percentage of population and y-axis represents percentage of respondents. This chart can be used to compute a lift score and compare the performances of different models. If the dataset has segments, then this chart is highly useful to determine till what percentage of the population the model is working well, and then predicts skewed results.

As is seen in Figure 5.1, the model is ideal fit until 25% of the population, after which its prediction accuracy decreases. The accuracy until 25% of the population is 100%, while it decreases thereafter. Therefore, if it is known which segment represents the first 25% of the dataset, the model can be used for highly accurate predictions here. Further, this lift chart can also be used to determine the threshold used for prediction. Typically, in a two-class dataset, the threshold is set at 0.5, but this is not always the case. By using the lift chart, model accuracy can be enhanced by varying the thresholds as interpreted from a lift chart. For example, in Figure 5.1, 0.25 can be used as one threshold value.

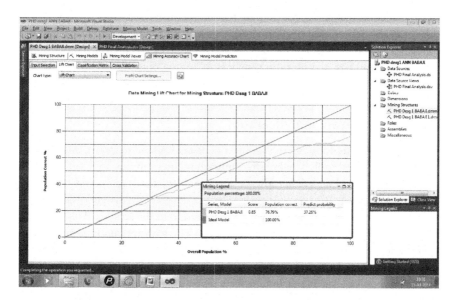

FIGURE 5.1   Lift chart

Area under ROC curve

Now that the reader is acquainted with sensitivity and specificity, it becomes easier to understand the ROC curve. ROC (receiver operating characteristics) curve is a plot between sensitivity and specificity. It is a widely popular performance evaluation metric, as it doesn't account for the percentage change in population characteristics, as was the case with the lift chart. Typically, sensitivity and specificity are inverses of each other, obviously since sensitivity = 1−specificity. By determining sensitivity and specificity from ROC curve at the threshold, the user may compute the AUC (area under the curve), which is simply the ratio of area under the curve and total area. AUC values close to 1 are considered good, while values below 0.7 generally indicate a poor model.

Gini index

Although widely used for evaluation of the performance of decision trees model, Gini index measures the area between cumulative response rate (used to draw a lift chart) and the ideal model line (a 45-degree angle). Its values range between 0 and 1. Again, a value close to 1 depicts a good model.

Validating the results of KNN

For KNN, the measures used to evaluate performance are RMSE (root mean squared error), R^2 (R squared), and mean absolute error. In addition, ROC and AUC are also used to determine prediction accuracy of the model and determine the optimal value of K. These functions are available in R in mlbench and caret package. For ROC, class probabilities are required. For this purpose, twoClassSummary() function is used which computed area under ROC curve for the two classes present in the dataset. It also computes sensitivity and specificity which can be used for performance evaluation. By default, accuracy (MAE) is used to compute the optimal K. However, the user can supply ROC as the optimality deciding criteria through selectionFunction(). These concepts are practically illustrated in Chapter 7.

Basis to choose an analytical tool

Often a major issue for any analyst is to understand where to begin, and how to choose an analytical tool. The holistic approach followed in this book suggests that the user understand and define the business problem thoroughly, and only then attempt to model it. When a user clearly defines the problem, half of his confusion fades away as he gets an idea as to what is required from the analysis. This aids a lot in the identification of the right analytical tool. The basis for choosing an analytical tool depends on some criteria, and an exhaustive list is presented in Table 5.2. Often, analysts apply many suitable analytical techniques and then identify which would be the most suitable technique for a given business problem.

TABLE 5.2 Basis to choose analytical tools for business problems

S.No.	Basis	Choice of analytical tool
1	Availability of labelled data	Supervised/unsupervised tool
2	Purpose of analysis	Classification/clustering/prediction/association
3	Technical knowledge	Analytical platform with user interface/platforms that require coding
4	Budget	Proprietary analytical software/open access
5	Design considerations	Accuracy, precision, sensitivity, etc., required
6	Type of data	Structured/unstructured/semi-structured data
7	Volume and rate of change of data	Big Data tools/routine algorithms
8	Need for integration of different platforms	Choice of platforms to implement an analytical tool which supports multiple platforms like web data, databases, voice data, etc.
9	Availability of resources	Choice of platform based on hardware, types of equipment, storage, etc. required
10	Budget	Choice of open-access or proprietary analytical services

These criteria are not exhaustive. Table 5.2 is simply a suggestive list of various dilemmas faced by a user while deciding on an analytical platform. It is also to bear in mind that the choice of the tool also affects the choice of the platform where the tool will be implemented. As discussed in previous chapters, several paid and open-access software products offer support for a variety of analytical algorithms. Therefore, if the user doesn't have adequate technical knowledge, then there is no point in applying an open-source tool. Also, when the data is adequately labelled, then it is possible to apply supervised learning tools like KNN, ANN, etc., while unsupervised techniques have to be used otherwise. Further, if the volume and rate of change of data are very high, then Big Data analysis techniques have to be utilised. Sometimes, the application involves integrating data from multiple platforms like web data, historical data from databases, call log data, etc., all of which should be supported as an interface by the platform of choice. R and Python have robust interface capabilities with almost all types of data sources, and SAS also has robust interface capabilities but is paid software. If the user is interested in the application of Big Data analytics, then adequate storage space, hardware, and server support is required. Besides this, open-access software also poses installation requirements for the device. All of these should be taken into consideration for the accurate implementation of analytics.

Conclusion

This chapter emphasises the need for validating analytical outcomes. It presents a thorough discussion of various techniques used to evaluate the performance of a model. In addition, a discussion on various deciding criteria to choose among analytical algorithms has been presented. The market is flooded with analytical algorithms, all of which have their niche areas of application and benefits. Choosing one of these models becomes tedious for a naïve user. In this context, the chapter offers a way to equip the layman with the knowledge to choose from different algorithms. Further, unless an analytical tool provides the right result, its outcome is of little importance for the decision-maker. Therefore, accurate performance evaluation of the model also needs to be carried out.

Glossary

Accuracy   the proportion of accurate total predictions made by algorithm viz. the total number of predictions

Compactness   is a measure of the homogeneity of a cluster that is an assessment of the similarity of the data points belonging to a particular cluster

Confusion matrix   is an N × N matrix used to depict the accuracy of the prediction algorithm, where N is the number of classes in the dataset used for training and prediction

Connectivity   is a measure of the predictive effectiveness of clustering, in the sense that how effectively the tool can place a data item in the same cluster as its nearest neighbour

External validation   of cluster implies comparison of the computed clusters against a reference

Gini index   measures the area between cumulative response rate (used to draw a lift chart) and the ideal model line (45-degree angle)

Lift chart   a graphical technique to determine how well the model can distinguish between different classes in the dataset

Misclassification error   the error made by predictive algorithms in wrongly predicting a data item as belonging to a target class, where its actual class is different than the one predicted

Negative predict value   the proportion of class 2 predictions

NoInformation rate   an outcome of implementing confusion matrix in R which depicts the proportion of the largest class present in the dataset

Overfitting   implies that the model has accounted for all the features in the dataset to such an extent that now generalisation from the model for other data samples becomes difficult

Pareto's rule   the most widely used rule for splitting the dataset into training and test data, in a proportion of 4:1, reserving 80% for training and 20% for testing

Precision   the proportion of class 1 predictions

ROC curve   abbreviation for 'receiver operating characteristics' curve, a plot between sensitivity and specificity of a classification algorithm

Sensitivity   the proportion of actual positive cases predicted (total class 1 actual predictions viz. total class 1 observations)

Separation   is a measure of the heterogeneity of a cluster that is an assessment of the distinctness of the clusters from each other

Specificity   the proportion of accurate negative cases predicted (total class 2 actual predictions viz. total class 2 observations)

Review material

1   Discuss the three reasons explaining the need for validating the analytical outcomes.
2   What is Pareto's rule?
3   Define overfitting.
4   Discuss the need to split the dataset into training and test data.
5   Why is overfitting a big problem in data analytics?
6   Discuss the two ways in which data can split in R.
7   List the purpose of cross-validation of data.
8   What is k-fold cross-validation?
9   Explain in simple terms how cross-validation of data works.
10   Write code for implementing cross-validation in R, with and without repeats.
11   What is the basic objective of K-means clustering?
12   List the three clustering indices and their purpose.
13   Define compactness.
14   Define separation.
15   Define connectivity.
16   List the two most widely used clustering indices and the functions used to implement them in R.
17   Define external validation of cluster.
18   What is the purpose of corrected Rand index?
19   Define confusion matrix.
20   List and explain the five metrics derived from the confusion matrix.
21   What is NoInformation rate?
22   Write the code for manually building a confusion matrix in R.
23   Which R package has inbuilt confusion matrix function? What are the outcomes of this function?
24   Define misclassification error.
25   Write the code in R to compute misclassification error.
26   List the purposes that the lift chart serves.
27   What is understood by ROC curve?
28   What is the benefit of using ROC curve?
29   What is the relation between ROC and AUC?
30   Define Gini index.
31   Discuss different measures used for validating KNN.
32   List different basis used for the choice of an analytical tool and platform.

Problem exercises

1   For a business data classification, the algorithm was able to classify 322 as HighPerforming (out of which 210 were correct), and 154 as NonPerforming (81 correct classifications). Create a confusion matrix for the described scenario.

2   From the confusion matrix created in Problem 1, determine the misclassification error and the five metrics used to evaluate the model performance, derived from confusion matrix. Comment on the usability of the model for classification in the future.

Bibliography

Bhattacharya, S. (2018, December 6). *Model evaluation techniques for classification models.* Retrieved 2019, from Towards Data Science: https://towardsdatascience.com/model-evaluation-techniques-for-classification-models-eac30092c38b

Cawley, G. C., and Talbot, N. L. (2010). On over-fitting in model selection and subsequent selection bias in performance evaluation. *Journal of Machine Learning Research*, 2079–2107.

Charrad, M., Ghazzali, N., Boiteau, V., and Niknafs, A. (2014). NbClust: An R package for determining the relevant number of clusters in a data set. *Journal of Statistical Software*, 1–36.

Dataman. (2018, December 5). *How to determine the best model?* Retrieved February 2019, from Towards Data Science: https://towardsdatascience.com/how-to-determine-the-best-model-6b9c584d0db4

Fankhauser, D. (2018, June 26). *4 key learnings on HR analytics from SHRM 2018.* Retrieved 2019, from Reflektive: www.reflektive.com/blog/hr-analytics-shrm/

Kassambra. (2018, March 11). *Cross-validation essentials in R.* Retrieved March 2019, from Statistical tools for high-throughput data analysis: www.sthda.com/english/articles/38-regression-model-validation/157-cross-validation-essentials-in-r/#k-fold-cross-validation

Kodra, A. (2019, June 26). *Momento: Animating memories with immersive GIFs powered by mobile machine learning.* Retrieved 2019, from HeartBeat: https://heartbeat.fritz.ai/momento-animating-memories-with-immersive-gifs-powered-by-mobile-machine-learning-81ff52806ae3

Mutuvi, S. (2019, April 16). *Introduction to machine learning model evaluation.* Retrieved May 2019, from HeartBeat: https://heartbeat.fritz.ai/introduction-to-machine-learning-model-evaluation-fa859e1b2d7f

Nighania, K. (2018, December 30). *Various ways to evaluate a machine learning model's performance.* Retrieved October 2019, from Towards Data Science: https://towardsdatascience.com/various-ways-to-evaluate-a-machine-learning-models-performance-230449055f15

Ritchie, N. (2017). *Evaluating a classification model.* Retrieved 2019, from Machine Learning: www.ritchieng.com/machine-learning-evaluate-classification-model/

Santafe, G., Inza, I., and Lozano, J. A. (2015). Dealing with the evaluation of supervised classification algorithms. *Artificial Intelligence Review*, 467–508.

STHDA. (2016). *Clustering validation statistics: 4 vital things everyone should know – Unsupervised machine learning.* Retrieved 2019, from Statistical tools for high-throughput data analysis: www.sthda.com/english/wiki/wiki.php?id_contents=7952#external-clustering-validation

6

PREDICTIVE HR ANALYTICS IN RECRUITMENT AND SELECTION

After reading this chapter, users will be able to understand the following key concepts:

- Review the basic concepts of recruitment and selection
- A practical step-by-step illustration of the application of predictive analytics (holistic approach) to selection
- How to install packages and import datasets
- How to normalise a dataset using min-max transformation or z-transformation
- How to split a dataset into training and test data manually and using the Sample function
- Areas of application of analytics to recruitment

Opening case

A lot of information is present in the data itself, but only the proper analytical tool can discern it and present a significant insight for management. Organisations, in all functional areas of management, are collecting voluminous data. But the question is: do they mine it to generate unprecedented insights? Many firms, in the wake of increasing competition, have identified the necessity of applying analytics to their historical data (collected and stored over many years, but rarely mined). One such firm in the chemicals industry, Dow Chemical, has started applying analytics to its historical data for workforce planning. The firm employs more than 40,000 employees and has been able to gather massive historical data for all of its business units. It applies a classification technique to make predictions of future employee requirements at different positions in each of its business units. Utilising a custom modelling tool, it segments its employees for each business unit based on their age groups and job levels. It has been able to generate five classes for age groups and ten classes for job levels. For each of these classes, it can project future employee requirements based on historical headcount data, and aggregation of these yields overall workforce requirements of the company. These future headcount projections have saved the firm huge money since the chemical industry has highly dynamic and fluctuating business cycles. Further, these forecasts enable the firm to proactively plan for high-risk positions such as succession planning. Also, the firm can forecast promotion rates, internal transfers, and overall labour availability. By applying 'what if?' scenario planning, the firm can gain insight on the effect on these workforce forecasts, in case internal organisational factors like staff promotions or external environmental factors like political considerations change. With this scenario analysis, the firm can timely staff up in key growth areas or identify high-risk areas, which is those employees who have key organisational knowledge and are vital to its functioning. Therefore, the application of analytics to historical HR data can allow organisations to proactively plan for the workforce and curb the risk (Isson and Harriott, 2016; Way, 2017).

Introduction

As rightly stressed by John Spence, a leading global management consultant, the success of a firm is directly influenced by the quality of people who are hired, trained, and retained by the firm (Spence, 2015).

HRM encompasses a variety of processes starting from recruitment and selection to separation from the company to manage these resources. This process also deals with matching knowledge, skills, and abilities (KSAs) of candidates with those required by the job in the organisation. In the present business times, HRM departments are faced with the challenge of justifying their investments in human capital. Therefore, HRM teams need to devise ways to calculate and demonstrate how HR functions contribute to the overall strategic objectives of the organisation. For this purpose, human resources executives (Cipolla, 2005) in the 21st century do not need to downsize their departments, but rather narrate a success story with each investment in human capital – and validate that story with numbers. One way to do that is to measure hROI, the human return on investment, and industry experts believe that one possible solution to generate guaranteed returns is to invest in the right people (Pareek and Rao, 2003). Since it's not the people who are the rights assets for a firm, it's the right people who are the most important assets (Collins, 2001). Therefore, the process which finds and selects the right people should be rightly modelled to ensure that only the best enter the firm for a job.

The question is: how does the organisation define who these right people are? The definition will vary from one organisation to another and one job role to another. This is because the roles and responsibilities vary by different job profiles and job profiles vary by organisations and industry. For hiring and selection, 'people' can be defined in terms of their KSAs, psychometric traits, previous job experiences and profiles, and so on. But it is worth pondering how a hiring manager will decide which definition would best fulfil the job role in question. Interestingly, analytics can provide a solution. By identifying the people who best fit a particular job profile from the existing employees of the firm, future hiring profiles can be built. However, the adoption of such an approach would require remodelling of the process of recruitment and selection being carried at the organisation.

Many factors have led to redefining the role and conduct of employees in the workplace, ultimately changing the nature of HR practices. It is often rightly said that employees today need to do both smart work and hard work to succeed. Globalisation has led to a higher competition which requires mobile employees (for example, those who need to move to other countries for work) who think quickly, act quickly, and are more productive even with low job security and income. Changes like work have also affected the change in skills required of an employee. For example, most of the jobs today are technology oriented. Firms are largely knowledge intensive, and employees work with automated machinery. Besides this, a rising trend is towards the delivery of services where employees play a front-facing role where they need to take action on the spot or face loss of consumer. So, to manage such a changing nature of work, employees need to be managed. This also suggests that the firms (Dessler and Varkkey, 2008) today need sophisticated HRM selection practices which focus on acquiring employees who are motivated, fit with their jobs, and are committed towards better performance.

First, let us recall the concepts of recruitment and selection and how they were being administered in the firm conventionally. Traditionally, firms followed a time-consuming and capital-intensive selection process which did not guarantee a perfect fit for employees. A popular conventional method for selection of candidates as defined by Flippo (1984) involved the following steps: initial or preliminary interview, application blanks or blank, check of references, psychological tests, employment interview, approval by the supervisor, physical examination, and induction or orientation. Such an approach has several limitations. First, not all jobs require such elaborate hiring process. Second, when the number of candidates for hiring is large, this process would become tiring and cost ineffective, and would also not ensure quality (Dessler and Varkkey, 2008). While earlier, candidates were just selected based on their academic performances or past experiences, what was missing was whether or not the employee would fit into the organisation and the job. This missing link was a major cause of concern for employees, since this leads to an inflow of largely poor performers in a firm. Although these poor performers satiated the basic selection criteria and filled the vacancies in the firms, they were not able to deliver beyond the assigned tasks. The firms today seek to hire passionate workers who can add value to the tasks that they are assigned and suggest ways to improvise them. For this purpose, the selection process requires alteration to accommodate this missing link. With the advent of technology, firms are now looking for more effective ways to shorten this process of hiring, while at the same time not reducing their effectiveness. The Internet and automation and information systems are changing the previous ways processes were designed.

In light of this, some challenges which selection process has to encounter, and therefore adapt to, are discussed. The foremost challenge is related to the concept of flexibility. This implies that employees now stay with a firm for shorter periods, while more output and performance will be required of them. Further, selection devices should also appropriately address individual differences. In addition to this, it is seen that in the present business times, either the employer or the employee can end the contract of employment at any point in time, so the selection process has to be modelled accordingly to address all these issues and decide on the right selection tool (Beardwell and Holden, 1994) (Chaudhary, Rangnekar, and Barua, 2012). The leading organisations globally now use broader criteria of hiring, including external environmental inputs, adapting the hiring process to the changing needs of the environment. For example, Google, which initially used only average GPAs (grade point averages) to hire candidates, used analytics to redefine their hiring criteria (Anderson, 2014). IBM (International Business Machines) goes beyond traditional psychological tests, and seeks candidates with situational judgement and thinking appraisal skills (Lightfoot, 2007).

Holistic approach – predictive modelling of selection

Having understood the basics of recruitment and selection, and how the processes are changing in the dynamic times, the following discussion presents one illustration of the practical application of predictive analytics to the problem of selection at IT organisations in the Indian IT industry. This section discusses in steps about how to implement a holistic approach to apply predictive analytics in HR.

Step 1: identification of the problem

Many facts and figures have led to defining this business problem that process of selection needs to be remodelled and made predictive, so that the right people can be hired by firms for the right positions at the right time. The discussion is based on the statistics of the Indian IT industry, specifically of tier 1 IT industries (which have annual revenue greater than 1 million INR and employ more than 50,000 employees). It has been seen that poor selection practices, without ensuring an appropriate fit of the candidate for the hired position, leads to high rates of turnover. This is especially pertinent to new hires, in their first year of hiring in the Indian IT industry (Bhatnagar, 2007), as well as for the experienced and senior-level employees. As the figures suggest, the Indian IT industry suffers from high voluntary turnover rates, fluctuating between 17% and 20% yearly (PTI, 2018) (Basu and Sarkar, 2019). Voluntary turnover refers to employees voluntarily leaving the firm, not including layoffs made by the firm. Second, statistics also suggest that India is a major global outsourcing hub for the IT sector, largely because of the availability of skilled English-speaking workers. However, although substantial new talent in the field of information technology accrues to industry annually – compounded annual growth rate for Indian IT graduates from 2008–2015 was 9.4 percent – IT businesses are reluctant to tap this talent pool because of quality concerns and retention issues (SectoralReport, 2016) (PTI, 2018). Again, if the hiring is done properly, the quality concerns can be managed and fixed 'at the source' (at the time of selection) itself. This defines the business problem that firms need to remodel their process of selection of candidates, to both curb turnover (the extreme outcome of poor hiring) and manage quality concerns (the immediate outcome of hiring). When organisations plan strategically and utilise appropriate analyses, they can improve the effectiveness of their HRM processes (Elkjaer and Filmer, 2015).

Step 2: model the problem

Now that the reader can comprehend the business problem and also the limitations of the traditional process of hiring and selection undertaken at the organisations, an illustration of the use of predictive modelling for effective hiring of individuals will be presented.

To predict who to select to manage quality concerns and turnover issues, the objective of predictive modelling is to select the candidates in such a way that turnover and quality concerns can be managed appropriately. But first, the question that needs to be answered is: what candidates for which position? Since the job roles and responsibilities vary with job positions, a generalised solution for selection would not be feasible. Therefore, for this illustration, three different positions of software engineers in tier 1 Indian IT firms will be considered. That is, predictive models of selection for the first three positions of software engineers will be developed.

Now the reader should recall that to develop a predictive model, one needs to apply the theoretical framework, experience (if any) and systems view/process approach. The reader should start by answering the following two questions.

1   **First, who will be a good hire for IT firms?**

   •   Common sense suggests that the characteristics of successfully performing employees in the existing employee pool of the firm at each position of software engineers would serve as a good answer to this question. Now successful performers can be identified by their performance rankings (conducted at least once every year by all tier 1 Indian IT organisations), their total experience in the industry, their previous grades, and additional performance indicators like patents, contributions, and so on.
   •   Further, backing it up with a theoretical framework, successful performers also differ in their job attitudes. Therefore, following the literature review, those employees can be termed as good hires who are satisfied with their jobs, since job satisfaction is further predictive of many job outcomes.

2   **Second, how can it be ensured that these good hires will not leave the firm shortly?**

   •   Although considering the present business environment, it cannot be ensured that the employees will continue to stay with a firm until retirement, but firms should engage them in such a way that they stay for a substantial period so that a firm can reap maximum from their talent. Therefore, firms need to continually monitor job satisfaction of the employees as a good practice for retaining the employees.

So, based on this discussion, the reader can conclude that to build the predictive model for selection, the target is to first determine how to identify successful performers among existing employees. This can be done by classifying the existing employee pool at each position into 'good' and 'bad' performers, based on the range of values of target variables identified above. Then utilise this classification to predict who will be a successful performer from the pool of candidates who have applied for the process of hiring at a particular position.

For each of the three levels, data on these target variables will be gauged from the existing employees to train the predictive model, so that it learns the criteria of classifying a good and a bad hire.

3   **Now the question is how to predict these target variables for the pool of candidates who are applying for the job, and therefore, make this model more robust.**

- It is understandable that for new applicants, job attitudes and outcomes cannot be gauged. But that is the core reason for applying predictive HR analytics – we are predicting these outcomes to suggest whether the applicant will be a good or bad performer in the future. Therefore, as an HR analyst, one needs to rethink ways through experience, knowledge, or based on theories, in which this predictive model can be enhanced. So, the reader needs to ascertain what can predict these target variables, that is, job satisfaction, performance ranking, and grades.
- Recall that based on experience, selections have traditionally been made based on psychometric traits. Consider whether these psychometric traits (individual differences) affect an individual's work outcomes. If the answer

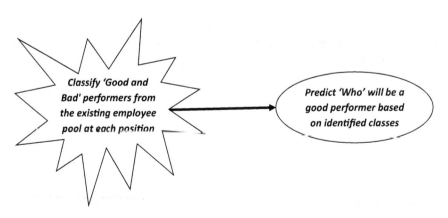

FIGURE 6.1   What the predictive model for selection is expected to do

is yes, then these too need to be included in the model. Theories on individual differences and attitudes (Cooper, 2010; Judge and Kammeyer-Mueller, 2012) suggest that individuals vary significantly in their behaviour as an outcome of the variation in their traits (Cooper, 2010). Researchers studying organisational behaviour often consider measurement of individual differences in employees since they are predictive of many work outcomes (Cooper, 2010), like levels of job satisfaction and job performance (Judge and Bono, 2001) and work behaviours. To summarise, variability in job attitudes can be explained through individual differences, which in turn lead to differences in behaviour; therefore, individual differences should also be included in the predictive model.

- Again, from experience, discussion with HR managers, and review of literature on individual differences, one would be able to list the individual differences currently used by tier 1 IT employers for hiring. A good data source for such enlisting is leading magazine articles presenting discussion with HR managers of IT firms regarding selection and hiring. Some of the findings based on excerpts from such articles have been presented next. Leading firms such as Wipro, TCS, HCL, Infosys, etc., are on the lookout for several new traits in their employees (Phillips, 2015). Instead of relying on just psychometric tests like MBTI which assess personality, the IT firms are now moving forward to talent analytics, whereby they attempt to identify the key traits possessed by top performers and then look for same in recruits. Leadership, resilience, and detachment are some of the key traits desired by employers in the IT industry, owing to the fast pace of change in the sector, requiring employees to be risk-takers and be adaptable to change. Deloitte and KPMG look for analytical and evaluation skills, while PwC tests reasoning and situational judgement abilities. Leading IT firms look for logic, reasoning, language, and analytical abilities, problem-solving skills, quantitative aptitude, and general computer science and programming skills (Wadhwa, DeVitton, and Gereffi, 2008). Besides, since none of these is a good indicator of logical ability, ability to work under pressure, emotional intelligence, and several other soft skills such as leadership, communication, and decision-making, which are considered by recruiters before hiring, laying more emphasis on the journey taken to achieve the degree (extra-curricular activities) or soft skills (Lightfoot, 2007). Google looks for five key attributes a candidate should possess to be hired (Vincent, 2014; Anderson, 2014) – learning ability, emergent leadership, humility, intellectual humility, and good grades. Facebook looks for proactive behaviours, teamwork, autonomy, and self-motivation, along with leadership skills. Apple hires employees who are hospitable, agreeable, humble, and can connect with people. Other key traits in demand with such leading firms are resilience, adaptability, and communication (McGraw, 2015). Based on this review, readers can well comprehend the use and importance of inclusion of individual differences in the process of selection of IT software engineers. Now, based on the availability of historical data on such traits, and the possibility of gauging this data through surveys, the traits to be used in selection can be short-listed. For illustration in this chapter, the traits shortlisted are integrity, intellectual humility, resilience, self-esteem, self-efficacy, and personality.

Hence, to enhance the predictive model for the selection of new applicants, we add a step, that predicts the target variables based on the previously mentioned traits and then uses these relationships to classify the applicant as good or bad hire.

Summarising the preceding discussion in simple terms, to build the predictive model for selection, first gauge the data on individual traits and the target variables mentioned, for existing employee pools at each of the three positions, and then apply classification to label them as good or bad performers. This classification would be used later for prediction. Then for the new applicants, gauge data on individual traits and predict the values of target variables to classify each applicant as a good or bad performer in the future. Applying the system view/process approach to these understandings, one can summarise for generating classification (Table 6.1).

Applying the system view/process approach to data for new applicants looks like what is seen in Table 6.2.

It is worth mentioning here that while developing a predictive model, the analyst or the manager can also ascertain the data sources. For example, a lot of data required in developing a predictive model for selection is readily available with a large firm, such as data on most of the job attitudes as part of organisational health surveys. If not, then this data can be collected by administering a

TABLE 6.1 Summary based on the system view/process approach

Input	Transformation	Output
• Integrity • Intellectual humility • Self-esteem • Self-efficacy • Big Five personality • Resilience	Determine the combination of values of input variables for each class of output variables – job satisfaction, grades, performance ranking	Classify as a good or bad performer based on a range of values of target variables

TABLE 6.2 Applying the system view/process approach to data for new applicants

Input	Transformation	Output
• Integrity • Intellectual humility • Self-esteem • Self-efficacy • Big Five personality • Resilience	Determine the combination of values of input variables to predict values of target variables	Use the predicted values of target variables to classify applicant as a good or bad performer in future

questionnaire-based survey. The standardised questionnaires for all the traits discussed here are readily available on the Internet for open access. Some other demographic variables included in the work for analysis are gender and marital status.

Step 3: selecting the tool

While developing a predictive model for the business problem, one gets clarity as to what needs to be done to apply prediction to the data collected. As is with the case of developing a predictive model for selection, the reader gains an understanding that model needs to classify. Recalling the techniques of classification presented in the earlier chapters, most of the techniques would fit here, viz. regression, decision trees and artificial neural networks (ANNs). For illustration in this chapter, ANN would be applied using neuralnet package in R software. For the sake of simplicity of illustration, we will use output variable job satisfaction as the target variable for classifying performers in the firm and using all input variables including gender, marital status, performance ranking, and grades for predicting this target variable.

Step 4: applying the tool

For the application of the tool, Version 3.2.6 of RStudio has been utilised. This software can be easily downloaded from the website rstudio.com, which hosts the latest version and recommended as per the operating system – Windows or Mac OS – of the device. A brief overview of RStudio is presented in Chapter 5, and for greater details, users may go through the references listed at the end of this chapter for further reads. The dataset used for analysis is available with the book. The dataset is an Excel worksheet titled 'Selection'. Please note that all the datasets and R scripts used throughout the book are attached for reference in the appendices available on the eResource site. The R package used for implementing ANN is neuralnet package. Two other packages available in R and popular for implementing ANN are nnet and AMORE (Gunther and Fritsch, 2010). Neuralnet package (nnet) is comparatively more flexible since it allows customisation of some parameters and package contains inbuilt functions to view the results of ANN implementation.

About neuralnet package in R

The ANN model used in neuralnet package is multilayer perceptron, which is one of the most widely used models of ANN in all software design. The representation is the same as illustrated in the chapter section on ANN, such that there are three layers – input, hidden, and output layers. Neuralnet package offers flexibility to switch between three algorithms for implementation of ANN – backpropagation, resilient backpropagation, and without weight backtracking. It is dependent on two other R packages, MASS and grid. The function neuralnet takes the following arguments (Gunther and Fritsch, 2010, p. 33):

- **Formula** – specifies the description of the ANN model.
- **Data** – specifies the data frame on which ANN is to be applied.
- **Hidden** – represents the number of hidden layers to be used in the ANN model. The default is set at one. To supply multiple hidden layers, c(#layers, #nodes in each layer) is to be provided in the 'hidden' argument. For example, hidden c(2,1) implies two layers with one node each.
- **Threshold** – specifies the minimum partial derivative of the error term to be used to converge the iterations of the analytic process.
- **Rep** – number of times training has to be repeated.
- **Algorithm** – default is rprop+ (resilient backpropagation with weight).
- **Err.fct** – how to compute the error, using either 'ce – cross-entropy' or 'sse – sum of squared' errors.
- **Linear.output** – when set to true, it applies activation function. Else set to FALSE. When the output is categorical, set to TRUE – and vice-versa.

To model the network with the variables in the analysis, the following structure is used:

```
Neuralnet (output ~ Input1 + Input2 + Input3
+. . . . ., data=datasetname, hidden = # of hidden
nodes, err.fct = "specify anyone within quotes",
linear.output = FALSE)
```

A step-by-step illustration with screenshots of loading the dataset and implementing and interpreting ANN in R has been presented in what follows (Figures 6.2–6.10).

1   Open RStudio. Open a new script from the extreme left corner of the upper ribbon. Click on R script and a new window will open in the upper left portion of RStudio.
2   Now import the dataset 'Selection' from the location where you have stored it on your device. For this, click on Import Dataset from Global environment tab in RStudio, and select From Excel, since our dataset is an Excel file.
3   This will open up a new window. In this, browse to the location where the dataset has been saved. Select it, the 'sheet' in the lower pane of this 'Import Excel data' window is selected to default. Since our Excel sheet has only one worksheet, keep it as default. A preview of the dataset is also generated. Then click on the Import button.

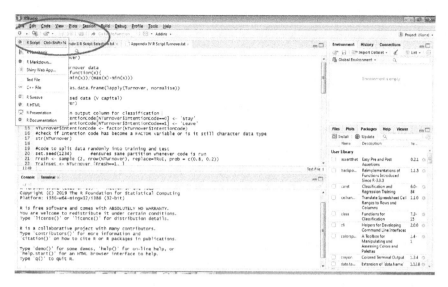

FIGURE 6.2   Opening a new R script

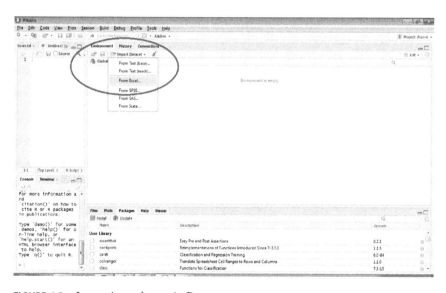

FIGURE 6.3   Importing a dataset in R

4   So that you don't need to repeat using the dataset name for all operations or fetching specific columns, simply type and execute the command attach(dataset_name). This will attach it to the global environment such that user doesn't need to refer to dataset name repeatedly. To execute, select the specific command line and click Run. Remember to type the name of the dataset here as 'Selection', initial capital, since R is a case-sensitive language.

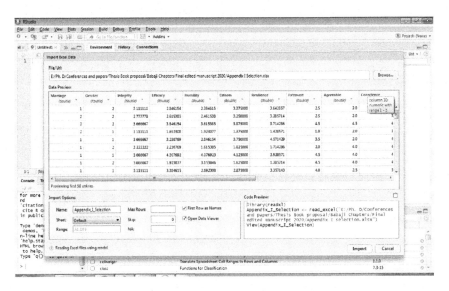

FIGURE 6.4   Importing a dataset preview

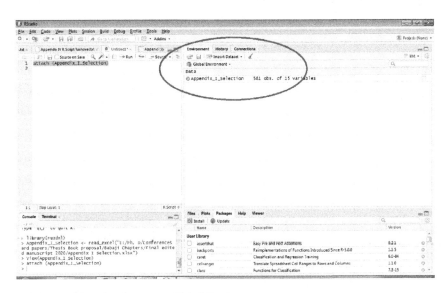

FIGURE 6.5   Attach a dataset to Global Environment

5   Now, the reader needs to install and use the neuralnet package. All packages in RStudio, as discussed in Chapter 5, appear under the Packages tab. However, you can use only those packages which have been checked from the Packages tab. Either search for the package name and then check it as shown, or simply type library(neuralnet) and execute this command.

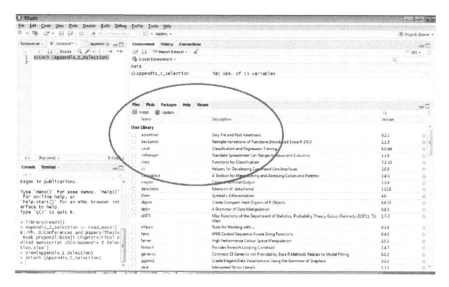

FIGURE 6.6   Using the Packages tab

FIGURE 6.7   Normalising dataset

In case the package you require is not available under the Packages tab, simply type install.packages("neuralnet") and execute it. This will simply fetch the package from community supported websites on R and install it on the device.

6   After this, you need to work on the dataset. To improve the predictive accuracy of R, it is best to normalise the dataset so all the extreme values in the

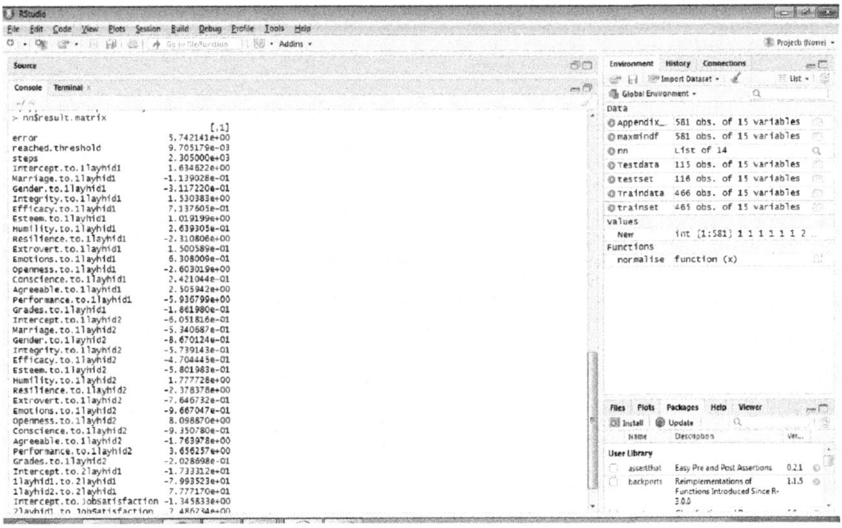

FIGURE 6.8 Output display of nn model

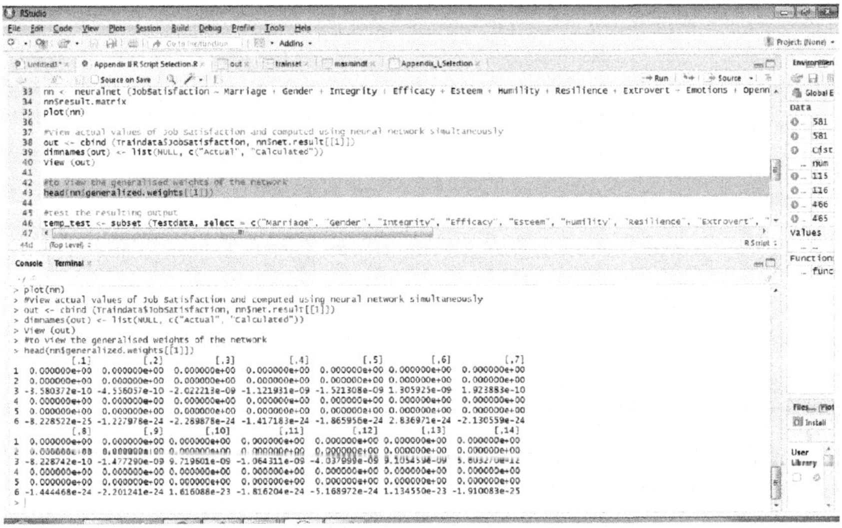

FIGURE 6.9 View of generalised network weights

dataset are resolved. Several numerical methods of normalising data are available, but the widely used ones are min-max normalisation and applying Z transformation. The formula used for each follows:

For min-max normalisation $= (X-\min(X)) / (\max(X)-\min(X))$

For z-transformation $= (X-\text{mean}(X)) / sd(X)$, where sd implies standard deviation

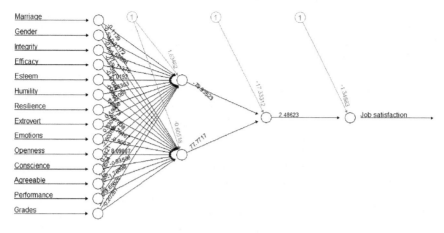

FIGURE 6.10 PLOTTING THE NEURAL MODEL

Inbuilt scaling in R doesn't allow for either of these normalisations, so code is presented for the aid of the users to compute min-max normalisation values for each variable in the dataset and scale it between 0 and 1.

```
#normalise data
normalise ← function(x){
    return ((x-min(x))/(max(x)-min(x)))
}
maxmindf ← as.data.frame (lapply(Selection, normalise))
```

Here the function takes x as input and returns the value after applying min-max normalisation on it. These returned values are stored temporarily in 'normalise'. Now the function lapply takes selection dataset, applies normalisation on it, and returns the values as a list, and as.data.frame will replicate the structure of selection dataset and store these values in another dataset named maxmindf which has similar data frame as selection dataset. Hence, to apply to normalise the dataset, type the set of commands in script and execute it.

You can also view the new scaled dataset maxmindf by typing the command View (maxmindf) and executing it.

7   As consistent with advanced analytical algorithms, you need to split the data into test and training dataset. For this, Pareto's 80:20 rule has been used to split the data. If the number of data points in a dataset is already known to the user, then by manually computing 80% and 20% of the dataset, following code may be used to split the dataset. Since selection dataset has 581 points, 465 and 116 form 80 and 20 percent of the data, respectively.

```
trainset ← maxmindf[1:465,]
testset ← maxmindf[466:581,]
```

In the above code, trainset contains rows 1–465 from the maxmindf dataset (the normalised version of selection), while testset contains approximately 115 remaining rows. Leaving a space after the comma in the above function specification implies to include all columns of the dataset. An alternative way to split the data into 80:20 without involving manual computation is by using Sample function in RStudio. The code for splitting is as under:

```
New ← sample (2, nrow(maxmindf), replace=TRUE,
    prob = c(0.8, 0.2))
Traindata ← maxmindf [New==1,]
Testdata ← maxmindf [New==2,]
```

Here, the Sample function takes the arguments (x, size, replace, probability). The function picks up a sample of the mentioned size, values of which are picked from the first argument (can be a list, a vector, etc.). Probability argument specifies how many times a given element has to be picked from the sample. In the preceding case, the sample will contain either 1 or 2, size of the whole sample is equal to the size of maxmindf dataset, and sample will include 80% of 1s and 20% of 2s. Then a new dataset Traindata will be created containing all elements from maxmindf dataset, with index numbers similar to the index number of 'New' dataset, wherever it contains 1s and Testdata where New contains 0s.

8   The next step is to build the neural network using Training dataset. For this, first call the neuralnet package, and then build the model using the following code:

```
#Build Neural network model
library (neuralnet)
nn <- neuralnet (JobSatisfaction ~ Marriage +
Gender + Integrity + Efficacy + Esteem + Humility +
Resilience + Extrovert + Emotions + Openness +
Conscience + Agreeable +Performance + Grades,
data=trainset, hidden=c(2,1), linear.output=FALSE)
nn$result.matrix
plot(nn)
```

In the preceding code, neuralnet takes the arguments job satisfaction, which is the predictor variable for our work, and marriage, gender, integrity, efficacy, esteem, and so on, which are the independent variables; dataset is specified using data argument, and a number of hidden layers are used using hidden argument. Hidden=c(2,1) implies creation of two hidden layers containing one node each. Linear.output is set to False for categorical variables, while if being set to TRUE applies the activation function on the generated output.

The output of the neural network model is stored in 'nn'. It contains the following details:

```
net.result - the output of the dependent variable
for each record in the dataset, as computed by
application of ANN
weights - list of weights fitted to the network for
each iteration of the model
generalised.weights - list of generalised weights
fitted to the network
result.matrix - final output summarised, containing
threshold, steps or iterations for convergence of
solution, shown for each replication (each column)
```

The outputs of nn$result.matrix are shown in the corresponding Figure 6.8, can be seen in the console. It depicts minimum error reached for convergence, the number of steps required to converge, weights from variables to hidden nodes for each hidden layer in the network. As the model shows, weights range from −6.33 to 9.67. For example, intercept to the first neuron of the first hidden layer is −6.34 and the weights leading to the first neuron for covariates marriage, gender, and efficacy are −0.13, 0.71 and −4.3, respectively.

For additional analysis, the generalised weights for each covariate are also shown, and it can be analysed to see if the variable has a linear effect. If the variance in weights is small, it implies a linear effect (Intrator and Intrator, 2001). As shown in Figure 6.9, for each covariate of the study, the first few generalised weights are shown, here [,1] [,2] and so on, representing marriage, gender, integrity, and so on.

RStudio also allows visualisation of results. The output of plotting the neural model as shown in Figure 6.10 can be seen from Plots in the lower right tab of RStudio. It can be extracted as a pdf file, as an image or simply copied on the clipboard.

The plot simply depicts the topology of the network, trained synaptic weights, and basic information like all variables of the study. To view the actual values of job satisfaction and computed values, use the following code:

```
#View actual values of job satisfaction and com-
puted using neural network simultaneously
out ← cbind (Traindata$JobSatisfaction, nn$net.
result[[1]])
dimnames(out) ← list(NULL, c("Actual", "Calculated"))
View (out)
```

Step 5: interpret and validate the outcomes

Once the model gets fitted to the training data, it has to be tested on test data. For this purpose, first, a new temporary dataset is created with all fields of test data except job satisfaction. Then using the **compute function** of R, the following code is applied to compute the neural output using nn model for the test dataset.

```
temp_test <- subset (Testdata, select = c("Marriage",
"Gender",    "Integrity",    "Efficacy",    "Esteem",
"Humility", "Resilience", "Extrovert", "Emotions",
"Openness",  "Conscience",  "Agreeable",  "Perfor-
mance", "Grades"))
head (temp_test)
nn.results <- compute (nn, temp_test)
```

To determine the accuracy of the nn as applied on test data, a confusion matrix can be generated.

```
#check accuracy – confusion matrix
results <- data.frame (actual=Testdata$JobSatisfaction,
prediction=nn.results$net.result)
results
roundedresults <- sapply (results, round, digits=0)
roundedresultsdf=data.frame(roundedresults)
attach(roundedresultsdf)
tab <-table(actual, prediction)
table(actual, prediction)
```

This depicts the confusion matrix as shown in Figure 6.11.

As the confusion matrix shows, the accuracy percentage is approximately 81% (computed as sum of all predicted correctly, here 39+62, divided by total number of observations, here 125). It misclassifies seven 0s as 1s and seven 1s as 0s.

	actual	prediction	Freq
1	0	0	39
2	1	0	7
3	0	1	7
4	1	1	62

FIGURE 6.11   Depicting a confusion matrix

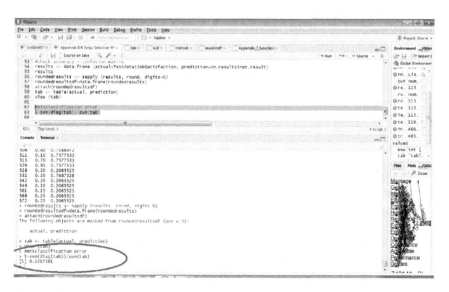

FIGURE 6.12   Displaying misclassification error

Further, the user can compute misclassification error, using the following code:

```
#misclassification error
1-sum(diag(tab))/sum(tab)
```

Step 6: generate recommendations

To generate recommendations, first, the user needs to interpret the contribution of covariates towards prediction. Since generalised weights for all covariates lie within the same range, they all contribute towards prediction and therefore play an important role in the selection of candidates. Further, the confusion matrix shows that the predictive accuracy of the model is high since it generates few false negatives. With a larger dataset, this number can be further reduced, and using test data, predictions could be made for future inputs. Therefore, to select a candidate, an organisation can take input on all the previously mentioned covariates, feed it into this model abbreviated nn and then generate output value to infer how his levels of job satisfaction would vary. Based on the output, the closer the value of predicted job satisfaction to 1, the better would be the candidate for the organisation. This way, the firm can use prediction for selection of candidates.

Step 7: optional – future prospects

This is the final step of the holistic approach. In case a variable doesn't show a strong contribution towards final output, then a new network model needs to be run excluding that variable from the model. Additionally, the organisation can also include other variables for prediction as appropriate for their organisation and job positions that they are analysing. Users may also add many hidden layers, and test for a reduction in misclassification error. Deciding on the number of hidden layers is by hit-and-trial method. You keep on varying the hidden layers and the number of nodes in each, and then decide the optimal one based on reduction in misclassification error.

Predictive analytics in recruitment

The primary game-changer in the area of recruitment in the present business environment is the advent of the Internet and social networking sites. Digitalisation has had far-reaching consequences for recruitment in organisations. Many websites now offer the opportunity for the candidates to register and float their résumés on the website to be picked up for the selection process by firms seeking to hire candidates possessing certain skill sets. Many websites today work on this business model, and the leading ones are Monster.com, JobSearch.com, and so on. Other professional websites allow candidates to build a public profile and display their skill sets and achievements for prospective employers. Also, such sites allow candidates to build their professional networks, which can aid them in career progression. A leading website in India which features these traits is LinkedIn. Firms have also admitted to searching an individual's social media profile before hiring to gain an insight into his personality through his social media posts, likes, and dislikes. All of these have completely changed the scenario of recruitment and hiring in organisations. Firms have deployed their automatic web search engines which scrape résumés from such websites, containing skill sets that are in demand for a particular job opening in the firm.

CORPORATE SNAPSHOT: PREDICTIVE ANALYTICS IN WORKFORCE PLANNING

Predictive HR analytics aids in conducting a comprehensive supply analysis of the current workforce. It can aid in the identification of gaps in the current supply of employees or indicate likely areas of future shortages. Typically, it inculcates the following steps to implement analytics:

- For each function, for each job position and role, specify the headcount and gender, maybe through a dashboard.
- Now categorise each job position and function on as many variables as possible, such as job title, job level, education, performance rating, experience, gender, age group, etc.
- Next, conduct a leave analysis by types of leaves, types of job functions and positions, and location; for example, casual leaves by a job function, a job position, a location.
- Include external environmental variables like commuting distance variations for late reporting.
- Further conduct analysis based on similar variables on sources of hiring, turnover rates, and retention rates.
- Now conclude from the entire analysis where current or probable future skill gaps can occur. Also, deduce the strengths and weaknesses of the current supply chain.

Source: Isson and Harriott (2016)

HR analytics plays a key role in this scenario. The following are some major areas where predictive analytics can make an impact on HR recruitment practices:

1   Primarily, predictive analytics has had an impact on enhancing the quality of the process of hiring. As demonstrated through a practical example in this chapter in the previous section on the application of analytics in the selection, firms are now gaining unprecedented insights into the definition and composition of a successful employee at a firm. Firms collect a lot of data regarding attrition, performance, absenteeism, engagement levels, training programmes, and feedback, all of which can be combined to yield meaningful information about a high-performing individual in an organisation. This can form the basis for future hiring, such that analytics can predict whether a particular employee is going to be a high performer or not. In addition, firms can build profiles and refine job descriptions for particular job roles, based on the analysis of

high-performing candidates, and future hiring can be based on these refined definitions.

2   Besides this, firms can also scrape the web to mine out the job offerings made by competitive firms. This can allow them to understand the kind of diversification adopted by competing firms. For example, how many job offerings are made by competing firms for the roles of business analysts? Answering these questions based on analytics would strengthen the case for a firm addressing the dire need to inculcate analytics in its business functions. Therefore, such an analysis would not only justify the job offerings made, but also be in line with the competition.

3   A major area of deploying analytics in recruitment is to assess the effectiveness and efficiency of hiring sources. The firms don't hire from a single channel or source; rather they first build a pool of candidates to be called for the selection process who will be then screened and tested for final hiring. To build this pool, firms base past hiring decisions on a number greater than an actual number of hires and then splits this number among the available sources of hires. For example, if a firm is seeking to hire 20 engineers at first level, then from past data analysis, it decides to build a pool of 100 candidates, out of which 20 will be finally hired. Now to call these 100 candidates, it will divide it into hiring sources, like 50 to be called from engineering institutes, 20 from third-party recruiting services, ten from in-house referrals, ten from job board evaluations, and ten from websites. But the question is how the firm is going to decide on splitting this among various sources. Analytics provides a solution to this situation. Analytics allows the firms to analyse the effectiveness and efficiency of these sources – such as ranking them based on the performance of hired candidates from each source, their tenure and engagement with the firm, number of hires from each source, and so on. Additionally, analytics can also be used to eliminate sources hosting 'bad' profiles such as with incomplete information or misleading information, unauthentic or those who turn out to be poor hires – low in performance or leaving the firm too quickly.

4   Another major impact is on the speed of hiring. Automation and text analytics are the key to creating this impact. Since many candidates now apply online through professional websites or applications invited online by firms through their web portals, text analytics allows quick screening of information on these incoming job applications. This allows eliminating all the forms which don't match the eligibility criteria, contain incomplete information, or don't fit with the job profile. This accelerates the process of hiring because only such short-listed candidates are then called for further process of hiring, saving both time and money for the employers.

5   Analytics can also be used to assess skill levels, gaps, and therefore, the need for probable hiring in jobs. An emerging area of HR analytics, interaction analytics or people analytics, analyses the conversations of employees on the company's digital platforms. This area of analytics looks out for keywords associated with dissatisfaction with the current functioning of the firm, and

thereby assesses any shortcoming in terms of skills up-gradation, or skill shortage in the firm. For example, exchanges in IT department of a firm often contained words like 'unable to perform', 'slow functioning', 'no assistance', 'need to learn', 'training', and so on. It implies that some working in the IT department are being impacted owing to maybe introduction of new software, which employees are not conversant with, or lack of new software such that old software is performing slow. This predicts of a skill gap or skill upgrade or lack of skill set in the IT department. The HR department can then investigate to gauge the actual situation and plan for hiring or training accordingly.

Besides deploying analytics, many firms can now predict the likelihood of their existing employees quitting the firm. This way, they can predict the skill gap likely to occur in the future and plan for it proactively. For example, Hewlett-Packard (HP) computes a flight risk score for each of its 30,000+ employees. Google also predicts candidates likely to leave the firm and thereafter their success in other firms (Way, 2017). Some of the parameters used by such predictive algorithms may include employee-related variables like tenure, absenteeism, and performance ratings, and company-related variables like company health, turnover rates, stock fluctuations, and external variables like economic health, and so on.

6   Another aspiring area in this stream of analytics is to define work as per people's needs and not find people who match to job openings. The idea is to apply analytics to dynamically understand the career choices of individuals, and suggest to them career paths to follow. This is only possible when analytics can assess the actual skill sets of employees, and their choices, passions, and interests, and then generate individualised recommendations so that employees are enabled and empowered to reach their full potential.

CORPORATE SNAPSHOT: PREDICTIVE ANALYTICS IN RECRUITMENT

Several customisable software platforms and solutions are present in the market which provide analytics solutions for recruitment. One such product is Koru, which enables organisations to define what would make a quality hire for their firms. Applying analytics on the business data of the company, its jobs, and employees already working in the firm, Koru builds a unique hiring profile for each job and a fit score which represents the ideal candidate for each job. Then it conducts automated online interviews of all applicants, also generating customised feedback and an individual fit score for each applicant at the end of the session. Thereafter, the top prospects who have the highest fit scores are identified. A client of Koru experienced a change in the role of an accountant at its firm from being more of a consultant than a transactional role. However, they were experiencing difficulty in developing a suitable hiring profile for this changing job role. However, Koru identified the performance drivers of the changed role of accountants in the client firm and built a hiring profile for them. All of the new hires based on this profile are a strong fit with the firm and high performers.

Source: Koru (2019)

Conclusion

The chapter begins with a basic discussion of the concepts of recruitment and selection, stressing on the changing role and nature of HR practices. It explains the limitations of the tedious traditional selection process followed in firms and why there is a need to make it more flexible and adaptive to accommodate environmental dynamics. Thereafter, by building a practical case for the application of predictive analytics in the selection, a step-by-step illustration of the holistic approach using the software package R has been presented. The chapter also lists various data sources which can be used to build a predictive model for selection. The chapter also illustrates how to install packages and import datasets. Also, it presents how to normalise a dataset using min-max transformation or Z transformation, how to split a dataset into training and test data manually, and how to use Sample function. The code for generating confusion matrices and computing misclassification error has also been explained to validate the accuracy of the model. The chapter also highlights the various areas in which predictive analytics can be applied to recruitment, such as for improving the quality of hires, improving the efficacy and effectiveness of hiring, improve the speed of hiring, and identify skill gaps for workforce planning. It also presents small cases on implementation of analytics in areas of recruitment and selection.

Glossary

Arguments of neuralnet   formula, data, hidden, threshold, rep, algorithm, err. fct, linear.output

Compute function   used to apply the results of neuralnet model built using training data, on test data for validation of the model

Confusion matrix   a technique to check the accuracy of the model by depicting false positives and false negatives in a tabular format

Misclassification error   a quantified value of wrong predictions made by application of the model to test data

Neuralnet   a statistical package in R to model and apply artificial neural networks, based on multilayer perceptron model

Normalising the dataset   involves scaling the values of dataset within a particular range; typically, min-max normalisation or z-normalisation is used

Pareto Rule   the most commonly used rule for splitting the dataset, establishing the norm as 80:20; that is, 80% of the dataset is to be used for training and 20% for testing

Recruitment and selection   the first process of HRM which generates and attracts the required pool of candidates to fill a job opening in a firm and then choose the right person who fits into that role perfectly; this process also deals with matching KSAs of candidates with those required by the job in the organisation

Splitting the dataset   A dataset used to build mining model is split into test and training data so that training data can be used to build and train the model, while test data can be used to validate the outcomes of the model

Steps in traditional selection process   initial or preliminary interview, application blanks or blank, check of references, psychological tests, employment interview, approval by the supervisor, physical examination and induction or orientation

Review material

1   What is the purpose of recruitment and selection?
2   Why it has become important for the HR department to quantify its performance?
3   Explain the meaning of the 'changing nature of HR practices'.
4   List the steps followed in the traditional selection process.
5   Detail the limitations of following a traditional selection process.
6   List a few challenges selection process has to face in the current business environment.
7   Summarise the application of a holistic approach to the problem of predictive selection in your terms.
8   Justify how classification is an appropriate prediction technique for the problem of selection, as discussed in the text.
9   Explain the application of system view/process approach to the problem of predictive selection.
10   List the data sources which can be used to build a predictive model for selection.
11   Discuss the characteristics of neuralnet package in R.
12   Explain min-max normalisation and z-normalisation.
13   Discuss the need to split data into test and training data.
14   What is the Pareto Rule? How is splitting as per the Pareto rule implemented in R?
15   Explain how Sample function works in R.
16   Discuss the components of the output of a model built using neuralnet package.
17   What is the role of the compute function in validating the outcomes of neuralnet?

18 List the steps used to build confusion matrix and generate misclassification error for checking the accuracy of the model.

19 Briefly explain how to generate recommendations from the model results.

20 List some probable future aspects emerging from the application of the model.

21 Explain the environmental dynamicity which has led to changes in recruitment practices.

22 List the six steps implemented in organisations to generate a comprehensive supply chain analysis using predictive analytics.

23 How can predictive analytics improve the quality of the hiring process?

24 How can predictive analytics be used to gauge a competitor's job offerings?

25 How can predictive analytics be used to assess the effectiveness and efficiency of the hiring process?

26 How can predictive analytics improve the speed of hiring?

27 How can predictive analytics be used to identify and address the skill gaps in hiring and supply of employees in a firm?

28 Why is it becoming all the more relevant now to generate individualised career growth recommendations for employees?

Problem exercises

1 Using the code for min-max normalisation, write a code for z-normalisation and test it see if results are different.

2 Collect a small sample of about 100 data points on age, gender, academic grades, and performance ranking from employees working at the same job position at the same level in similar organisations. Now build a neural network to predict performance ranking based on three covariates – age, gender, and grades. Normalise the dataset and generate a confusion matrix, as well.

Bibliography

Anderson, M. (2014, March). *5 traits Google looks for in new hires*. Retrieved May 2019, from Code Fellows: www.codefellows.org/blog/5-traits-google-looks-for-in-new-hires

Basu, S., and Sarkar, B. (2019, August 16), *IT companies go all out to stop attrition of skilled young staff*. Retrieved September 2019, from ET Bureau: https://economictimes.india-times.com/tech/ites/it-companies-go-all-out-to-stop-attrition-of-skilled-young-staff/articleshow/70693130.cms?from=mdr

Beardwell, D., and Holden, L. (1994). *Human resource management – a contemporary perspective*. New Delhi: Macmillan India Ltd.

Bhatnagar, J. (2007). Talent management: Strategy of employee engagement in Indian ITES employees: Keys to retention. *Employee Relations, 29*(6), 640–663.

Chaudhary, R., Rangnekar, S., and Barua, M. K. (2012). HRD climate, occupational self efficacy and work engagement: A study from India. *The Psychologist-Manager Journal, 15*(2), 86–105.

Cipolla, V. (2005, October 10). *HR ROI means metrics CEOs want* (Guest Commentary). Retrieved from HR Reporter: https://www.hrreporter.com/news/hr-news/hr-roi-means-metrics-ceos-want-guest-commentary/310450

Collins, J. C. (2001). *Good to great: Why some companies make the leap and others don't*. New York: Harper Collins.

Cooper, C. (2010). Introduction to individual differences. In C. Cooper (Ed.), *Individual differences and personality* (pp. 1–6). Oxon and New York: Routledge, Taylor and Francis Group.

Dessler, G., and Varkkey, B. (2008). *Human resource management* (11th ed.). Manipal: Pearson Education, Inc.

Elkjaer, D., and Filmer, S. (2015). *Trends and drivers of workforce turnover*. New York: Mercer (Health Wealth Career).

Flippo, E. B. (1984). Recruitment and hiring. In E. B. Flippo (Ed.), *Personnel management* (pp. 141–164). Singapore: Mc-Graw Hill Book Company.

Gunther, F., and Fritsch, S. (2010). neuralnet: Training of neural networks. *The R Journal*, 30–38.

Intrator, O., and Intrator, N. (2001). Interpreting neural networks: A simulation study. *Computational Statistics and Data Analysis*, 373–393.

Isson, J. P., and Harriott, J. S. (2016). Workforce planning analytics. In J. P. Isson and J. S. Harriott (Eds.), *People analytics in the era of big data: Changing the way you attract, acquire, develop, and retain talent* (pp. 99–129). Hoboken, NJ: John Wiley & Sons, Inc.

Judge, T. A. and Bono, J. E. (2001). Relationship of core self-evaluations traits – self-esteem, generalized self-efficacy, locus of control, and emotional stability – with job satisfaction and job performance: A meta-analysis. *Journal of Applied Psychology, 86*, 80–92.

Judge, T. A., and Kammeyer-Mueller, J. D. (2012). Job attitudes. *Annual Review of Psychology, 63*, 341–367.

Koru. (2019). *Predictive hiring for fit*. Retrieved 2019, from Koru: www.joinkoru.com

Lightfoot, L. (2007, July). *Firms use personality tests for the best graduates*. Retrieved February 2018, from The Telegraph: www.telegraph.co.uk/news/uknews/1556982/Firms-use-personality-tests-for-best-graduates.html

McGraw, M. (2015, May). *Finding leaders early*. Retrieved June 2018, from Human Resource Executive Online: www.hreonline.com/HRE/view/story.jhtml?id=534358666

Pareek, U., and Rao, T. (2003). Matching the role and the person: Recruitment and placement. In U. Pareek and T. Rao (Eds.), *Designing and managing human resource systems* (pp. 84–98). New Delhi: Oxford & IBH Publishing Pvt. Ltd.

Phillips, M. (2015, May). *Could you handle the big four's psychometric tests?* Retrieved 2018, from In the Black: http://intheblack.com/articles/2015/05/01/the-rise-and-rise-of-psychometrics

PTI. (2018, January). 2018 to see more hirings, salary rise of 10%: Mercer's pay survey. *The Economic Times*. Retrieved 2018, from https://economictimes.indiatimes.com/jobs/2018-to-see-more-hiringssalary-rise-of-10-mercers-pay-survey/articleshow/62455032.cms

SectoralReport. (2016, August). *IT & ITeS industry in India*. India Brand Equity Foundation. Retrieved 2019, from www.ibef.org/industry/information-technology-india.aspx

Spence, J. (2015). Retrieved May 2019, from http://associationsnow.com/2014/03/important-invest-talent-acquisition/

Vincent, J. (2014, February). *Want a job at Google? Internet giant reveals the 'five attributes' necessary for all employees*. Retrieved December 2018, from The Independent: www.independent.co.uk/life-style/gadgets-and-tech/features/work-for-google-internet-giant-reveals-the-five-attributes-necessary-to-get-a-job-9151897.html

Wadhwa, V., DeVitton, U. K., and Gereffi, G. (2008, July). *How the disciple became the GURU*. Retrieved 2018, from Harvard: www.law.harvard.edu/programs/lwp/people/staffPapers/vivek/Vivek_HowDiscipleBecameGuru.pdf

Way, P. (2017, April 10). *The HR analytics revolution*. Retrieved October 3, 2019, from O Platform Leader: https://blogs.oracle.com/platformleader/the-hr-analytics-revolution

Further readings

1 *R for Dummies* by Andre D. Veris and Joris Meys, Wiley Publishers.
2 *R for Data Science* by Hadley Wickham and Garrett Grolemund, O'Reilly Publishers.
3   www.rdocumentation.org

7

PREDICTIVE HR ANALYTICS IN TURNOVER AND SEPARATION

After reading this chapter, users will be able to understand the following key concepts:

- Revise the basic concepts of turnover and define turnover intent
- Understand the role of turnover intent and job attitudes in the prediction of turnover
- Use a practical step-by-step illustration of the application of KNN to predict turnover in IT firms using holistic approach
- Understand how to view the KNN model performance and interpret optimal K
- Understand how to view variable importance in predicting turnover
- Understand how to predict turnover using test data using KNN model built in R
- Understand how to change the metric for assessing model performance from accuracy to ROC
- Learn about different areas of application of analytics to the management of separation
- Understand the use of exit interview data for analytics
- Grasp how analytics can be used for workforce planning and supply analysis
- Discuss the role of analytics in effective management of retirements

Opening case

Lean manufacturing is a relatively new concept in production industries and requires a specific skill set for the managers to effectively perform and reap results from its teams under these circumstances. A metal manufacturing firm operating globally decided to incorporate lean manufacturing in its operations and hired supervisors who were experienced in this field. While the company was apprehensive about the success of lean manufacturing with the workforce, it was faced with a new challenge. In a large number of its plants, the company witnessed high attrition among the workforce. The firm assumed that since supervisors hired for implementing lean manufacturing at each plant were new to the firm, the workforce was probably resisting change, and this was contributing to increased attrition at the plants. So it implemented analytics to understand how supervisor related with team results at each plant. For this purpose, they collected data on the number of parameters like quality, delivery performance, safety, innovations in processes improvements, supervisor behaviour, and so on. The firm discovered that the plants where attrition rate was low exhibited 150 percent better results than corresponding plants with high attrition rates. In all these plants, supervisor performance was very high and exhibited critical behaviours predictive of success in each plant. These behaviours included many factors such as beginning the job with an orientation, defining the behavioural norms for the team, providing coaching on the use of new technology, viz. lean tools, and on problem-solving to the team members. Therefore, they found that switching to coaching rather than directing was the key to success for a supervisor to implement lean manufacturing and also resulted in lower attrition rates. This further led the firm to create a competency model for predicting the success of leaders in lean manufacturing, which proved to be useful in hiring for future positions in lean manufacturing, as well (Grillo and Hackett (2015).

Introduction

Separation is the final HRM process in managing the employees of a firm. Separation of an employee form an organisation may occur owing to his demise, retirement, voluntary early retirement, resignation, or termination. When the process of separation occurs before the expected date of retirement, it is termed as turnover and may be voluntary or involuntary. Turnover has also been termed as quitting, attrition, exit, mobility, migration, succession, and so on. Involuntary turnover is often initiated by the firm. Of concern to the management is voluntary turnover. Separation of an employee often involves the management of several other activities such as payment of benefits like gratuity, provident fund, finding a successor to fill in the role, management of successors, and so on.

Turnover can be predicted by turnover intent. Turnover is prevalent across all employee categories and varies with factors such as age, skill level, and experience.

A general measure defined to measure attrition in an organisation is the number of employees leaving in a year divided by the total or an average number of employees in the firm that year and is often expressed as a percentage, but this measure is seldom used. Turnover is defined as:

> Individual movement across the membership boundary of an organization.
>
> *(Perez, 2008, p. 11)*

Here, individuals refer to employees of the firm and movement can be due to any reason such as separation, succession, etc. Turnover is further classified into two types: voluntary and involuntary. Voluntary turnover is the form addressed in the research and is a prominent cause of concern in firms. It occurs when an employee resigns from the firm. Involuntary turnover occurs when an employee does not initiate the process of separation and can occur due to dismissal, death, and so on. It is widely accepted that voluntary turnover is avoidable by timely interventions by the management. For example, if an employee resigns because they are unable to live together after the transfer of either spouse, the firm can relocate the employee. Further, it is said that turnover can be functional if it causes the movement of unproductive employees, else it would be dysfunctional. Although figures at the end of a year reflect the actual turnover of a firm, it is very difficult to gauge if employees intend to leave the firm. This is termed as turnover intent.

> Turnover intent is defined as the reflection of the probability that an individual will change his/her job within a certain time period.
>
> *(Sousa-Poza and Henneberger, 2002, p. 4)*

Many firms periodically gauge the turnover intent of their employees to determine or predict the likelihood of employees planning to leave the firm in the upcoming year. Therefore, for the prediction of turnover, turnover intent can be used as the target variable.

Holistic approach: predictive modelling of turnover

Now that the concept of turnover is clear and how to measure it, an attempt has been made to apply a holistic approach to predictive modelling of turnover.

Step 1: identification and definition of the problem

To illustrate how step 1 can be implemented, the example which will be discussed in this chapter involves the turnover prediction of software engineers in the IT industry. This section of the chapter begins with a brief overview of the IT sector in India to acquaint the user with the same, followed by a brief on the problem of turnover in this sector.

As per (IBEF, 2018), India is the world's largest sourcing destination for the information technology (IT) industry, accounting for approximately 67% of the US$124–130 billion markets. The industry employs about 10 million workers.

More importantly, the industry has led to the economic transformation of the country and altered the perception of India in the global economy. India's cost competitiveness in providing IT services, which is approximately 3–4 times cheaper than in the US, continues to be the mainstay of its unique selling proposition (USP) in the global sourcing market. However, India is also gaining prominence in terms of intellectual capital, with several global IT firms setting up their innovation centres in India. The total contribution of the Indian IT sector to India GDP was 8% in 2018 (FE Bureau, 2018).

The development of the software services/IT sector in India has a long history (Arora, Arunachalam, Asundi, and Fernandes, 2001), starting from the Sino-Indian conflict in 1962. Some Indian policies of major importance contributing to the growth of the Indian IT sector are the Computer Software Export, Software Development and Training Policy in 1986, 10-crore rule in 1987, IPSS (International Packet Switching Service) in 1989, and development of software technology parks (STPs).

Notably, the domestic production of software products for the domestic market in India is growing slowly, and it is the only industry in which exports account for 65% of revenue. However, the IT sector in India has the highest hiring capacity or is the largest employer in the private organised sector in India, forms the largest share in terms of Indian exports, has the highest number of entrepreneurs in the world as well in India, and attracts the largest investments. Majority of these exports are related to coding, testing, low-level design, while domestic projects span almost all stages of the software development lifecycle. Also, executives agree that the experience gained from domestic projects does not fetch as much experience as an outsourced project. All the firms, whether big or small, do indulge in similar activities – maintenance projects such as maintaining legacy systems or mainframes, migration to client-server systems, and delivering solutions. Besides this, the duration of export projects is also small, lasting an average 150 months. The US outsources IT projects to India owing to a lesser amount of investment in staff and resources in less critical activities, the ability of the staff to work 24 hours every day, and considerably lower salary than US counterparts. The difficulty arises when professionals are required with more than four years of experience. There is no dearth of such candidates in India, but they tend to shift abroad after almost four years of service. Employees not sticking with the same firm after this amount of experience also accounts for the inability of the country to move beyond coding, development, and maintenance.

Although figures suggest a promising road ahead for Indian IT firms, the industry has consistently experienced environmental uncertainties attributed to the economic slowdown, technological changes, and political pressure, among other factors. In particular, the Indian IT industry suffers from high turnover rates, fluctuating between 13% and 15% yearly (PTI, 2018; Dasgupta, 2017). Also, although substantial new talent accrues to the industry annually – compounded annual growth rate for Indian IT graduates from 2008–2015 was 9.4% – IT businesses are reluctant to tap this talent pool because of quality concerns and retention issues (SectoralReport, 2016; PTI, 2018).

In recent years, as the Indian economy has grown, so has turnover (Yiu and Saner, 2008). Turnover is prevalent across all categories of employees, and the higher the skill level of the employees, the higher would be the rate of turnover. The report on Indian employee turnover suggests that the maximum rate of attrition is among the knowledge workers (11% to 20%) because they indulge in job-hopping due to high demand for their skills. Following them, managers demonstrate the next highest level of attrition, between 6% and 15%, followed by employees at executive ranks at about 5%. An increased rate of attrition is also seen in clerical and line staff, although it is much lower than all the other categories at 2%–10%. Other than job categories, another factor which impacts the rate of turnover is experience or seniority that is maximum turnover occurs between one and four years of employment. Another study (Elkjaer and Filmer, 2015) averaged the trend over five years from 2011–2014, and it too suggests that highest turnover is among medium-performance workers, while it is lesser for high-performance and low-performance workers. Besides this, the rate of turnover is negatively linked to the age of workers. Therefore, firms should devise strategies to curb turnover accordingly, taking into account all these factors.

Turnover has several consequences for the firm since it is negatively associated with the business unit and organisational success. However, when an organisation plans strategically and utilises predictive analytics, it can curb turnover (Elkjaer and Filmer, 2015). Conceptual models can be applied to explain turnover in the IT industry. The resource-based view (RBV) (Holland, Sheehan, and Cieri, 2007) suggests that a firm gains competitive advantage from three resources – physical, organisational, and human resources, with the highest importance attributed to human resources in the present era (Ostroff and Bowen, 2016). In this context, retaining employees has become a major issue for IT firms (Murray, 1999), where employers face a 'seller's market' and therefore seek to become an 'employer of choice' (Bellou, Chaniotakis, Kehagias, and Rigopoulou, 2013), so that if one worker leaves, many other skilled workers are willing to enter the firm. 'Employer of choice' is a strategy adopted by companies to strategically manage their workforce by enhancing the ability of the company to attract, retain, and motivate its key employees (Bellou et al., 2013; Backhaus, 2016).

Issues of retention and management of it vary significantly among industries and organisations (Sheridan, 1992), due to differences in organisational culture values, which in turn has an impact on the policies and procedures of a firm. 'Person-organisation fit' (PO fit) theories (Kristof, 1996) adopt a multidimensional approach to evaluate the fit of an employee with the firm – value congruence, personality congruence, and work environment congruence. These theories posit that people who have been 'hired' for an organisation, and not just given 'jobs', display significantly better work attitudes, lower turnover intention, and higher work performance (Westerman and Cyr, 2004). It has also been seen that voluntarily turnover in employees occurs (Yiu and Saner, 2008) due to dissatisfaction with organisational factors such as salary, career advancement, relationship with supervisor, economic growth and talent competition, job content, recognition, and training and development opportunities. External factors, organisational practices and individual characteristics, each influence employee turnover (Elkjaer and Filmer, 2015). Therefore PO fit can play a significant role in explaining high turnover (McCulloch and Turban, 2007), and through creation of organisational factors which encourage environmental and value congruence of employees with the firm, their turnover intention (Amos and Weathington, 2008; Van Vianen, DePater, and Dijk, 2007) can be lowered, thus aiding in employee retention.

> Attitudes like organisational commitment and job satisfaction have been consistently used to predict turnover.

Attitudes like organisational commitment and job satisfaction have been consistently used to predict turnover. When employees perceive that they are tied in the form of the social web to the organisation, they are embedded in the job and are less likely to quit the firm. Turnover in the IT industry can be mitigated through effective management of job attitudes and HR practices, and monitoring individual characteristics of the employees. An important aspect to look for embeddedness is whether or not they find themselves fitting with the organisation and the job. The unfolding model of turnover explains turnover intention by describing that when employees perceive some sort of shock, then they start looking for alternative job opportunities. However, also in such cases, when they weigh other aspects to be favourable, then despite the perception of a shock, their intention to quit diminishes. Therefore, when employees perceive that they fit with the organisation and the job, they continue to stay, despite perceptions of organisational shocks. In this context, it can be said that HR practices moderate the relationship between perception of organisational shock and turnover intent. When a firm indulges in high-involvement practices, turnover tendencies are less influenced by environmental shocks. Therefore, to mitigate turnover in IT industry, the conceptual foundations assert that if the job fit, organisational fit, and job attitudes like quality of work life and job satisfaction are appropriately managed and utilised to build a predictive turnover model, this can aid in timely prediction of turnover intent.

A predictive attrition model would be able to highlight the employees who are going to leave the organisation soon, and this can aid the firm in making proactive arrangements such as counselling, indulging in retention strategies, or coming up with a plan to fill the vacancy. This would also have implications for screening candidates; it should be taken into account while hiring if a candidate is one of those who has high predicted turnover intent – that is, the characteristics of such individuals.

Following from the preceding discussion, we can summarise the following points to implement step 1 of a holistic approach to the application of analytics:

- Facts and figures support that the high rates of turnover in the Indian IT industry are a prominent business problem.

- Theoretical and conceptual models describe the story behind the building up of turnover intent. It aids the reader in building an overview of the problem and steering in the direction of modelling the problem.
- A predictive system for prediction of turnover intent would be the best-fit analytical solution for the current problem of turnover.
- This prediction can be based on job fit, organisation fit, and job attitudes carried out by the IT firms.

Step 2: modelling the problem to predict who is going to leave the firm

As the reader is acquainted with the theoretical and experiential background now, turnover intent of the software engineers working in tier 1 IT industries can be used to predict turnover of software engineers. Therefore, the input variables used would be: person-job fit (PJ fit), person-organisation fit (PO fit), job satisfaction, quality of work life, gender, marriage, and performance ranking. To collect data on each of these variables, standard questionnaires freely available on the Internet have been utilised. Person-job fit and person-organisation fit was measured using a four-item scale developed and validated in (Saks and Ashforth, 1997). Intention to quit within one year measures turnover. This was measured using three items scale that assesses the tendency of an employee to continue with the current organisation (Chatman, 1991). Job satisfaction has been measured using a five-item scale given by Brayfield-Rothe (Judge, Van Vianen, and DePater, 2004). This data may be available to HR managers if they periodically conduct organisational health surveys and employee engagement surveys; else, they can collect the data by administering a questionnaire as a survey instrument.

The output variable intention has been coded as 1 and 2, where 1 implies 'intention to quit' while 2 implies 'intention to stay'. The 'intention to quit' scale has been averaged, and the values less than 3.5 are coded as 2, else 1.

Step 3: selecting the tool

While developing a predictive model for the business problem, one gets clarity as to what needs to be done to apply prediction to the data collected. As is with the case of developing a predictive model for turnover, the reader gains an understanding that model needs to classify. Recalling the techniques of classification presented in the earlier chapters, most of the techniques would fit here, viz. regression, KNN, decision trees and artificial neural networks (ANN). For illustration in this chapter, KNN would be applied using class and caret package in R software. For the sake of simplicity of illustration, we will use output variable 'intent to stay' as the target variable for classifying employees in the firm who have intent to stay or leave, and use all input variables including gender, marital status, performance ranking, job satisfaction, PO fit, PJ fit, and job satisfaction for predicting this target variable.

Step 4: applying the tool

For the application of the tool, RStudio has been utilised. The dataset used for analysis is available with the book. The dataset is an Excel worksheet titled 'Turnover'. The R package used for implementing KNN is class and caret package.

KNN model in R can be broadly built in two ways. One way, in which you use the package class, and then pass on the K value by yourself to the KNN function in r. This function has the format:

```
Pred ← Knn(training dataset, test dataset, class
labels, the value of k)
```

This will store the output in pred, which will contain the predicted values for each row in test data. Then you can check for the accuracy of this model. Here either you type in a code to compare the observed values and predicted values of the target variable or install another package like gplots, which allows you to directly cross-tabulate. Also, using hit and trial, you have to keep changing the K values and observe how the accuracy of the model varies.

This becomes tedious when you have to recall different package names and even supply K values of your own. For this purpose, it is necessary to install another package, caret, abbreviated for classification and regression training. Caret is an extensive package and contains a large number of algorithms. If the reader is interested in gaining an insight into the packages contained in caret, simply execute names(getModelInfo()).

To build a KNN model, caret package has inbuilt train function, which takes the arguments – training data, target variable to be predicted, and method to be used for training the model. This package also has inbuilt function to plot a confusion matrix and tabulate predicted results. The train function has an argument metric which allows the evaluation of the performance of various models run using this function. By default, for regression problems, RMSE, R squared, and mean absolute error are computed as performance metrics, while accuracy and Kappa are computed as classification problems. By default, the train function is designed to choose the best model which has the highest reported performance metric. However, the user can change the optimality criteria by supplying the algorithm used to compute the final model in the selectionFunction argument of train function. The three criteria can be: 'best', which chooses the largest or smallest value; 'oneSE', which chooses the simples model within one standard error of best mode; or 'tolerance', which selects the least complex model with tolerance for the best value. Another important and useful function in this package is trainControl function, which is simply a resampling function. This function takes the arguments specifying how many times resampling is to be done and using which method it should be done. By using set.seed, we ensure that same resamples are drawn every time the code is executed. To predict the values of test data using the output of the model previously implemented, predict.train function can be used. By using argument type of this function, it can be specified whether probabilities are to be predicted or classes have to be predicted.

Application of KNN in R

To apply KNN in R, the libraries used in for application are caret, pROC, and mlbench. For this, packages which need to be installed have been specified in the code discussion as follows.

1   The first step is to import data from an Excel file. Use the Import Dataset function from global environment tab of RStudio. Attach the dataset to a global environment.
2   Normalise the dataset, using min-max normalisation. Upon normalisation, coded values of intention (2) also have been scaled to 0, therefore intention = 1, implies an intention to leave, while intention = 0 implies an intention to stay.
3   It is important to note that target variable be specified as factor variable for implementation of KNN for classification. The code for this is as follows.

```
#Use factor in output column for classification
NormTurnover$IntentionCode[NormTurnover$Intention
Code==0] ← 'Stay'
NormTurnover$IntentionCode[NormTurnover$Intention
Code==1] ← 'Leave'
NormTurnover$IntentionCode <- factor(NormTurnover$
IntentionCode)
#check if Intention code has become a FACTOR vari-
able or is it still character data type
str(NormTurnover)
```

As is seen in the console output, the data type of IntentionCode which is the target variable has been changed to factor.

4   Split the dataset into training and test data using the Pareto rule. The code used for partitioning the data is as follows.

```
set.seed(1234)  #ensures  same  partition  whenever
code is run
New ← sample (2, nrow(NormTurnover), replace=TRUE,
prob = c(0.8, 0.2))
Traindata ← NormTurnover [New==1,]
Testdata ← NormTurnover [New==2,]
```

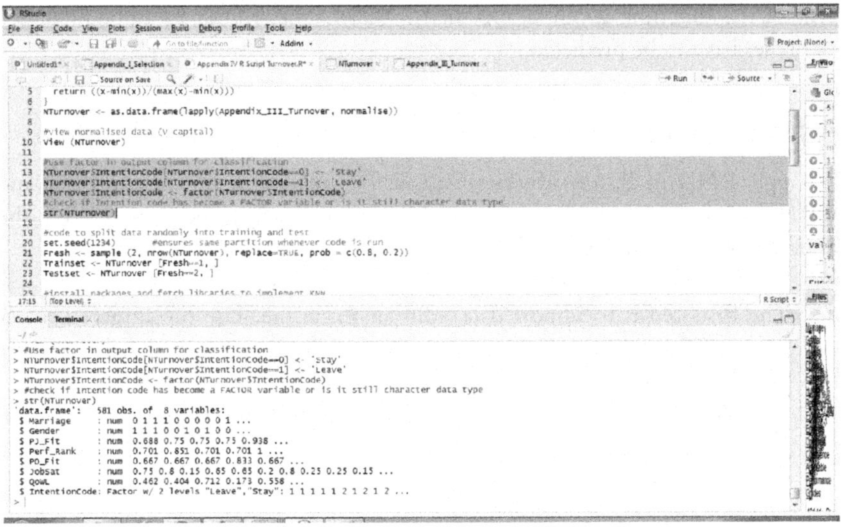

FIGURE 7.1 Specifying target variable as factor variable

FIGURE 7.2 Splitting the dataset

On execution, the summary has been presented as shown in the right-hand side of the global environment of R. The code has created a dataset titled 'Testdata' with 116 observations and a 'Traindata' with 465 observations.

5 Install packages required to implement and execute KNN model and fetch libraries. As discussed earlier, packages used to implement KNN are class, caret, pROC, mlbench, and e1071.

```
#install packages and fetch libraries to implement
KNN
install.packages("class")
library (class)
install.packages("caret")
library (caret)
install.packages("pROC")
library (pROC)
install.packages("mlbench")
library (mlbench)
```

6   Build and execute the KNN model using train function

```
#KNN model
Control <- trainControl(method = "repeatedcv",
number = 10,
repeats = 3)
set.seed(222)
KNNfit <- train(IntentionCode ~.,
data = Trainset,
method = 'knn',
trControl= Control)
```

Step 5: interpreting and validating the outcomes

After building and implementing the KNN model, user can check for model performance by typing in the code:

```
#model performance
KNNfit
```

This displays a summary of the model in the console window.

1   The results depict that optimal model has been selected based on accuracy, and the K = 5, which implies that for future predictions, the distance of the item from five nearest neighbours would be evaluated to generate the predicted class.
2   The summary clearly shows that there are seven predictor variables: gender, marriage, PO fit, PJ fit, job satisfaction, quality of work life, and performance ranking. There are two classes in the output variable: leave or stay. For

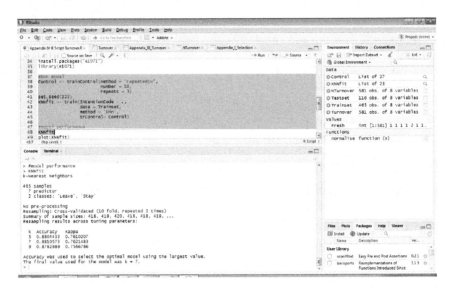

FIGURE 7.3   Model summary

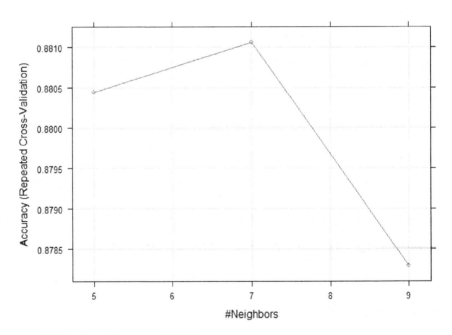

FIGURE 7.4   Graph depicting KNN fit

resampling, tenfold cross-validation, repeated three times, has been utilised. This implies that for each sample, tenfolds or 10 splits of the data have been created, where nine folds have been used to build the model and the tenth fold has been used to validate the model. this entire process has been repeated three times. Model accuracy and Kappa values have been assessed.

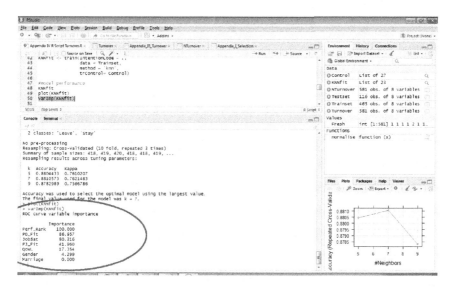

FIGURE 7.5   Variable importance

To gain a better understanding, plotting of fit can also be done using **plot (KNNfit).**

3   As is seen in the graph, the highest accuracy value is at K = 5, after which it progressively decreases.

4   Next, one can infer the varying levels of importance of predictor variables towards the prediction of the target class. For this, simply type in the code varImp(KNNfit) and execute. It displays the predictors with their importance in decreasing order of importance. The most significant predictors of turnover intent of software engineers are performance ranking, PO fit, and job satisfaction (more than 80 importance). Another interesting revelation is that gender and marriage are the least important in predicting the turnover intent of software engineers.

5   Use the previously trained model to predict for Testdata. Here one can make use of the predict function.

```
#use the model for prediction
pred <- predict(KNNfit, newdata=Testset)
pred
```

The preceding code will run KNNfit model built previously on test dataset, and store it in pred. Then simply all predictions for each row of the dataset will be displayed by executing pred.

6   Plot the confusion matrix. You can use the inbuilt confusionMatrix function.

```
confusionMatrix (pred, Testset$IntentionCode)
```

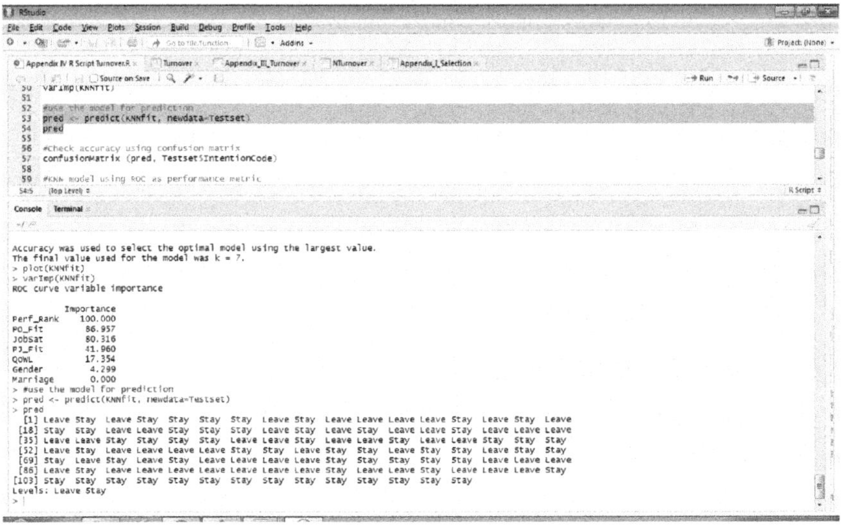

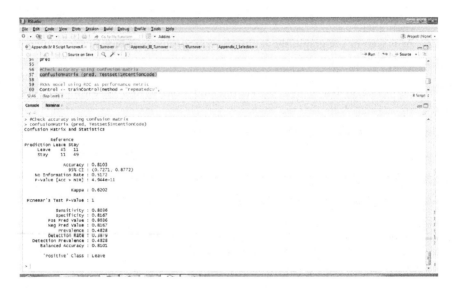

FIGURE 7.6 Using the model for prediction

FIGURE 7.7 Confusion matrix

As can be seen, the accuracy of the model is quite high, at 81.03%. The testset has 116 observations. There are 45 observations which have an intention to leave the firm, and model also predicts that they have the intent to leave. Similarly, there are 49 observations which have the intent to stay and predicted the same by the model. Therefore, accuracy = (49 + 45)/116 = 0.8103, as depicted in the preceding summary. The 95% confidence interval goes from 72.71% to 87.72%. If the model had no information about intent to stay, then model accuracy had been about 51.72%.

Step 6: generating recommendations

To generate recommendations, first, the reader needs to interpret the contribution of covariates towards variable for prediction. This can be gauged in KNN using varImp code. Next, the model can be re-run by removing the variables with least importance. The accuracy of the model can be further removed, by changing the optimality assessment metric.

Let us attempt to **further improve the performance** of the model by changing the metric from accuracy to ROC. For this, trainControl has to be revised by including class probabilities and summary function, as shown following.

```
#KNN model
Control <- trainControl(method = "repeatedcv",
number = 10,
repeats = 3,
classProbs = TRUE,
summaryFunction = twoClassSummary)
set.seed(222)
KNNfit <- train(IntentionCode ~.,
data = Trainset,
method = 'knn',
trControl= Control,
metric = "ROC",
tuneGrid = expand.grid(k=1:60))
```

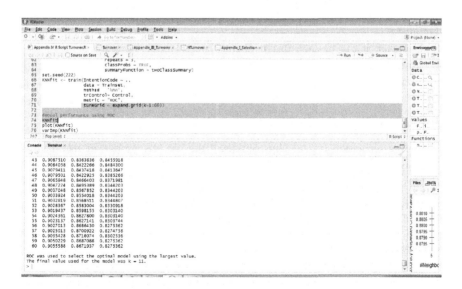

FIGURE 7.8 Model summary using ROC as performance metric

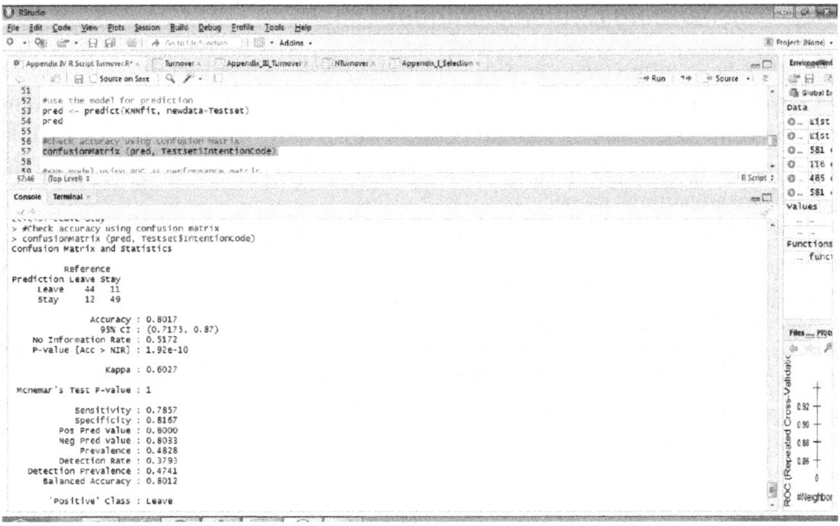

FIGURE 7.9   Confusion matrix with ROC

Again testing the model performance by typing and executing KNNfit, the model has been executed for K ranging from 1–60 and the ROC values for each K has been computed. Now the optimal model has been selected based on ROC value, and optimal K is 11. Again using plot(KNNfit), it can be seen that as values of K increase, the area under curve first increases until K = 11, after which it decreases. Also running variable importance, it can be seen that it is similar with minor variations as the previous one.

Again doing predictions and executing confusion matrix, results are shown in Figure 7.9.

However, it can be seen that performance and model accuracy has decreased by using ROC as a performance metric. Therefore, the best model prediction is based on K = 5.

Predictive analytics in separation

Employee separation is generally considered the last HR process in an organisation and involves multiple activities for smooth separation of the employee from the firm. Separation may occur due to retirement on completing tenure with the firm for a stipulated period as per job offer, due to voluntary resigning, termination, layoffs due to downsizing of the firm, or mergers and acquisitions. The process of separation also creates a lot of administrative burden for the firms. Besides paperwork for a formal separation from the firm fulfilling all legal obligations, the process involves ensuring the proper return of company assets, providing the post-exit benefits such as gratuity, informing the third-party service providers such as

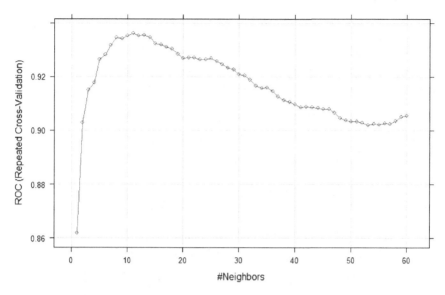

FIGURE 7.10   Graph depicting KNN fit (using ROC)

insurance providers to stop coverage, and so on. Post-exit from the firm, employees may seek referrals for future employment, which also needs to be managed. There is an increasing pressure on the firms to manage separation properly to ensure smooth employee experience to preserve the image of the firm. This is because the employees carry that experience to other organisations, where they will be seeking future jobs, and it is important to ensure proper emotional connection even at the time of separation from the firm. Collecting appropriate employee data is very important at this stage, as it would be very difficult to gain any missing information once the employee leaves the firm. Predictive HR analytics on separation data can aid the organisations in many ways as discussed in the following parts of this section.

Managing retirements through analytics

An interesting trend visible in the workplace has been the change in retirement patterns. Many organisations are witnessing either a delay in retirement by people seeking extensions in their tenure even at lesser wages, or a trend towards increasing the contractual or part-time workforce. Understanding these changing trends and identifying patterns, if any, early on, before they can create an organisational impact, is imperative for the organisations. Therefore, this is one field where prediction is becoming valuable and important for companies. The role of analytics to predict the trend of the pattern of retirement behaviour becomes especially crucial at higher positions or key roles of the organisation. When people in key roles delay their retirement, it directly impacts the organisational behaviour of a potential successor to that role. Hence, application of analytics in this area has twofold benefits – one, identifying the trend in retirement and ensuring business continuity by pipelining probable positions with potential successors; and two, managing the successors in case there is a delay in retirements by identifying that delay in a timely manner. HR departments now deploy analytical algorithms which inculcate factors additional to age and tenure to predict retirements, such as recent changes in role, pay level, rates of change in pay, and incentive eligibility. It has been seen that these factors are more predictive of who will retire than the conventional metrics of age and tenure. Such firms have been able to effectively deal with retirement cycles, ensuring timely pipelining of key roles with a potential successor.

Supply analysis and workforce planning

Since separation is the end process in HRM, streamlining the process of gathering of data for each HR process from recruitment to separation sets the ground for implementation of analytics for effective workforce planning. In this scenario, predictive HR analytics aids in conducting a comprehensive supply analysis of the current workforce. It can aid in the identification of gaps in the current supply of employees or indicate likely areas of future shortages. Typically, it inculcates the following six steps to implement analytics:

- For each function, for each job position and role, specify the headcount and gender, maybe through a dashboard.
- Now categorise each job position and function on as many variables as possible, such as job title, job level, education, performance rating, experience, gender, age group, etc.
- Next, conduct a leave analysis by types of leaves, types of job functions and positions, and location. For example, casual leaves by a job function, a job position, a location.
- Include external environmental variables like commuting distance variations for late reporting.
- Further conduct analysis based on similar variables on sources of hiring, turnover rates, and retention rates.

Now conclude from the entire analysis where current or probable future skill gaps can occur. Also, deduce the strengths and weaknesses of the current supply chain.

CORPORATE SNAPSHOT: PREDICTIVE ANALYTICS IN SEPARATION

A leading analytics firm analysed a firm to depict how a change in retirement patterns affects the workforce and its planning. The firm deduced that one of the key factors in influencing retirement plans of the employees was the reception of workplace pension. Since most employees perceived this to be their only financial support once they leave work, this had the largest impact on their retirement plans. In this context, many firms have now initiated defined contribution (DC) plans for retirement, whereby a fixed percent of investment for pension is done by both employer and employee. The analytics firm analysed employee savings in the DC pension plan and projected it against targeted savings. These employees were then classified into red and green bars, with red were unlikely to reach their projected targets. The classification depicted that the majority of those employees who were in their 50s or 60s were highly unlikely to reach their projected savings target, and hence impact retirement plans. Taking a cue from these findings, the firm then implemented analytics to determine 'retirement readiness' for each of its employees and also to predict the composition of the workforce over the next few years, in terms of an ageing workforce and its abilities and likely market dynamics at the time. This would aid the firm in understanding how retirements will affect the younger workforce in the firm and plan accordingly.

Source: Singleton (2018)

Using analytics on exit interviews

Exit interviews have become a commonplace in firms today, owing to their benefits in providing valuable insights on organisational features driving the employees to quit the firm. Exit interviews are typically conducted immediately before the employee is leaving the organisation. The data collected from exit interviews can be categorised by factors like age group, department, supervisor, location, client, gender, and so on. Such insights are extremely helpful in understanding if some specific factors within the organisational control are driving the employees to leave the firm. Such reports can be compared with organisational benchmarks, industrial benchmarks, and global best practices to adjudge the position of a firm in managing its employees. Important outcomes of the application of analytics on exit interview data are:

- Creation of retention strategies.
- Insights on working conditions and satisfaction with various components of the job, such as salary, supervision, career growth.
- Insights on job-related parameters such as workload distribution and schedule flexibility.

Conclusion

In a nutshell, the dynamic business environment calls for adoption and implementation of innovative solutions in the organisations to sustain a competitive edge.

HR analytics, despite being in a nascent stage of adoption, has fetched enormous benefits for adopting firms. Although the demonstration of direct ROI on human capital investments is not possible, design of HR metrics and predictive models based on the same can be inculcated by the firms, since HR investments translate into worker efficiency and productivity, and job attitudes, ultimately manifesting in work or business outcomes. All the leading firms globally have adopted HR analytics frameworks. There are many barriers reported for its adoption – namely, a dearth of skilled professionals, lack of support from top management, lack of availability and access to data, outdated and disparate HR systems, and lack of integration with other organisational systems, to name a few. This book is an attempt to equipping managers with the skills to apply predictive analytics in any business area, through the example of building a predictive turnover and selection screening system. This chapter explains the different models and frameworks used by the organisations to implement HR analytics, while also explaining the holistic step-by-step approach to the application of analytics. Through the illustration of adoption of a systems approach and process view, the book clearly explains the first step in the step-by-step approach, which is how problem identification and definition can be carried out to apply analytics to solve the problem. The following chapters practically demonstrate the other steps in the framework through the same example of turnover and retention management.

Glossary

Benefits of application of analytics in management of Separation one, identifying a trend in retirement and ensuring business continuity by pipelining probable positions with potential successors; and two, managing the successors in case there is a delay in retirements by timely identifying that delay

'Employer of Choice' strategy adopted by companies to strategically manage their workforce by enhancing the ability of the company to attract, retain, and motivate its key employees

Exit interview conducted when an employee is about to leave the firm and is typically conducted immediately before the employee is leaving the organisation

The resource-based view (RBV) suggests that a firm gains competitive advantage from three resources: physical, organisational, and human resources, with the highest importance in the present era attributed to human resources

selectionFunction an argument of train function used to change the optimality criteria for computation of the final model; the three criteria used to assess best model can be 'best', which chooses the largest or smallest value; 'oneSE', which chooses the simplest model within one standard error of best mode; and 'tolerance', which selects the least complex model with tolerance for the best value

Separation generally considered the last HR process in an organisation and may occur due to retirement on completing tenure with the firm for a stipulated period as per job offer, due to voluntary resigning, termination, layoffs due to downsizing of the firm, or mergers and acquisitions

Turnover Intent   the reflection of the probability that an individual will change his job within a certain time period

Turnover   "Individual movement across the membership boundary of an organisation"

Train function   an inbuilt function in caret package which allows the evaluation of the performance of various models run using this function; by default, for regression problems, RMSE, R squared, and mean absolute error are computed as performance metrics, while accuracy and Kappa are computed for classification problems

Unfolding model of turnover   explains turnover intention by describing that when employees perceive some sort of shock, they start looking for alternative job opportunities

Review material

1   What do you understand to be the meaning of turnover?
2   Define turnover.
3   List the types of turnover.
4   List the causes of separation in an organisation.
5   Define turnover intent.
6   List some facts and figures depicting how turnover is a problem for IT firms.
7   What is meant by resource-based view of the firm?
8   Define employer choice strategy.
9   Discuss the role of PO fit in explaining turnover intention.
10   Discuss the role of job attitudes in explaining turnover intention.
11   Explain how a predictive model can be used to predict turnover in organisations.
12   Discuss the ways in which KNN model can be built in R.
13   List the benefits of using caret package in R.
14   How can a user change the optimality criteria used for the selection of model using train function?
15   What is the purpose of trainControl function in R?
16   List the steps used to define a variable as factor variable for implementation of KNN.
17   How can user view performance model of KNN model?
18   What is the purpose of plot() and varImp() functions?
19   Which package enables the user to directly plot confusion matrix? Also, write the syntax for the same.
20   Elucidate how the user can change the metric used to assess model performance from accuracy to ROC.
21   List some ways in which retirements can be managed through the application of analytics.
22   Elucidate the steps to implement analytics for supply analysis and workforce planning.

23 How can reports be generated from exit interview data, and what are the benefits?
24 List some outcomes of the application of analytics to exit interview data.

Problem exercises

1 Based on your understanding from the text and cases, attempt to build a simple model to predict who will retire from those who are eligible to retire.
2 For the illustrated example in this text for prediction of turnover, use different criteria in selectionFunction() to compute optimality.

Case study

Analytics to inform effective retirements

Retirements, whether voluntary such as due to resignation or otherwise, are often valued in terms of financial loss and resultant risk. Relatively little focus is given on labour productivity or impact on workforce alignment – how the separation of one individual affects the workflow tailored around the individual when he was part of the firm. If this impact is assessed quantitatively, it will enable the firm to gauge actual workforce risk and create retirement plan accordingly. One such case in point is that of a global retail firm which conventionally implemented rich promotion packages and sought to enrich and retain talent within the firm. However, owing to the economic slowdown and decrease in demands of goods offered by the retailer, the firm witnessed a new challenge. A large number of its senior executives delayed retirement since they lacked significant work opportunities elsewhere in a slow economy. This led to stalling of career growth prospects of junior talent, where the highly talented were remunerated well while others were forced to leave the firm owing to lack of career progress. This had serious negative consequences for the business of the retailer, and it therefore had to redefine its retirement programme.

The firm was initially implementing a so-called build strategy, whereby it offered incentives to its employees for working within the firm and building on their talent. However, once the individual left the firm, no incentives were offered. This probably led to stalling of career progress at the junior level, since senior employees were unwilling to retire. Economic slowdown added to this pile of miseries for both the firm and its employees. To substantiate this finding and gain deeper insight, implemented analytics on the movement of employees from new hires to exit at each job level. It discovered that employee movement in terms of promotion was significantly high at the first two job levels, and dropped significantly at higher levels. The ratio of new hires to promotes further dropped at the next promotion level (less than one), creating 'choke points' in the organisation. These chokepoints were especially pertinent at job levels 4 and 5 (middle management level) of the firm. This implied that beyond a professional level, the rate at which talent movement occurs in the firm is very low.

Such an analysis had several important implications for the firm. This implied that for each retirement delay, a backup of more than five employees due for promotion was created. For example, analytics revealed that if 4% of employees in the firm were due for retirement and almost half of them choose to delay their retirement plans, about 10% of employees would experience choke points that were blockage in promotions.

Gaining wisdom from this outcome of analytics implementation, the firm decided to redesign its retirement plan. It decided to align outcomes of analytics with the functioning of its business. Since the retailer endorsed products which had long life cycles, it was important to ensure employee continuity. And also, since retail firms are relationship-driven, it is important to ensure employee tenure to maintain relationships. Therefore, the firm inculcated retirement benefits and health benefits programmes, enabling the employees to retire since they would receive incentives at retirement, and also paving way for promotions in the firm. Strengthening the point in the implementation of such a retirement programme, metrics were introduced to implement analytics to assess the impact of the new retirement programme and also quantify turnover behaviour. The firm realised that the most important predictor for turnover in the firm was lack of promotion and lateral moves within the firm such as job rotation. Further participation in the retirement and health benefits programme also decreased employee turnover and managing retirements effectively. Despite other organisational factors like pay differences, leaves, disciplinary actions, etc., the single most important contributor to retention for employees at junior levels was participation in these benefits programmes.

To enhance understanding of the factors that affect an employee's decision to retire, the firm also conducted the empirical analysis. It conducted a conjoint analysis to discover the degree of importance employees attach to different organisational and individual factors when contemplating retirement. It also built a statistical model to predict whether or not an employee will retire at the point of eligibility, based on factors on employee behaviour. As a result, the firm's performance metrics suggest that almost all the CEOs spent their entire tenure at the firm itself, and a majority of its employees in senior leadership positions hold a service record of more than 15 years. The firm has been able to significantly reduce turnover by enabling timely retirements and promotions.

Source: Bulvid and Nalbantian (2014)

Case questions

1 Discuss the challenges faced by the retailer in managing retirements.
2 List the issues in organisational strategies which led to the challenges identified in Problem 1.
3 How did analytics and use of metrics improve the situation at the firm?

Bibliography

Amos, E. A., and Weathington, B. L. (2008). An analysis of the relationship between employee-organisation value congruence and employee attitudes. *The Journal of Psychology: Interdisciplinary and Applied*, 615–632.

Arora, A., Arunachalam, V., Asundi, J., and Fernandes, R. (2001). The Indian software services industry. *Research Policy*, 1267–1287.

Backhaus, K. (2016). Employer branding revisited. *Organization Management Journal*, 193–201.

Bellou, V., Chaniotakis, I., Kehagias, I., and Rigopoulou, I. (2013). Employer brand of choice: An employee perspective. *Journal of Business Economics and Management*, 1201–1215.

Bersin, J. (2017, December 17). *People analytics: Here with a vengeance.* Retrieved May 2019, from Forbes: www.forbes.com/sites/joshbersin/2017/12/16/people-analytics-here-with-a-vengeance/#48dad6332a14

Bulvid, J., and Nalbantian, H. R. (2014). *How workforce analytics can inform retirement plan design: The case of J&J.* Retrieved May 2019, from Mercer Human Resource Consulting LLC: www.mercer.com/content/dam/mercer/attachments/global/webcasts/mercer-how-workforce-analytics-can-inform-retirement-plan-design-the-case-of-JandJ.pdf

Bureau, F. E. (2018, July 11). *India IT-BPM sector revenue expected to touch $350 bn by 2025, says IT minister.* Retrieved 2019, from Financial Express: https://www.financialexpress.com/industry/india-it-bpm-sector-revenue-expected-to-touch-350-bn-by-2025-says-it-minister/1239509/#:~:text=The%20revenues%20of%20India's%20Information,Ravi%20Shankar%20Prasad%20has%20said

Chatman, J. A. (1991). Matching people and organisations: Selection and socialisation in public accounting firms. *Administrative Science Quarterly*, 459–484.

Cook, I. (2019). *Real examples of HR analytics in action and data scientists in HR.* Retrieved 2019, from CPHR Alberta: www.cphrab.ca/real-examples-hr-analytics-action-and-data-scientists-hr

Dasgupta, S. (2017, February). *Trends in top Indian IT companies – from hiring to attrition.* Retrieved 2018, from NDTV Profit: http://profit.ndtv.com/news/tech-media-telecom/article-trends-in-top-indian-it-companies-from-hiring-to-attrition-1659231

Elkjaer, D., and Filmer, S. (2015). *Trends and drivers of workforce turnover.* New York: Mercer (Health Wealth Career).

Grillo, M., and Hackett, A. (2015, Spring). *What types of predictive analytics are being used in talent management organisations?* Retrieved January 2019, from Cornell University, ILR School Site: http://digitalcommons.ilr.cornell.edu/student/74

Holland, P., Sheehan, C., and Cieri, H. D. (2007). Attracting and retaining talent: exploring human resources development trends in Australia. *Human Resource Development International*, 247–262.

IBEF. (2018, February). *IT & ITeS industry in India.* Retrieved 2018, from IBEF – Indian Brand Equity Foundation: https://www.ibef.org/industry/information-technology-india.aspx

Judge, T., Van Vianen, A., and DePater, I. (2004). Emotional stability, core self-evaluations, and job outcomes: A review of the evidence and agenda for future research. *Human Performance*, 325–346.

Kristof, A. (1996). Person-organization fit: An integrative review of its conceptualizations, measurement, and implications. *Personnel Psychology*, 1–49.

McCulloch, M. C., and Turban, D. B. (2007). Using person – organization fit to select employees for high turnover jobs. *International Journal of Selection and Assessment*, 63–71.

Menezes, B. (2015, February 11). *Indian IT services exports seen growing 12–14% in year ahead.* Retrieved December 2019, from Livemint.com: www.livemint.com/Industry/bCLO-gyalLGili6TuhmN0S7J/Indian-IT-services-exports-seen-growing-1214-in-year-ahead.html

Murray, J. P. (1999). Successfully hiring and retaining IT personnel. *Information Systems Management*, 18–24.

Ostroff, C., and Bowen, D. E. (2016). Reflections on the 2014 decade award: Is there strength in the construct of HR system strength? *Academy of Management Review*, 196–214.

Perez, M. (2008, June). *Turnover intent* (Diploma thesis). University of Zurich, Zurich.

Phillips, M. (2015, May). *Could you handle the big four's psychometric tests.* Retrieved April 2019, from In the Black: http://intheblack.com/articles/2015/05/01/the-rise-and-rise-of-psychometrics

PTI. (2018, January). *2018 to see more hirings, salary rise of 10%: Mercer's pay survey.* Retrieved 2018, from The Economic Times: https://economictimes.indiatimes.com/jobs/2018-to-see-more-hirings-salary-rise-of-10-mercers-pay-survey/articleshow/62455032.cms

Saks, A. M., and Ashforth, B. E. (1997). A longitudinal investigation of the relationships between job information sources, applicant perceptions of fit, and work outcomes. *Personnel Psychology*, 395–426.

SectoralReport. (2016, August). *IT & ITeS industry in India.* Retrieved from India Brand Equity Foundation: www.ibef.org/industry/information-technology-india.aspx

Sheridan, J. E. (1992). Organisational culture and employee retention. *The Academy of Management Journal*, 1036–1056.

Singleton, S. (2018, September 18). *Using retirement analytics to predict the shape of the future workforce.* Retrieved October 2019, from HRD Connect: www.hrdconnect.com/2018/09/18/using-retirement-analytics-to-predict-the-future-shape-of-the-workforce/

Sousa-Poza, A., and Henneberger, F. (2002). Analysing job mobility with job turnover intentions: An internal comparative study. *Research Institute for Labour Economics and Labour Laws*, 1–28.

Spence, J. (2015). Retrieved March 2019, from http://associationsnow.com/2014/03/important-invest-talent-acquisition/

Van Vianen, A. E., DePater, I. E., and Dijk, F. V. (2007). Work value fit and turnover intention: Same-source or different-source fit. *Journal of Managerial Psychology*, 188–202.

Visier. (2019). *5 L+D questions you can't answer without analytics.* Retrieved 2019, from HR Curator: https://hrcurator.com/post/59

Wadhwa, V., DeVitton, U. K., and Gereffi, G. (2008, July). *How the disciple became the GURU.* Retrieved July 2019, from Harvard: www.law.harvard.edu/programs/lwp/people/staff Papers/vivek/Vivek_HowDiscipleBecameGuru.pdf

Westerman, J. A., and Cyr, L. A. (2004). An integrative analysis of person – organization fit theories. *International Journal of Selection and Assessment*, 252–261.

Yiu, L., and Saner, R. (2008). *Indian employee turnover report.* Confederation of Indian Industry, Switzerland.

8

PREDICTIVE HR ANALYTICS IN OTHER AREAS OF HRM

After reading this chapter, users will be able to understand the following key concepts:

- Identifying different areas where predictive analytics can be applied for learning and development of employees in organisations
- Understanding various data sources and LMSs used for the implementation of learning analytics
- Understand how to identify the causes and predict absenteeism in the firms
- Learn various ways in which analytics can be applied for performance management of employees
- Interpret how outcomes of applications of analytics to employee performance can be useful in succession planning, workforce planning, retaining, and hiring of candidates
- Understand how wearable technology can be used for prediction of employee performance and employee safety
- Understand how analytics can be used to optimise the rewards package and ensure pay equity
- Identify different sources and ways in which employee safety incidents can be predicted using the application of analytics

Opening case

A leading European entertainment and communications company, serving more than 20 million customers and employing approximately 30,000 workers, was facing a budget crunch for its training programmes. These programmes were largely delivered face to face, and typically an employee had to wait for almost three months to undergo a particular training course. This traditional approach consumed both time and money, and reaped few benefits, so the firm decided to eliminate this conventional approach and replace it with conversation-based experiences as a learning strategy. They termed this the 'agile approach'. The firm started searching for potential next-generation learning content providers and shortlisted four such providers. As a pilot test run, it deployed the solutions of all four and assigned employees to undergo learning from each solution. To determine the best out of these solutions, the firm deployed cameras which could track eye movements of the employees while they were exploring the solution for learning, to observe where and how they navigated, how long the screen could retain individual attention, and when and where they got lost. They conducted the exercise for an entire course for all four solutions and collated the eye movement data in a report. Based on the report, for each solution, a usability score was generated and Looop was selected as the digital unconventional learning tool for the firm.

The firm has integrated learning analytics into all its aspects of functioning, even in its communication channels, to identify any opportunity which can be a potential trigger for learning. For example, in monthly emails from managers, learning contents are embedded. And analytics tracks various metrics such as click-through rates of the content, number of views of content, the pattern of on-screen content engagement, and so on. Assume, for example, that analytics determines that the number of employees who simply looked at the content but didn't enrol for learning is high, then additional data regarding that content would be analysed to ensure improvement in user engagement. By simply driving on analytics applied on content and feedback, the firm ensures iterative improvements in its overall learning experience, while also keeping the cost low (Fosway, 2017).

Introduction

Commenting on the wide scope of application of analytics in HRM, Deloitte Analytics reports that in some firms, HR departments are way ahead of other functional areas in application of analytical methods like predictive and prescriptive models (Davenport, 2019). If there is data or the possibility of collection of data, there is scope for the application of analytics. However, one should always keep in mind that analytics yields answers for only the questions that have been posed to it. If an analyst doesn't ask the right set of questions, the results or outcomes will also be ambiguous. In this context, there is no area of HRM which has been untouched by the application of analytics. Right from the starting point in HRM, that is, HR planning till the endpoint of separation from the company, each small process has scope for implementation of analytics. Digital means of data collection, use of information systems for collection, storage and dissemination of HR data, and availability of relevant tools and techniques have led to the emergence of analytics as a strong discipline in business management. The stream has wonderful implications, resulting in newer ways of managing HR functions and processes. Payroll data, attendance and time record data, HRM data, case management systems, learning management systems, and use of surveys are some of the vast sources of

HR data to which analytics can be applied. Some of the pertinent themes to which analytics have been applied in firms have been to model workforce promotions and career paths, workforce turnover, and employee engagement. As per an Oracle survey (Davenport, 2019), encompassing 1,510 senior HR, finance, and marketing personnel from across 23 countries, more than half of the respondents opined that their workforce is skilled enough in application of analytics to model basic HR issues like turnover prediction, identifying high performers, and recruitment of best-fit candidates. However, advanced analytics and application of analytics in other areas of HRM still seem challenging to most of the workforce. In addition, they don't understand how to act on the data or build a story about the same. If these limitations are worked upon, HR analytics will lead the way. Given the skill shortage and fierce competition for talent, HR analytics is the only solution which can provide a competitive edge to the firms. This chapter, therefore, sheds light on various areas of HRM, other than recruitment and selection, where HR analytics can be applied. The chapter discusses the application of predictive HR analytics in learning and development, absenteeism, employee performance, compensation and benefits, and employee safety.

Predictive analytics in learning and development

In the end, it all comes down to driving business performance and consistency with organisational strategy. Be it any functional area of HRM, it is said to be optimal only when it contributes to the organisational strategy with best results. The purpose of applying HR analytics by the function of learning and development in organisations is also the same. Organisations globally recognise that people are their greatest assets, and therefore need to realise the value of learning and development (Visier, 2019). Learning and development programmes in the organisation deal with promoting the development of the employees, which is consistent with the overall development of the organisation. This is often done through providing timely training programmes for upskilling of employees. The question typically faced by managers is how to decide which programme would be useful for which employee. This question, and many others, can be answered by application of analytics. The fundamental premise for applying analytics is that the performance of employees is measurable as a consequence of imparting learning and development programmes in the organisation. Therefore, some areas in learning and development where analytics can shed a light are:

1   Identifying top performers of the firm and then associating their training received from the organisations with resultant performance improvements.
2   Identifying performers who have made a point in a short period and then mining out the skills and associated training programmes of the firm which ensure such performance.
3   Predicting training programmes for individual employees – personalised predictive analytics – most suitable for ensuring their success by associating skills

possessed, experience, work allocated in the past, and past training undertaken, then using this data to predict future career possibilities and recommend training programmes.

4   Mining the success rate of different training programmes offered by the organization by associating each programme with consequent improvements in performance can also be used to remove redundant programmes in light of organisational and environmental dynamicity.

5   External environment analysis to predict the need for the development of new training programmes and also identifying components to be included in each such programme.

6   Learning and development as a retention tool – past work has determined that organisations which offer training interventions for their employees see lower rates of turnover. Training as a metric is often associated with organisational commitment, loyalty, and job satisfaction.

For most of these points, the data already exists within the organisation. Primarily, the data to implement analytics in learning and development, and LMSs (learning management systems), is adopted in the organisations.

LMSs are used to keep track of all activities related to learning and development occurring in the organisation, and they also provide metrics such as learner satisfaction, enrollments, cost of training, demographics of the learner, and so on. LMSs are capable of recording the data, but are not equipped with analytical and reporting capabilities. Using the data from LMSs, predictive analytics can help with the following:

1   Identify the individuals who are the best performers after receiving training.

2   Identify the individuals who have received the highest benefit in terms of promotion and appraisal in a short time, as a consequence of training.

3   Identify the individuals who have not undergone any training, or are due to receive training for the first time in a long time, and this has impacted their performance.

4   Measure the effectiveness of training programmes.

5   Use employee feedback and course performance metrics to improve training programmes.

Some of the predictive analytical techniques typically used to answer these questions are cohort analysis and classification techniques like KNN, ANN, etc. The existing performance and training data can be used to identify the attributes of high-performing employees. Then cohort analysis or KNN can be used to determine the employees who share these attributes of high performers. Their career paths can then de developed, and they can be offered a tailored training programme. This is a highly demanded area of HRM and a powerful retention tool for employers, since employees seek targeted career development – and when firms aid them in achieving their full potential and lead the way, employees are tethered to the firm to deliver their best.

On the flip side, analytics should also be used to study the characteristics of those who have never undergone training and relate it to their performance and career growth. For such individuals, a different career development strategy and learning programmes could be developed. Firms are now also switching to cloud-based HR systems, which enables them to get a complete picture of the working of business systems and HR systems and strategy. This integration of HR systems like LMSs with business systems allows the firms to answer critical questions such as how learning and development at the firms contribute to overall business goals.

CORPORATE SNAPSHOT: PREDICTIVE ANALYTICS IN LEARNING AND DEVELOPMENT

A software services firm was keen to improve the course content of the training programmes designed to enhance the skill sets of its employees, based on learner feedback. The firm delivered the learning through e-learning solutions and sought continual improvement in the same to stay updated with current market demands and also satiate learner interests. The firm, therefore, discovered that to achieve optimal content improvement, it needed to gauge performance metrics of its e-learning courses on two different streams – one, related to the measurement of changes in individual employee performance post-reception of the training course, and two, the rate of overall retention of knowledge.

Although the two metrics were related, their separate observations were important, since knowledge retention rate varies with individual learning style and preferences. Depending on the employees' current skill set, his takeaway from the course would be different since it has a direct impact on the 'knowing-doing' gap. Therefore, by implementing learning analytics on individual employee data such as skill set, learning preferences, educational background, etc., and test results and feedback, the firm was able to answer the following:

- **Individual-level answers** – Identify different learning styles prevalent among employees
- **Programme-related answers** – What should be the duration of a course? What should be the course use rate to determine frequently used and rarely used courses? Does the course require improvement, or does it need to be phased out from current delivered programmes?

Also, by specifically targeting analytics at metrics of learning programmes offered during the incubation period, and relating it with employee performance, a firm could gain many useful insights such as for successful and high performing employees, what was their learning orientation during incubation period? Did they report on the first day of training? How is their tenure linked with learning performance during the incubation period?

Another important area where learning analytics has been useful is in the improvement of learning programmes, which is consistent with employee demands and organisational goals. Most of the course content is now designed and delivered using e-learning technologies. Such courses also enable firms to collect data regarding course content and collect feedback. Many parameters are observable or measurable in this context, such as feedback of learners, programme evaluation score of employees, number of people enrolled, attendance, the duration for course completion, and so on. Besides, data regarding individual employee level skills, achievements, career path, programme preferences, and so on are also available and can be aggregated to generate performance report of the delivery and design of the course. Learning analytics implemented at the highest level will allow tailored recommendations at an individual level, matching with the interests and learning styles of the individual. Establishment of such a framework of learning at a firm will deliver the best possible results for both the employee and the firm.

In a nutshell, it can be said that the implementation of learning analytics would benefit both the employee and the firm. It will introduce improvements in both the work environment and work experiences, thereby improving overall employee engagement and retention at the firm.

Predictive analytics in absenteeism

India labour laws require employers provide leave to the employees for every 20 working days. Absenteeism refers to the prolonged or recurring absence of an employee from the workplace, which may be habitual or arising out of genuine personal concern. Absenteeism grows into a concern for the organisations when it is unplanned and repetitive. Organisations have uncovered many reasons for absenteeism in employees, some of which might be genuine and unavoidable, while some can be completely avoided if spotted in time. To curb absenteeism and monitor its causes and concerns, companies track overall health of the organisation, which can generally be assessed on five broad health components: physical, psychological, work-life balance, environmental, and economic. By identifying the key causes of recurring absenteeism, firms can provide an immediate fix. For example, an electricity distribution company periodically tracks the physical well-being of its employees at its workplace since the job is prone to injuries. In case an employee gets sick while on the job and due to the job, the firm immediately assists in providing medical aid, managing sick leave, modifying office space to accommodate the changing needs of the employee post-injury, and also, the work patterns of peers are adjusted as per needs of the employee. This way, the firm ensures that employees don't feel isolated and are being taken care of by the firm. Further, the firm has observed that none of its employees has demonstrated absenteeism for any other reason than this. The outcome, therefore, from this discussion is that reasons for absenteeism vary with the organisation and may even vary for different departments of that firm. The firm needs to proactively identify the cause of the same and work out a solution. Even the people with good attendance records can be incentivised (*HRMagazine*, 2001).

The major reasons cited for absence of employees in firms are childcare, accidents, sickness, bullying at the workplace, lack of flexibility at the workplace, poor leadership, bereavement, change in the work environment, stress and fatigue, travel, and ergonomics. Ergonomics-catering arrangement of office spaces to ease the workflow and employee movement has become a prominent factor in affecting employee absences. A Harvard study identified that while wellness programmes satiate only half of the workforce, ergonomics – especially ventilated office spaces offering natural light – can reduce absenteeism up to four days (Meister, 2019). Another persisting issue contributing to employee absenteeism is 'workation'. Employees are offered vacations by organisations; however, digital devices have blurred the boundary between office and personal lives. Even when employees are on vacation, use of digital devices doesn't allow them to mentally disconnect from the workplace, which builds up stress and fatigue among employees. Resultantly, despite being on a vacation, employees perceive that they are overworked and therefore feel entitled to avail a higher number of sick days to combat arising stress and tension. These reasons cover almost all aspects of the employee absence in organisations. The question is how to identify what is causing the problem and how to fix it once the issue is known.

The major effect of absenteeism is on financial aspects. The salaries of all employees are computed on a per hour basis, so each day of employee absence from the workplace contributes to loss of finance for lack of work. This financial loss increases with increase in the cadre and job level of workers. Especially in organisations involving teamwork or dependencies, overall productivity is also hit, as other team workers have to contribute to the missing worker tasks. Facts suggest that when an employee calls for unplanned absenteeism, it increases stress due to disruption of work among more than 55% of employees, which in turn hits their overall productivity and also their morale.

The first step in curbing absenteeism, therefore, should be to identify its causes. The question that needs to be addressed here is: where will the data come from to identify causes and report rates of absenteeism? Many information systems and surveys conducted by the firms periodically may provide the necessary data. Attendance management systems track daily attendance and reporting times of employees. Data from these systems can be categorised, along with different locations where the firm operates, by different departments, and by collating this data with employee record data in HRM information systems, many other features can be used to categorise absenteeism rates. For example, categorical assessment of variation in absence rates by supervisors, clients, promotion rates, skill levels, etc., can also be done. Firms can also conduct annual health surveys to monitor employees' mental, physical, and psychological health. Mental health has become a recurring cause of decreased organisational productivity and higher reported unplanned absence among employees. Using this data, the firms can then apply analytics in ways such as:

1   Simple descriptive figures depicting the state of absenteeism, by different departments, annual variations, variations by employee features, etc. For example, analytics can depict:

   a   The average rate of absenteeism.

   b   Comparison reports of absenteeism rates by industry or organisational benchmarks.

   c   Variation of rates by different departments.

   d   Variation by level, gender, tenure, performance rating, and age of different employees.

   e   Prediction of absence rates based on annual historical data.

2   Associate absence data with employee turnover data to determine how rates of absenteeism vary with attrition rates. This can be further explored to answer how these rates vary with location and departments and teams.

3   Identify the causes of absenteeism. For example, if absenteeism is high in a particular location, it may correlate with a particular manager or external environmental factor such as an economic slowdown in that particular region.

4   Mental health surveys and absenteeism data can be used to determine if an employee of a particular department or location is overworked, experiencing stress and fatigue, or prone to workations. Appropriate measures can be implemented in such cases.

5   Periodically assess how employees rate workplace ergonomics and how it relates to absenteeism data.

6   A firm can further use analytics to assess the effectiveness of the measures that it has taken to curb absenteeism, which was tailored to the cause identified by analytics.

CORPORATE SNAPSHOT: MEASURE TO MANAGE EMPLOYEE ABSENCE

VJS Foods (*HRMagazine*, 2001), which is a food wrapping company was experiencing high absenteeism rates in one of its regions of operation. The absence rate was so high that out of the 400-plus workforce in the region, only 50 were reporting each day consecutively for a month. On interviewing the employees, it was discovered that employees were not reporting to work owing to lack of motivation, as an outcome of overall economic slowdown and high rate of unemployment in that region. Therefore, to curb the high absence rates, VJS Foods implemented a reward scheme to appreciate a good attendance record. Each month, employees reporting consistently to work were entered into a monthly draw where winners were rewarded with cash prizes. And every six months, those who did not call for a single sick day were entered into a draw worth 50,000 Australian dollars for the winner.

Once the firms have identified the causes for absenteeism, a discussion of some measures that they can undertake to curb it is presented. If the major cause for absenteeism is childcare, firms can offer flexible working hours, extended maternity and paternity leave to take care of the child, creche facilities, and options to work from home. Some firms even provide helplines where an employee can communicate with a childcare worker like a nanny at their homes to enquire about the health and well-being of their child, while they are at the workplace. For absences occurring due to workplace or personal accidents and sickness, firms have developed their occupational health programmes which provide medical solutions like physiotherapy to facilitate early recovery of employees. Besides, firms also go the extent of workplace redesign and peer workload modification to accommodate employees who have sustained injuries causing permanent disabilities (like restricted employee movement). When employees perceive unjust behaviour like bullying or disrespect and harm to their dignity at the workplace, they have been known to report sick. Firms can offer counselling in such cases, and through programmes like anti-harassment initiatives, they can take action against those who bully at the workplace. Issues with leadership can only be identified through analytics applied to peer feedback and through the administration of employee attitudes' survey in the firms. The only way to correct this is through the creation of awareness and provision of training to leaders to develop the skills that they are lacking. Often, employees are prone to bereavement following the loss of a close family member, for which they can report a large number of absent days from the workplace. Firms offer counselling programmes through different means like telephonic, face to face, etc., to curb this issue. Also, firms have been known to invest significantly in transport like buses to ease the commutes of their employees, so that this doesn't become a concern for reported absenteeism.

Predictive analytics in employee performance

A central issue to HRM is the definition, quantification, and measurement of employee performance. The department of HRM in every organisation has faced the challenge to depict its productivity and thereby, the contribution it makes to overall business goals, and quantification of employee performance is one way in which HRM departments justifies their productivity in their firms. Not only does employee performance indicate the effectiveness of HRM in hiring and selection and ensuring proper placement of the candidate in the firm in a given job role, but it also benefits the employees since it provides timely feedback, thereby serving as reinforcement for proper organisational conduct. Conventionally, organisations have stuck to tedious methods of gauging employee performance which are biased and do not provide timely and real-time feedback. As per a survey conducted by Randstad India HR Game Changers (Jerath, 2018), around 30% of HR personnel perceive the need to redesign tools used to measure employee performance, so that it eliminates the previously mentioned drawbacks of conventional techniques. The conventional methods such as conducting surveys have poor outcomes, directly impacting employee morale and subsequent performance. Therefore, organisations are now leveraging on technology and digital methods to capture performance.

A major advantage of switching to digital means of data collection by the firms lies in the possibility of applying analytics to this data which can be used to predict the employee performance of existing employees in near future, as well as performance of the candidates to be hired in the firm. Both historical and real-time data can be used by the firms to make predictions about employee performance. It has been seen that the accuracy of performance ratings and prediction has a direct effect on employee morale. Such an application of analytics provides both retrospective and forward-looking analysis.

Some areas where predictive analytics can be useful when applied to employee performance data can be:

1   Analytics can be applied to the historical performance data of the workforce to identify individual characteristics which constitute a good or a bad performer in an organisation. Such an analysis can be carried out for each department, individual performance, and group performance, such as in a team. The traits of a good performer can be used to build a job profile for a particular job role which can be used for future selection and hiring processes. Google (Leonardi and Contractor, 2018) applies analytical algorithms on its employee data to determine what makes a good or bad performer, and then seeks new hires which match the qualities of a good performer.

CORPORATE SNAPSHOT: HR ANALYTICS DRIVING STORE PERFORMANCE

Interesting use of analytics is demonstrated by a large restaurateur which was witnessing a significant drop in its revenues despite offering best-in-class compensation packages and friendly HR policies. The restaurateur decided to hire analytics consultants, who would provide insights based on data to resolve the situation. Since the firm did not have any data of its own, the consultants decided to survey to collect data. However, they did not administer a normal engagement and attitude survey; rather, they designed and administered a survey which would link employee outcomes to relevant business outcomes. These business outcomes were identified as customer count, customer satisfaction, and employee satisfaction for each operating chain store. Then the employee outcomes which directly impacted these business outcomes were identified, such as job fit, teamwork, senior leaders, communication, compensation, career development, customer focus, and so on. The scores for each of these factors were mapped onto relevant business outcomes in a two-dimensional space. The techniques used for analysis were correlation, regression, structured equation modelling, and the use of heat maps to depict the results. The result of this activity was that they were able to visualise the business drivers that are those factors which had the highest impact on business outcomes. Then these factors were arranged as 'maintain', 'monitor', 'promote', and 'focus', such that the highest attention was given to 'promote' factors to increase the business performance. A total of six factors fell into the 'promote' category, and line managers at each store were asked to focus on these to generate maximum returns. Within one year of implementation of the outcomes of this analysis, the restaurant chain was able to increase customer satisfaction by 16% and the number of customers by approximately 20,000 annually, with a 10% reduction in employee turnover.

2   Inculcation of organisational and environmental factors to classify good or bad performers in an organisation can also provide an insight into the factors that drive individual performance in the firm; it also gives objective insight into work preferences and the factors that drive performance. Insights gained from this analysis can aid the firms in bringing out reforms in areas where employees consistently depict low performance. For example, a manufacturing firm experiencing low employee performance applied analytics to determine the cause for the same. It was established that the attitude of the supervisor lowered employee morale, resulting in poor performance. The management could intervene in a timely manner to prevent further deterioration in the performance.

3   Many organisations have been gauging the employee attitudes through periodic organisation-wide surveys. This data can be related to employee performance data through the application of analytics. For example, employee attitudes like employee engagement and job satisfaction have many prominent implications for work outcomes. With the help of analytics, the firms can identify how variation in the level of employee engagement affects their performance. Further analysis can yield which engagement activities conducted by the firm cause an increase in performance, and which activity causes a decrease in performance. Understanding this would allow the firms to invest in only those activities which result in enhancing performance.

4   Use of analytics on employee performance data can also aid in the timely prediction of employees who have a risk of leaving the firm. Leading firms globally use such analytics to identify 'red flags', indicating those employees who have shown a significant decrease in performance. Combined with some other metrics, it can be predicted if these red flags also have a high risk score of leaving the firm. For example, Hewlett-Packard (Leonardi and Contractor, 2018) computes a flight risk score for each of its 30,000-plus employees annually, which takes into account performance data, several leaves taken, and job attitudes, among other parameters.

5   Another area where the application of analytics on employee performance data has proven to be beneficial is in succession planning. Through analytics, probable job openings in a particular role or department can be indicated. Observable drop in employee performance in a given department or job role can be related with employee strength and may be attributable to an insufficient number of employees in the same. Also, it may indicate for lack of skills requiring new hires, promotions, or provision of training. Further analytics can also indicate employees suitable for promotion for a particular role based on their past experiences and skill sets.

6   A new trend in performance measurement is the use of wearable badges at the workplace. These badges adorned by the employees at workplace allow monitoring the activities that they indulge in, including time spent on leisure activities, which can be correlated with their job performance, thereby suggesting how employee movement affects job performance in the workplace.

Predictive analytics in compensation and benefits

The present job market worldwide is quite not pretty, due to economic slowdown. Digital innovations and the Industry 4.0 revolution has redefined the skill sets required by employees. As a result, the competition for hiring talent in the market is fierce and retaining key talent is an additional challenge being faced by firms. A key tactic to hire and retain key talent, therefore, is offering competitive compensation and rewards packages. Although firms believe that they are offering compensation as per industry standards, employees feel otherwise. As per a global survey conducted by Mercer Group in 2018 (Mercer, 2018), for every five employees surveyed, only two considered the compensation offered by their employer to be competitive. As a result, firms are looking for ways to redesign their rewards and compensation strategy.

1   One such strategy is the use of predictive analytics to predict the optimal reward programme customised for each employee. Although this is not realistic enough, firms often apply this technique to predict optimal reward by job categories or team of workers. This is termed as TRA, or total rewards strategy, which implies the use of analytics to determine an optimal mix of reward programmes considered highly desirable by employees while ensuring

the least cost for the firm. The firms conduct a joint survey in which employees are asked to rate the reward programmes on a relative rating scale (say from 1–10, where 1 is most desirable and ten is least). The results of the survey and the cost for each programme are used as inputs in the analytical algorithm. The analytical tool determines the optimal balance of reward mix, usually the one which contains programmes with the least cost and highest desirability. When the reward programmes are designed and delivered in such a manner, they ensure positive employee outcomes such as higher engagement and lower turnover. However, the results of such studies are to be considered with caution, as experience and judgement may be used in addition to the results. All the TRA outcomes may not be consistent with business outcomes; therefore, their relevance and implication for business performance should be adequately assessed. For example, a casino chain, consistent with results of the application of analytics, increased employee salaries as this was determined as the most significant contributor to enhanced employee performance and lowered turnover intent. However, this strategy only reduced turnover by 3%. The second most important contributor was providing employee autonomy, which lowered turnover by 34% following implementation. Therefore, simply designing a package as per employee preferences will not necessarily provide a sufficient solution; rather, the choice should also consider their impact on business outcomes.

2   Application of analytics to workforce data can aid the managers in making realistic decisions regarding the compensation that should be offered to employees. Analytical tools can compare the profile of a candidate, incentive rates, and their performance ratings relative to those of other employees working in similar positions or job roles.

CORPORATE SNAPSHOT: PREDICTIVE ANALYTICS FOR REWARD OPTIMISATION

Hitachi Data Systems has developed an Intelligence Platform called PANDA, which contains data for people and business systems for many organisations. This data has been in use to analyse the factors that drive business performance. One such area where the application of analytics on PANDA has been effective is on the determination of compensation and rewards for the Hitachi salesforce. Conventionally, the determination of reward or sales commission used to be a lengthy manual process. Besides this, on analysing the relation between sales commission and sales performance data from PANDA, it was discovered that the data were highly skewed, implying that overachievers were underpaid and underachievers were overpaid. This had repercussions for both employees and management, as it resulted in low morale and turnover of high achievers while bearing the high cost for underachievers by the firm. The firm, therefore, automated the computation of the sales commission which was now computed based on the absolute value of a customer (sales generated) and the size of opportunity with that client. By taking into account internal data from sales and finance, and external data from share of wallet from key customers and competitors' sales figures, the analytical tool automated calculation of sales commission such that, if absolute value of the customer is high, while size of opportunity is less, the total compensation will also be low. For example, if a client generated 50 million rupees of sales, while IT expenses for the client amounted to 2 billion rupees, the total share from customer wallet is very much less for the firm. Therefore, the sales force could target clients accordingly and be paid compensation as per their targets.

Application of analytics to compensation data of the workforce also allows the decision-makers to compare compensation profiles of different employees working in the same cadre and similar job positions. This way they can investigate 'pay equity'. Pay equity implies ensuring non-discrimination among employees on any basis while offering them compensation for a given job position and job roles in the firm. Analytics allow HR personnel to conduct internal compensation reviews, by which they can compare the compensation profiles by salary bands, ethnicity, caste, gender, religion, tenure, etc., and determine if there is any sort of discrimination occurring on any such basis.

3   Use of analytics in compensation and benefits also allows managers to identify the employees who excel in their field but are under-valued in the organisation, simply because they have low visibility. However, analytics enables digging out such profiles and ensuring that the right benefit reaches the right profile. Many factors can play a role in varying the compensation for candidates, such as workload, recognition, participation beyond workload, etc., all of which cannot be analysed independently by an HR manager without the aid of technology.

Predictive analytics in employee safety

Workplace safety has become a growing concern among organisations globally. Internationally recognised standards for safety management at the workplace have been developed like the OHSAS 18001 guidelines, and firms have also designed and implemented robust safety programmes consistent with these standards to prevent workplace injuries or harm to the employees. Occupational Health and Safety Management certification termed as OHSAS 18001 is an international standard which provides a framework for identification, detection, control, prevention, and reduction of the risks associated with workplace safety and employee health in the workplace. The biggest threat of workplace injury is to the reputation of the organisation, and firms have to then undertake ample damage control strategies, all of which result in incurring huge financial losses for the organisation, as well. Despite taking adequate measures, workplace fatalities and injuries have been reported to be on the rise globally (Knight, Solly, and Richardson, 2019), and now the firms are moving towards adoption of analytics to curb the same.

If organisations can identify the root cause of any such potential 'safety incident', it can predict the likelihood of its occurrence soon. Although descriptive analytics applied on historical data can identify the 'lagging indicators' and describe what happened, it has to be supplemented with additional data which can enhance the prediction accuracy, such that it can explain 'how' it happened. Such causal factors are often hidden in variables not included in incident reports like weather, equipment condition, geospatial data, demographic data, employee well-being data, and other HR and training-related organisational data. This has to be supplemented through additional data sources in the predictive model to predict the likelihood of occurrence of a workplace safety hazard.

Several disparate data sources can be included to enhance the accuracy of such predictions. Inclusion of a variety of disparate sources for analysis ensures understanding the root causes from multiple perspectives and predicting even bleak chances of occurrence of a safety incident. Some of the commonly used sources for prediction of safety hazards are:

1   Employee rosters depicting the schedule of work of employees, which can also indicate of employees are overworked and fatigued and not offered ample rest.
2   Performance records of the employees in HRM systems, which can provide a summary of past performance and any previous safety incidents for an employee, a particular plant, location, region of operation, machinery, etc.
3   Training received and skill sets would enable determination if a lack of skills led to the occurrence of the incident. This data can also be used to correlate with the degree of risk, that is, how lack of a particular skill contributes to a high degree of adversity in a safety incident.
4   Audits and investigations, and case management system.
5   Geospatial data, weather data, date and time data.
6   Organisational health record and culture of the company.
7   Task variation offered to the employees.
8   Equipment maintenance systems depicting the state of machinery and indicating the overall health of the equipment used in the organisation.

Another analytical technique which is relatively newer and gaining popularity to ensure employee safety is the use of wearable technology and IoT (Internet of Things) at the workplace. By equipping organisational equipment with sensors and asking workers to wear electronic badges to the workplace, potential safety concerns can be monitored and managed in real time. While the equipment sensors can indicate and aid in predicting faulty operation of the same, badges can generate warnings related to employee fatigue, stress, or potential danger, all in real time, so a safety incident can be proactively avoided. In addition, all this data can be backed up and stored for future analysis. Such an analysis can also aid in developing a complete lifecycle of occurrence of potential safety incidents – by indicating the first point of occurrences (useful as warning signs in future predictions) to corrective action and reporting the same.

CORPORATE SNAPSHOT: PREDICTIVE ANALYTICS FOR EMPLOYEE SAFETY

A huge mining firm (Knight et al., 2019) with international clientele was seeking to assess employee safety, owing to the recent increase in the number of workplace fatalities. The consulting firm to analyse employee safety collected 620 data points on various parameters related to employee safety incidents such as on weather, socio-demographics, residence proximity to mine site, shift schedule, experience and tenure, age, equipment conditions, incident reports, and so on. The consultants segmented the data points and developed a two-dimensional map which depicted the factors which correlated with the highest number of fatalities recorded in the data. The findings established that fatalities have a high probability of occurrence if the workforce stays on or near the site, is involved in equipment operation at the time of incident (from incident reports), has taken high number of leaves in the past, has long tenure with the firm, and has reported late for his shift. However, the least correlating factor which demonstrated rare occurrence of fatalities was when the workforce was part of the maintenance group, and had received safety training and was a top performer at the firm.

Conclusion

This chapter is an attempt to address all the prominent areas of HRM to which predictive analytics can be applied. The chapter begins with the application of predictive analytics to learning and development, explaining different sources for application and various areas in which analytics can be applied. Another area addressed in this chapter is the problem of absenteeism prevalent in many firms. Predictive analytics can be used to identify the causes and predict the likelihood of future absenteeism among employees. Further, the chapter outlines how predictive analytics can be of use in gauging and predicting employee performance. It also explains how the outcomes of the application of analytics in employee performance can be used for succession planning, for workforce planning, as a retention tool, and for future hiring and selection. The latest trends in HR analytics, such as the use of wearable technology for monitoring, collecting, and predicting employee performance data were discussed in brief. Predictive analytics can be useful in predicting optimal rewards package, analysing competitive compensation profiles and also identifying any possible discrimination in pay equity. The chapter also sheds light on the prediction of employee safety in organisations through analytics and identification of various disparate source useful in such predictions.

Glossary

Absenteeism   the prolonged or recurring absence of an employee from the workplace, which may be habitual or arising out of genuine personal concern

Learning and development programmes   in the organisation deal with promoting the development of the employees, which is consistent with the overall development of the organisation

Learning management systems or LMS   used to keep track of all activities related to learning and development occurring in the organisation; in addition, LMSs also provide metrics such as learner satisfaction, enrollments, cost of training, recording the demographics of the learner, and so on

Occupational Health and Safety Management certification (OHSAS 18001)   an international standard which provides a framework for identification, detection, control, prevention, and reduction of the risks associated with workplace safety and employee health in the workplace

Pay equity   implies ensuring non-discrimination among employees on any basis, while offering them compensation for a given job position and job roles in the firm

TRA or total rewards strategy   implies the use of analytics to determine an optimal mix of reward programmes considered highly desirable by employees, while ensuring the least cost for the firm

Review material

1 Explain the role of learning and development programmes in organisations.
2 List some areas where analytics can be applied in learning and development.
3 Explain how analytics applied in learning and development aid in predicting individualised training programmes for employees.
4 Explain how analytics applied in learning and development aid in retaining employees.
5 List some data sources useful for the application of analytics in learning and development.
6 What do you understand to be meant by LMS?
7 Elucidate how predictive analytics can be applied to data from LMSs.
8 How can learning analytics be useful in the improvement of learning programmes?
9 Define absenteeism.
10 When does absenteeism grow into a concern for the firms? Why is it important for firms to monitor and tackle absenteeism?

11 List some major causes of absenteeism in organisations.
12 List some effect of absenteeism on organisations.
13 Elucidate some data sources used to identify the causes of absenteeism in firms.
14 Explain how analytics can be applied to understand and curb absenteeism.
15 Discuss some measures taken by firms to address and curb absenteeism, once its cause is discovered using the application of analytics.
16 Explain how the measurement of employee performance benefits both the employee and the organisation.
17 Discuss the limitations of conventional employee performance methods and need to switch to digital means.
18 Explain how analytics can be applied to identify good performers in the firm. How can this be used for selection and hiring?
19 How can employee performance analytics be used to bring out reforms in organisational working?
20 Discuss how employee performance analytics aids the firm to optimise investment in organisational activities meant to enhance employee engagement.
21 How is performance analytics related to the prediction of turnover among employees?
22 What implications do performance analytics have for succession planning and workforce planning?
23 Explain the role of wearable technology in predicting employee performance.
24 Define TRA, or total rewards package.
25 Detail out how analytics can be used to optimise the rewards package.
26 Why there is a need to weigh the TRA outcomes against business relevance?
27 Define pay equity.
28 How can analytics be applied to compensation data of the workforce to ensure pay equity?
29 Explain the role of analytics in identifying under-valued yet high-performing employees?
30 What do you understand is meant by OHSAS 18001?
31 Why is employee safety a big concern for organisations?
32 How can predictive analytics aid in ensuring employee safety?
33 List various disparate data sources used for the prediction of safety incidents in firms.
34 Explain how IoT can be used for the application of predictive analytics to the field of employee safety.

Problem exercises

1 Collect attendance record data (maybe availed from teachers on request) and attempt to build a predictive model inculcating variables like student age, gender, academic grades, class participation, and so on.
2 Arrange a visit to a manufacturing firm near your vicinity. Interview the employees about workplace safety, awareness regarding measures for workplace

safety, and the provision of training for the same. Collect data on these parameters in addition to age, gender, job position, location, number of leaves availed, and safety incidents in the past month for each employee interviewed. Next, develop a predictive model useful to predict such safety incidents.

Case study

Lysithea – mental health predicting employee absence

Hitachi designed Lysithea (Morii and Hirayama, 2018), which is an employee management system inculcating modules on talent management, human resources management, and payroll management. It has been in operation since 2017 and has been adopted by more than 1,200 companies; it has a strong user base, approximating to 1.64 million people. A large number of Lysithea's adopter firms were looking at ways to increase employee productivity, and a major factor affecting it was the prevalence of high absenteeism rates. Hitachi further discovered from industry-wide surveys that poor mental health was a key cause of high absenteeism among employees. So, Hitachi undertook a programme to implement analytics to first, identify what caused poor mental health among employees, and second, design measures to improve mental health and prevent employees from taking leaves for those reasons.

Workplace physicians were invited to brainstorm on the underlying issues such as organisational, environmental, and work-related issues which may cause poor mental health among employees. Around 28 such factors were identified and categorised into two broad factors: individual factors and circumstances. Individual factors were further sub-divided into attributes, work practices, work, and private factors. Each of the 28 factors was placed under an appropriate heading and then probable sources and techniques to collect data for each were determined. In the process, it was found that there were approximately seven factors like age, gender, work output, place of work, etc., for which no data was available in the system; and four factors like sleep hours, job mismatch, life events and losses, which were deemed influential in affecting mental health, but data collection for the same was difficult for this large user base. For the remaining factors, data was taken from either the existing systems or physician data, and collected through surveys. Since the collected data contained records of employees who had reported in sick owing to poor mental health and had taken some days off, this data could be used to apply predictive analytics to predict employees who would report an absence in the future, owing to poor mental health.

A total of six predictive analytics algorithms were applied, which included logistic regression, random forest, gradient boosting, support vector machines, neural networks, and deep learning. The method of choice was a gradient boosting algorithm, as it had the highest accuracy. A one-month lag was introduced in the data to make predictions, and the algorithm could make predictions with more than 50% accuracy, such that out of 93 employees predicted to take days off owing to poor mental health, more than 45 actually reported sick for those reasons. Overall mean accuracy in making predictions using gradient boosting algorithm and features discussed previously was more than 30%, which was considered fairly accurate by the firm since the individuals labelled as high risk by the algorithm were those who had taken leave due to poor mental health. The algorithm describes the key features of the employee who report poor mental health, such as number of paid leaves availed, frequency of reporting late to work, and count of the days they worked on public holidays (workation). Through a dashboard for use by a personnel manager, Lysithea depicts those employees who have fluctuating or non-rhythmic variation in any of these features. By collating this data with their state of mental health, which managers can gauge from physician data or personal talks scheduled with these employees, early intervention to tackle the same and prevent absenteeism is possible. Within the first year of implementation, Lysithea has been able to reduce unplanned absenteeism due to mental health by 0.3%, which is significant at key positions, owing to the effect on productivity. For employees identified with poor mental health using this product, appropriate treatment, leaves, and monetary benefits were offered by the firm.

Hitachi has now commercialised this product Lysithea and incorporates data on the following to predict employees in organisations with poor mental health, requiring immediate care: HR data, morale data, work data, absence data, target management data, and daily survey data. All this data is captured and logged in the system by the system itself. The model makes monthly predictions and generates early intervention reports for immediate addressing by the firms. An ongoing concern with such systems is the use of physician data. Only when an employee gives written consent for use of this data for analysis is it incorporated in the model.

Case questions

1   Discuss the process by which a predictive model was developed to predict absenteeism.
2   Discuss the outcomes of the application of the predictive algorithm for managing absenteeism. What were the implications for the management for the same?
3   List data sources and data collection techniques used in Lysithea. Discuss its practical applicability in other firms.

Bibliography

Cook, I. (2018). *HR moments matter: 3 compensation challenges solved with people analytics.* Retrieved 2019, from Visier: www.visier.com/clarity/compensation-people-analytics/

Davenport, T. (2019, April 18). *Is HR the most analytics-driven function?* Retrieved October 2019, from Harvard Business Review: https://hbr.org/2019/04/is-hr-the-most-analytics-driven-function

Fosway. (2017). *Innovation profile: Sky – ripping up the rule book of people development.* Retrieved 2019, from Fosway Group: www.fosway.com/wp-content/uploads/2018/05/Fosway-Innovation-Profile_Sky_Final_Website.pdf

HRMagazine. (2001, November 1). *The top ten causes of absenteeism and what you can do about it*. Retrieved September 2018, from HRMagazine.co.uk: www.hrmagazine.co.uk/article-details/the-top-10-causes-of-absenteeism-and-what-you-can-do-about-it

Jerath, A. (2018, January 10). *The role of analytics in predicting employee performance*. Retrieved August 2019, from SHRM: www.shrm.org/shrm-india/pages/the-role-of-analytics-in-predicting-employee-performance.aspx

Knight, C., Solly, J., and Richardson, B. (2019). *Workplace safety analytics: Save lives and the bottom line*. California: Deloitte.

Leonardi, P., and Contractor, N. (2018, November). Better people analytics. *Harvard Business Review*. Vol. 88(10), pp.52-58

Meister, J. C. (2019, August 26). *Survey: What employees want most from their workspaces*. Retrieved November 21, 2019, from Harvard Business Review: https://hbr.org/2019/08/survey-what-employees-want-most-from-their-workspaces

Mercer. (2018, March 5). *Rethinking total rewards optimization*. Retrieved 2019, from Mercer: www.mercer.com/our-thinking/career/voice-on-talent/rethinking-total-rewards-optimization.html

Mondore, S. (2018). *People analytics case study: How HR made customers happy*. Retrieved 2019, from AIHR Analytics: www.analyticsinhr.com/blog/people-analytics-case-study-how-hr-made-customers-happy/

Morii, T., and Hirayama, J. (2018, September). *Using people analytics to help prevent absences due to mental health issues*. Retrieved 2019, from Hitachi Review: www.hitachi.com/rev/archive/2018/r2018_06/06b07/index.html

Visier. (2019). *5 L+D questions you can't answer without analytics*. Retrieved 2019, from HR Curator: https://hrcurator.com/post/59

9

EMERGING TRENDS IN PREDICTIVE HR ANALYTICS

After reading this chapter, users will be able to understand the following key concepts:

- Understand the concept of Industry 4.0 and how new technological advancements can disrupt HR practices
- Learn the meaning of people analytics and the core areas where it can be applied
- Interpret the use of nudges and interaction analytics at the workplace
- List different sources of voice data in firms, and its use to predict HR outcomes
- Review the need for disparate data for implementation of voice analytics
- Understand the concept and application of IoT analytics in HRM
- Define data visualisation and dashboards, and their role in informing HR decision-makers
- Understand the concept and role of Big Data analytics in HRM
- Discuss the impact of analytics on workplace ergonomics

Opening case

Indian startup inFeedo, based in Gurgaon, has been working in the area of predictive people analytics. Its recent product 'Amber' is a chatbot which is equipped with predictive analytical tools to predict disengaged employees in a company. The product is an outcome of dissatisfaction of HR leaders with annual engagement surveys, which they believe do not reflect employee's opinion completely. Amber, a chatbot enabled with artificial intelligence (AI), on the other hand, can be visualised as an employee confidante for almost all the client firms where it has been implemented.

Almost every 15 days, periodically, employees receive communication messages from Amber, asking them personalised questions designed to capture different dimensions of employee engagement. The questions may include asking the employee about his perception of satisfaction derived from the work assigned to him, support from supervisor, the company's role in realising employee potential, and so on. Amber simply modifies the question pattern as per the answers provided by the employee. Amber also analyses people's expressions and tones, and if an employee repeatedly expresses dissatisfaction over a few months, an alert is generated for HR to intervene. The data from Amber is not accessible by the employee-manager, and access to it is restricted to a few people in the company. Using the data, employees are categorised into three categories based on their risk of leaving the firm: high, medium and low. The outcome of analytics is interpreted by an inFeedo expert panel comprised of psychologists, statisticians, and HR leaders. An interesting revelation by an e-commerce company which implemented Amber was that more than half of the employees believed Amber to be real, since the questions posed by Amber seem like conversations, without abrupt endings. An additional benefit for the firm is that feedback from Amber is also used to identify organisational areas of improvement, where most of the employees have expressed unhappiness. This is just one area where AI has found application in HR functions, and analytics can then be applied for improvement of the HR function. Smart systems, AI, and Industry 4.0 is disrupting traditional HRM, paving the way for newer means of conducting business and managing employees (Bora, 2019).

Introduction

A senior director at Hitachi Group sums up three factors contributing to the emergent trends in HR technology. First is the use of newer ways to quantify human beings, and second is a shortage of adequately skilled labour, while the third factor is problem of long working hours and human machine interface issues (Hitachi-Group, 2018).

Since the world is getting smarter, so are the business functions. Here, smarter implies the use of AI and robotics in business functioning, changing how business used to function. Just as the advent of the Internet and social networking sites redefined many ways of doing business, similarly the emergence of new technologies like cloud computing, Internet of Things (IoT), etc., have brought about drastic change. The change is so compelling that it has been reckoned globally as a new Industrial Revolution – Industry 4.0 – and it all began with automation and digitisation of manufacturing. Industry 4.0 is an enhancement in Industry 3.0, whereby automation and information systems will be augmented or replaced by smart systems, capable of independent operation without human intervention. Global business leaders have acknowledged that Industry 4.0 will disrupt traditional HRM (Rana and Sharma, 2019). Consider the production facilities, where machines are interconnected with each other, exchanging data to optimise workflow and productivity. This data can be collected, stored, and analysed to improve performance of machines, fix issues in a timely manner, and implement predictive maintenance rather than preventive maintenance. While all this will happen in real time, it will surpass human capacities at an unprecedented scale. HR leaders are apprehensive that it will redefine work roles and eliminate some of the existing jobs in the market. For example, automated warehousing and order fulfilment has been in operation for quite a long time now. Facilities of market leaders like Amazon and Flipkart fulfil many orders without any human intervention through the use of robots, and initiatives like AmazonGo, which is a completely unstaffed retail store (working on the Internet of Things), are nascent examples of Industry 4.0.

All industrial revolutions have brought about disruptions in HRM. The idea is to understand how disruption can be timely managed so that the effect on employees and organisational productivity is minimal. These advanced technologies open up newer business avenues and new forms of communication among people. Although like any technology use in organisations, Industry 4.0 brings about its challenges like ethical issues, leadership vision to implement it, organisational siloes limiting application, etc., executives across the world agree that it is promising and will result in higher payoffs gradually. In HRM, this calls for the ability to visualise new work roles, the need for a new type of leaders with traits who can envision and lead the change, change in HR practices, and identification of skill gaps and providing effective training to overcome. Industry 4.0, smart systems, AI, and robotics are all entering into HRM functions, as well, and as a result, bring about newer data and newer areas in which analytics can be applied. Predictive analytics also has the potential to uncover how Industry 4.0 and related innovations can disrupt HRM, and therefore, HR leaders can rethink ways of conducting business and implementing their functions. Recalling from previous chapters, it has been rightly said that if you ask the right questions, analytics will deliver just the right results. Therefore, this book – and specifically, this chapter – expects to spark the curiosity of the reader in applying his mindset to ask questions which can be answered through analytics, especially the questions about understanding the cause and effect of such new advents which have the potential to disrupt HRM. The chapter, therefore, presents some contemporary areas of application of HR analytics which are still developing and have much to be explored.

People analytics

People analytics is simply the use of analytical tools and techniques to manage people at the workplace, where the people decisions are driven by data and factual insights rather than conventional means like intuition and judgement. People analytics utilises the data on people behaviour, traits and relationships to understand and predict organisational behaviour and making informed business decisions. This stream of analytics is redefining all aspects of people management at the workplace, be it recruitment and hiring, employee engagement, employee productivity, etc. What follows is a discussion of the three core areas in which people analytics finds a place for application in HRM functions (Nielsen and McCullough, 2018).

Transformation of core business functions

This application of people analytics is driven towards understanding how analytics applied to HR data has the potential to transform other business functions like marketing, finance, etc. One such example is of a global company which seeks to improve its financial process, however was unable to standardise it owing to differences in local accounting practices of each country and region of operation. Since it was difficult to engage people from across different countries of operation of the company, in a discussion on ways to improve the financial process, the firm took a different route. It used people analytics data to identify the number of people involved in the process by each country and region of operation, and also the time spent on the process. The firm was surprised to find that one country spent 16% less time, involved 40 fewer people, and completed the financial process in 71 fewer man-hours than the global average. In this way, the company involved representatives from only this country to optimise their financial process, which had not been a possibility without people analytics.

Transformation of culture – how processes were carried out

Using feedback and data-driven information, organisations have discovered new ways of transforming cultures. In one such application, a software services firm found that managers were willingly not inclusive in their approach. To change this perspective, the firm applied analytics to depict how managerial involvement affected employee performance. It showed managers that when they indulged in at least 16 minutes of one-to-one conversation with their employees, it increased their engagement levels by 30%.

People analytics can be further used to generate these 'nudges' for both managers and employees. Nudges are timely customised reminders for each employee, generated by the machines, to remind and to increase productivity and performance. Nudges have been in use to remind managers to interact with employees, provide feedback to better engage them, and provide a perception that the organisation cares for them. Using data analytics to track employee time spent at their workstations, and determining work contribution, the analytics algorithm can track whether they are losing focus. Analysis of such patterns allows the tools to predict when fatigue has set in the employees from continuous work, and accordingly, a nudge is sent across the screen as a reminder to take a break from work.

Analytics to support strategic transformation

Interaction analytics is a specialised area of people analytics focused on analysing the conversations and communications among employees in the workplace. By applying analytics to communications among people, employees can be better managed at the workplace. Slack, a messenger widely used globally for employee communications at the workplace, deploys a chatbot Engazify. Since Slack allows closed group conversations between members of a particular team, Engazify tracks these team conversations and builds a leaderboard depicting the weekly frequency with which each team member has received appreciation. Further, these weekly statistics are compounded to depict how happiness levels within the team have increased each week. Another company (Bora, 2019) struggling to bring about an organisation-wide transformation overheard some experiential stories of their knowledge workers discussing fatigue, overwork, and burnout due to change. To solve this situation, the firm empowered executives with analytics-driven dashboards, which depicted a number of hours spent by each worker in the team. This way over-utilised and under-utilised workers, and over-numbered and under-numbered teams, could be identified.

A huge challenge faced by people analytics at present is ethical concerns about overuse of employee data for third-party analysis. Many firms have been attempting to resolve this issue by securing consent from employees before analysis, and also communicating beforehand that all employee conversations at the workplace conducted using organisational channels can be used for data analysis.

Speech and voice analytics in HRM

Voice recognition and voice assistants are entering in abundance in the market, with top players being Google Assistant, Amazon's Alexa, and Apple's Siri. Each of these devices is creating abundant data which have now found multiple uses by organisations. In organisations, data created through call centre conversations, over conference calls, messages in voice mails, or commands passed through voice assistants at the workplace all form a few of the many voice data sources. While conventional chatbots were limited to text conversations, voice assistants and voice recognition devices are the game-changers. Although the complexity of decoding voice data and then using algorithms to analyse it is far more difficult than any other source of data, the advances in this field seem promising, with each day bringing in new possibilities. IoT- and speech-enabled platforms will be a common occurrence in the next few years, prevailing in even simple everyday tasks that humans perform, like turning on cars, operating phones, and surfing websites (Shrock, 2018).

Business management, especially in the marketing function, has been leveraging speech and voice analytics for quite a while now. The trend is expanding in other functional areas and has picked up pace in HRM, as well. In HRM, voice and speech analytics is currently limited to use as a hiring assessment tool. HR personnel have been leveraging the use of audio and video technology platforms like Skype and mobile calls to conduct virtual interviews with potential candidates for hire. Using voice analytics, the firms can record interviews and then analyse parameters beyond speech such as voice modulation, the pace of speech, areas of emphasis in the speech, and intonation, all of which can aid in deducing the personality characteristics of an individual. It is possible to identify temperament, co-operability, creativity, communication effectiveness, etc., through voice analytics. By comparing these features of the candidates with behavioural traits required for the job position for which they are being interviewed, the analytical algorithm generates a score indicating how well the candidate profile matches with the job profile.

In addition, voice analytics is also finding use as a means of evaluating the mental health of employees. Since employees being prone to stress is becoming a common occurrence at the workplace today, which affects their productivity and performance, it has become imperative for organisations to track their mental health, in order to intervene in a timely manner before the condition of the employee deteriorates. Human speech occurs due to the vibration of vocal cords in the throat. It has been seen that when a person is relaxed, their vocal cords are loose, while they become tense when the person is under stress (Yamashita, Higuchi, and Satake, 2018). These changes in vocal cords also lead to changes in the pitch of the human voice, which becomes sharper under stress. Therefore, to predict the occurrence of a mental issue among employees, the voice analytics platform quantifies the changes in vocal cords and voice pitch. One such analytics platform working on this principle is MIMOSYS, implemented by Hitachi Ltd. to gauge the mental health of its employees and provide primary treatment. The outcomes of MIMOSYS are presented as vitality and mental activity. Vitality varies with situation and surroundings. The idea is to look for variations or trends or decline in mental activity. If mental health is poor, then vitality stops varying due to lack of emotion and mental activity starts worsening.

The only limitation with this area of analytics is injecting bias with the use of specific data. Unless an organisation developing an analytical model using voice and speech data has abundant data encompassing all possibilities, it cannot be sure of arriving at unbiased results. For example, the performance of a voice recognition algorithm trained on US English would vary with data from Indian English and UK English. Unless the algorithm has been trained with this data, inculcating all linguistic variations, the predictions and detections cannot be accurate. This is a major concern, and that is the main reason why global giants like Google dominate this field, owing to rich and huge data that they can gather globally through their applications.

Internet of Things in HR analytics

Chief of IoT business at Reliance Group believes that it begins and ends with people (SHRM_India, 2018). IoT is a network of interconnected smart devices and the humans adorned with those devices, exchanging data and commands to maximise performance and minimise or eliminate human intervention. IoT has widespread implications for HRM, as it can change the way humans operate in an organisation. Just like machines are equipped with sensors to track and record their performance, to optimise production and minimise faults, humans at the workplace can also be made to be adorned with wearable gadgets equipped with sensors. These gadgets can then allow organisations to track human movement in the firm, which can be used to improve both workplace ergonomics, thereby causing improvements in employee safety and mobility in the firm, and also workplace performance, by monitoring the work performed by employees while in the organisation. Additionally, when these gadgets are equipped to record employee conversations, the data can be used to predict in real time workforce dynamics such as areas of dissatisfaction in the firm and employee behaviour.

IoT-enabled HR analytics is especially useful for firms with mobile workforces or workforces operating in critical conditions such as power generation firms, mining firms, the chemical industry, etc. The workforce of such organisations should be made to wear smart badges which track in real time vital statistics of the worker and generate an immediate alert if some undesirable pattern is detected. Also, by tracking changes in environmental conditions prevailing in the facilities of such organisations, probable variations such as rise in heat levels, drop in oxygen levels, etc., can be used to generate timely alerts to minimise the effects on worker health. One example of corporate implementation of IoT analytics to ensure worker safety is that of Nation Waste, Inc., which is a commercial waste disposal company headquartered in the US. It combines data from both environmental sensors and wearable sensors worn by its workforce. Some of the sensors deployed include sensors to track employee movement to detect collision or fall, heat sensors, and heartbeat monitoring sensors which can predict burnout or stress among the workers. Whenever a hazard is detected by these sensors, the analytics solution developed by IBM, 'IoT Safer Workplace', generates alerts such as vibration or flashing light for immediate notice by the workers. Additionally, this data is also communicated to dashboards so managers can view each worker's safety metrics. With fewer safety incidents at the workplace, Nation Waste seeks to reduce expenses incurred in employee litigation, medical aid, and insurance claims by 60%.

Data visualisation in HRM

Data visualisation is simply a depiction of outcomes from the application of analytical algorithms, graphically or pictorially. The major data visualisation tools used for the depiction of HRM or any business data is a dashboard. Since reports can become cumbersome, especially when the data is huge, organisations switch to a graphical representation of data. Dashboard refers to a graphical user interface depicting key data for easy interpretation by the decision-maker. It is a tool to simplify the presentation of information for the decision-maker, and generally presents a summary of key data of a business function for which the dashboard has been designed.

In HRM, HR metrics can be displayed for a given HR function using a dashboard. A brief overview of possible data visualisation for a few HR functions, listing the HR function and items that the dashboard may contain (Maalerud, 2019), have been discussed.

1   Recruitment

a   Workforce supply gaps by different departments, regions of operation, job levels, skill sets.

b   Fulfilment of supply gap by above parameters through either training, hiring, or promotion.

c   Sources of recruitment.

d   Number of previous hires and success of hires from each source.

e   Credibility rating of the source.

2   Hiring and selection

a   Summary of top performers of each department listing their traits like education, skills, and job attitudes, and the turnover rate.

3   Compensation

a   Listing of profiles for comparative analysis of compensation offered for similar job roles and positions.

b   Salary analysis offered to new and previous hires.

c   Visualising pay differences by gender, religion, etc., to determine pay equity issues, if any.

4   Career development

a   Training programmes delivered annually.

b   Number of training programmes undergone by key employees.

c   Number of employees who did not receive any training.

d   Department and region-wise comparison of training programmes conducted.

e   Number of promotions after undergoing a training programme.

5   Turnover analysis

a   Top reasons for attrition cited in exit interviews.

b   Department-wise and region-wise turnover rates.

c   Job position-wise turnover.

d   Turnover by gender and age group.

e   Performance ratings and turnover rate comparison.

These visualisations may be in the form of simple bar graphs and pie charts, which can be done using simple tools like Microsfot Excel. However, with an increase in data and complexity of adding more dimensions to visualisation, organisations use tools like R and Tableau. Tableau is a powerful tool used across the world by a plethora of organisations for data visualisation since it can connect with a large number of data sources and work with disparate data types. Besides this, firms may also use data visualisation for networking analysis in the organisation, which can address many concerns like:

1   How employees are connected.

2   Identifying the strength of employee networks.

3   Identifying candidates with strong networks (they can act as influencers on behalf of the firm to advocate their practices).
4   Identifying candidates with connections beyond their departments, and so on.

By empowering these dashboards with real-time data, HR managers can gain actionable insight from the dashboards to take proactive action for better management of personnel. SAP (Maalerud, 2019) has implemented a digital boardroom at its headquarters which depicts key metrics for all business functions of the organisations which change in real time. For example, the HR dashboard at the digital boardroom displays new hires by skill, department, the region of operation, annual turnover rates, and so on. By integrating data across the enterprise, the organisation can view the impact of activities in one business function over another in real time. For example, the learning and development activities undertaken by HR globally vis-à-vis the investments made by the finance department, and how these activities and investments vary with previous years. Dashboards also allow 'drilling down' into data; that is, looking at the variations in data outcomes for varying levels of data granularity. For example, region-wise turnover rates can be clicked to reveal departments for a given region, the departments can be examined to reveal turnover rates for different job positions in each department, and these positions can be further examined to reveal variations in turnover by gender and age groups.

Such detailed insights are not possible manually, and not through traditional reporting since reading through these is so tedious. Therefore, data visualisation allows the managers to view data summary of key organisational metrics at a glance and reach informed decisions in real time.

Big data in HRM

A buzz phrase in data analytics is Big Data. 'Big Data' simply refers to any data which fulfils three key traits: being high in volume, high in variety, and high in velocity. High volume data here implies that the data is available in bulk, such that the organisation is experiencing difficulty in storing it and it cannot be processed by traditional methods. High velocity implies that data is increasing exponentially at an unmanageable rate. High variety implies that data is composed of many structured and unstructured data types. The advent of new technological platforms like social networking sites for communication, the Internet, AI, and robotics, all have led to drastic changes in data collected for any business function including HRM. In HRM, consider any business function to understand the implication of Big Data. Consider the example of employee performance, which is measured using sources including the following:

- Performance reviews, which is structured data.
- Using wearable sensors adorned by employees at the workplace, which is unstructured IoT data.

- Quantifying the number of effective interactions at the workplace using voice and speech data.
- Chatbot conversations, which is speech and text data.

All of this data, when collected and analysed for one HR function – that is, employee performance – can be termed as Big Data since it satisfies the three Vs by including high-volume, high variety, and high-velocity data. Therefore, Big Data is simply a term coined for existing data, only with the differentiating element of the three Vs. However, since conventional analytical tools cannot work with the complexity of Big Data in terms of bulk data, analysis of different data content, both structured and unstructured, and requiring dynamic data updates, a separate team of analytics called Big Data analytics has emerged. Implementing Big Data analytics in organisations requires implementing or renting huge storage spaces like cloud solutions, and working on specially equipped platforms like Hadoop.

Organisational leaders globally have expressed concerns regarding the use of the term Big Data in the HR data context. Many believe that no such thing as Big Data exists in HRM (Cappelli, 2017). However, both the term and the application of Big Data analytics have found use in HRM and have fetched enormous benefits and a shift in the way different HR functions and activities have been carried out. For example, for management of employee engagement, traditional annual surveys, chatbot data, employee communications, absenteeism data, wearable sensors, etc., can be used for analysis. This is another example of Big Data. However, before the application of Big Data analytics, a firm must ensure that the data collected and model built are reliable and dependable for future prediction and analysis. Using Big Data analytics, the global software services solution company Geminian (Cappelli, 2017) improved its manpower forecasting. Each year, the company recruits employees in millions from across the world, and using analytics, it can plan for six months ahead for each of its region and department of operation.

A major limitation of Big Data analytics is the fallacy of the data itself. GIGO – 'garbage in, garbage out' – is a widely used term in data analysis, implying that if wrong or faulty data is fed into a system, it is going to result in faulty outcomes. This has led to the emergence of humanised Big Data, which simply implies humanising the outcomes of Big Data analytics – that is, the validation of application and outcomes of Big Data analytics by a human professional – so that faulty interpretations owing to fallacious reasoning don't lead to faulty decisions.

Analytics in workplace ergonomics

Workplace ergonomics involves the application of scientific and psychological principles to design the workplace according to the needs and limitations of the workers. A Deloitte study reveals that only 60% of the available workspace is utilised in any modern office setup (Rose, 2019). The primary aim of workplace ergonomics is to increase employee comfort at the workplace to boost productivity while reducing risks and injury to the employees. Environmental dynamicity and changes in work, workplaces, and workers have led organisations to rethink their office spaces. Technology has even questioned the existence of dedicated physical spaces for office work for employees as now employees can work from any location, even across the borders. Additionally, workforce diversity has increased, posing an urge to accommodate the different needs of this diverse section of workers. Besides this, research studies (Hogan, Lucker, Robertson, and Schafer, 2019) have revealed that office spaces have an effect on employee behaviour at the workplace, such as on their motivation, engagement, vitality, and so on. When workplace design fails to incorporate the interests of different stakeholders who use it, and organisations fail to continue improving it and see it as a one-time activity, it has been seen to negatively impact worker productivity. Therefore, it is suggested that the workplace should be designed to accommodate a variety of reasons individuals come to the workplace. For example, some may come to the workplace for training and learning alone, some for client meetings, some for market activities, some for individual private work, and some for collaboration. Each of these requires a different sort of workspace, and the design should offer some space for each such sort of need.

To redesign workspaces, data from wearable sensors can be used to understand how office spaces like conference rooms, workstations, meeting rooms, and so on, are being utilised in the organisation. By quantifying the use of different office spaces and furniture, daily activity allocation and workspace arrangement can be made as per the frequency of use of the same. Studies have also shown that on average, around 60% of workers spend way more time to find a conference room than would be normally required (Rose, 2019). This can also be answered through analytics. By monitoring many employees, size of office space used for work, meeting, collaborating, and scheduling of different activities can be changed accordingly. If the analysis depicts a large space not being utilised, organisations may consider trimming down that workspace, saving money spent on maintaining it. The firms can also opt for 'co-working', allowing remote workers for other business partners to work from their office spaces, thereby earning more revenue for the firm. Sensors can also be installed in the workplace to monitor humidity, temperature, the number of people in a given area or room, etc., and can be used to improve the comfort and safety of the workplace. By monitoring workplace activity, organisations can use analytics to vary environmental conditions in the workspace such as temperature variation by the number of people present.

Conclusion

Technological innovations like AI and robotics have disrupted many business functions and redefined how they were conducted. HRM has also been hit by this disruption, and the impact is dual – fetching benefits for the firms and some sections of the employees, while others are bearing the brunt of the change. However, it is a given that organisations sooner or later will have to adopt these changes and accept the contemporary application of HR analytics, as well. The advent of smart systems, AI, and IoT have led to what has been coined as Industry 4.0, and will fetch widespread consequences for the workforce. Automation and autonomous systems – which due to advances in AI are being implemented and improvised for non-repetitive functions of HRM, as well – will potentially endanger existing job profiles. This doesn't imply that the need for manual workforce will end; however, it certainly means that their tasks in the organisation will be redefined, requiring a completely different skill set. This field of analytics is still evolving, with many new developments occurring each day. For effective and successful implementation of the same in any business function, visionary leaders who can foresee and lead the change will be required by organisations. As has been seen in many examples and discussions presented in this chapter, these technological advancements have had an unparalleled impact on HR functions and have completely changed the way they are managed in the organisations. Analytics allows real-time monitoring, which paves the way for newer means of workforce, work, and workplace management. Repeating its introductory lines, this chapter is an attempt to spark curiosity among readers about the many ways in which HR analytics can find an application in HR functions. Reminding the reader here that wherever there is data, there is analytics, and whenever there are right questions, analytics will provide the right answers. The chapter simply lists a few ways in which different areas of HRM can benefit through analytics, but the list is simply suggestive and not exhaustive. The era of the data revolution is here to stay, and analytics is not a fad. The sooner organisations (whether big or small) accept it, the better it will be for their sustainability.

Glossary

Big Data   any data which fulfils three key traits: high in volume, high in variety and high in velocity

Dashboard   a graphical user interface depicting key data for easy interpretation by the decision-maker; a tool to simplify the presentation of information for the decision-maker, generally presenting a summary of key data about a business function

Data visualisation   a depiction of outcomes from the application of analytical algorithms, graphically or pictorially

'Drilling down'   –implies looking at the variations in data outcomes for varying levels of data granularity

Humanised Big Data   implies humanising the outcomes of Big Data analytics; that is, to validate application and outcomes of Big Data analytics by a human professional so that faulty interpretations owing to fallacious reasoning don't lead to faulty decisions

Industry 4.0   an enhancement of Industry 3.0, whereby automation and information systems will be augmented or replaced by smart systems, capable of independent operation without human intervention

Interaction analytics   a specialised area of people analytics focused on analysing the conversations and communications among employees at the workplace

Internet of Things (IoT)   a network of interconnected smart devices and of the humans wearing those devices, exchanging data and commands, to maximise performance and minimise or eliminate human intervention

Nudges   timely customised reminders for each employee, generated by machines, to increase productivity and performance

People analytics   the application of analytical tools and techniques on people data like their behaviour, traits, and relationships, to better manage people at the workplace, understand and predict organisational behaviour, and make informed data-driven people decisions, rather than relying on conventional means like intuition and judgement

Three core applications of people analytics   the transformation of core business functions, the transformation of culture, and supporting strategic transformation

3 Vs of Big Data   volume (referring to a high amount of data), velocity (meaning the high rate of growth of data), and variety (implying diverse data types)

Workplace ergonomics   involves the application of scientific and psychological principles to design the workplace according to the needs and limitations of the workers

Review material

1 Define Industry 4.0.
2 How will Industry 4.0 disrupt conventional HRM?
3 List some challenges posed by Industry 4.0 and how HRM can overcome it.
4 Define people analytics.
5 List the three core areas in which people analytics finds an application.
6 Explain how people analytics can drive transformations in other business functions.
7 Define nudges.
8 Explain the use of nudges to increase employee performance and engagement.
9 Define interaction analytics.
10 Explain how interaction analytics aid in better management of employees at the workplace.
11 Discuss the challenge faced by people analytics.
12 List some voice data sources prevalent in firms.
13 Elucidate some ways in which voice and speech analytics has been used in HRM.
14 How can voice analytics be used to predict employee health?
15 Discuss a major limitation of voice analytics and how it provides dominance in this field to global leaders like Google.
16 What is meant by the Internet of Things?
17 Explain the role of IoT data analytics in improving workplace ergonomics.
18 Why is IoT data analytics especially useful for the mobile workforce? How does it ensure employee safety?

19 What is data visualisation?
20 Define dashboard.
21 List some HR functions and how data visualisation can inform the decision-maker for each function.
22 How can data visualisation aid in networking analysis?
23 What is the advantage of empowering dashboard data with real-time data?
24 Explain drilling down data on dashboards.
25 Define Big Data.
26 List and explain the three Vs of Big Data.
27 Explain how employee performance data is Big Data in HR.
28 What organisational changes need to be addressed to implement Big Data analytics?
29 Explain how employee engagement data is Big Data in HR.
30 Define humanised Big Data.
31 List the limitation of Big Data analytics and emergence of humanised Big Data.
32 Define workplace ergonomics.
33 Discuss the need to redesign the office spaces.
34 Explain how analytics can be used for workplace redesign.

Problem exercises

1 Surf the Internet to identify how Industry 4.0 affects HRM functions. Attempt to prepare a report on how analytics can be used to mitigate these effects.
2 Use the Internet to find how voice data and speech data are stored by organisations. Explain your findings in simple words in a report.

Case study

Quantifying employees differently: insights from Google and Deloitte

Generally, the performance of the team can be measured using simple metrics such as team performance rating after periodic performance appraisal, milestones reached, and so on. However, these are lag indicators and do not completely reflect how effective and productive a team was. As a result, Google (Schneider, 2017) sought to understand why some teams failed despite having the best of the workforce, while others win. In this direction, Google set out to evaluate team performance differently. It implemented Project Aristotle for two years to analyse the data collected from 180 teams at Google and more than 200 interviews, thereby including 250 team attributes in its analysis. The outcomes of the analysis were evaluated by data science experts, psychologists, sociologist, and experts in collective intelligence. To measure team effectiveness, they deduced that any trait that increases the collective intelligence of the team is deemed to contribute to effectiveness. Therefore, quantification of team effectiveness is based on measurement of five key features: dependability, structure and clarity, meaning, impact, and psychological safety.

Inspired by the use of smartwatches athletes to track their performance, Deloitte (2019) coined a term 'corporate athletes', stressing on the need for a present-day employee to deal with an enormous amount of business activity like responding to emails and making work decisions. Deloitte suggests that this multitude of activity has an effect on worker productivity, and just like athletes, the productivity of an employee at the workplace needs to be monitored using smart devices like wearable sensors. Further, the firm suggests that data from such smart devices can provide information about work patterns, communication patterns, travel patterns, trends in collaboration, and teamwork for the employees. All of this provides different means of employee communication, leading to a 'quantified employee'. Executives recognise the power of such quantification and the enormous consequences that it has for the effective management of employees.

One such application is at Deloitte Canada (Rose, 2019), involving workplace redesign using data analytics on data collected from wearable sensors. Deloitte Canada hired a few volunteers who were asked to wear sociometric badges at the workplace which could track location, voice, and movement of the employees. Using voice data, analytics could deduce the mental state of the employee and correlate it with location data to assess what activity the individual is involved in, who he is working with, and so on. As a result, the firm was able to generate a lot of useful insights. Deloitte has a culture where workers work independently in their field of work. However, analytics revealed that employee productivity increased when they worked in interdisciplinary teams. Employees are happier when their office spaces are large and allow natural light. Also, large conference rooms are preferable for effective meetings to smaller ones. Further, the firm discovered that employees were happier when they worked in smaller groups and physically closer to one another.

Case questions

1   From your understanding from the text and this case study, discuss why quantifying employees differently proves to be beneficial.
2   Why is the present-day workforce termed as 'quantified employee'? Explain.
3   How did Deloitte Canada redesign its workspace using data analytics?

Bibliography

Bora, G. (2019, August 28). *This chatbot is helping HR identify unhappy employees before they quit*. Retrieved December 2019, from Economic Times: https://economictimes.india times.com/small-biz/startups/features/this-chatbot-is-helping-hr-identify-unhappy-employees-before-they-quit-infeedo-amber/articleshow/70852705.cms?from=mdr

Cappelli, P. (2017, June 2). *There's no such thing as big data in HR*. Retrieved October 2019, from Harvard Business Review: https://hbr.org/2017/06/theres-no-such-thing-as-big-data-in-hr

Deloitte. (2019, March 26). *How leaders are navigating the fourth industrial revolution.* Retrieved August 2019, from Harvard Business Review: https://hbr.org/sponsored/2019/03/how-leaders-are-navigating-the-fourth-industrial-revolution

HitachiGroup. (2018). *HR-tech that boosts productivity and makes people shine: New value creation in HR achieved through data analysis.* Retrieved 2019, from Hitachi Review: www.hitachi.com/rev/archive/2018/r2018_06/activities1/index.html

Hogan, S. K., Lucker, J., Robertson, R., and Schafer, F. (2019, July 29). *If these walls could talk.* Retrieved October 2019, from Deloitte Insights: https://www2.deloitte.com/us/en/insights/focus/technology-and-the-future-of-work/workplace-of-the-future.html

Maalerud, E. (2019). *Data visualization is now essential for HR.* Retrieved 2019, from SAP Analytics: www.sapanalytics.cloud/data-visualization-hr/

Marr, B. (2018, September 2). *What is industry 4.0? Here's a super easy explanation for anyone.* Retrieved January 2019, from Forbes: www.forbes.com/sites/bernardmarr/2018/09/02/what-is-industry-4-0-heres-a-super-easy-explanation-for-anyone/#4adb8959788a

Nielsen, C., and McCullough, N. (2018, May 17). *How people analytics can help you change process, culture, and strategy.* Retrieved October 2019, from Harvard Business Review: https://hbr.org/2018/05/how-people-analytics-can-help-you-change-process-culture-and-strategy?referral=03759&cm_vc=rr_item_page.bottom

Rana, G., and Sharma, R. (2019). Emerging human resource management practices in industry 4.0. *Strategic HR Review*, 176–181.

Rose, G. (2019, March). *How real-time data is revolutionizing workplace design.* Retrieved November 2019, from Work Design: www.workdesign.com/2019/03/how-real-time-data-is-revolutionizing-workplace-design/

Schneider, M. (2017, July 19). *Google spent 2 years studying 180 teams. The most successful ones shared these 5 traits.* Retrieved November 2019, from Inc.com: www.inc.com/michael-schneider/google-thought-they-knew-how-to-create-the-perfect.html

SHRM_India. (2018, May 10). *What's IoT got to do with HR and people?* Retrieved February 2019, from The SHRM South Asia Blog: https://blog.shrm.org/sasia/blog/what-s-iot-got-to-do-with-hr-and-people

Shrock, E. (2018, April 20). *Why human voice is data's next frontier.* Retrieved November 2019, from Forbes: www.forbes.com/sites/forbestechcouncil/2018/04/20/why-human-voice-is-datas-next-frontier/#2a27091b4d6f

Yamashita, K., Higuchi, Y., and Satake, K. (2018). *Mind monitoring service: A simple check on people's state of mental health from their voice.* Retrieved September 2019, from Hitachi Review: www.hitachi.com/rev/archive/2018/r2018_06/06b06/index.html

SUBJECT INDEX

COMPANY INDEX

Printed in the United States
By Bookmasters